THE PROBLEM OF EVIL

The Problem of Evil

The Gifford Lectures Delivered in the
University of St Andrews in 2003

PETER VAN INWAGEN

CLARENDON PRESS · OXFORD

OXFORD

UNIVERSITY PRESS

Great Clarendon Street, Oxford OX2 6DP

Oxford University Press is a department of the University of Oxford.
It furthers the University's objective of excellence in research, scholarship,
and education by publishing worldwide in

Oxford   New York

Auckland   Cape Town   Dar es Salaam   Hong Kong   Karachi
Kuala Lumpur   Madrid   Melbourne   Mexico City   Nairobi
New Delhi   Shanghai   Taipei   Toronto

With offices in

Argentina   Austria   Brazil   Chile   Czech Republic   France   Greece
Guatemala   Hungary   Italy   Japan   Poland   Portugal   Singapore
South Korea   Switzerland   Thailand   Turkey   Ukraine   Vietnam

Oxford is a registered trademark of Oxford University Press
in the UK and in certain other countries

Published in the United States
by Oxford University Press Inc., New York

© Peter van Inwagen 2006

The moral rights of the author have been asserted
Database right Oxford University Press (maker)

First published 2006

British Library Cataloguing in Publication Data

Data available

Library of Congress Cataloging in Publication Data
van Inwagen, Peter.
The problem of evil : The Gifford lectures delivered in the University of St.
Andrews in 2003 / Peter van Inwagen.
p. cm.
Includes bibliographical references (p.   ) and index.
ISBN-13: 978-0-19-924560-4 (alk. paper)
ISBN-10: 0-19-924560-6 (alk. paper)
1. God—Proof. 2. Good and evil—Religious aspects—Christianity. 3. Theodicy. I. Title.
BT103.V35 2006   214—dc22   2006006153

Typeset by Laserwords Private Limited, Chennai, India
Printed in Great Britain
on acid-free paper by
Biddles Ltd., King's Lynn, Norfolk

ISBN 978-0-19-924560-4

3 5 7 9 10 8 6 4 2

For Lisette

Preface

These lectures were delivered in the University of St Andrews in April and May of 2003. It is difficult for me to find words to express my gratitude to the members of University of St Andrews for giving me the opportunity to deliver a series of Gifford Lectures in their university. Having attempted and discarded several more elaborate expressions of gratitude, I will say only that I am very grateful indeed for the honor they have done me. I am also grateful to many individual members of the university for all they did to make my stay in St Andrews a pleasant and productive one, and for their many acts of kindness to me and to my wife Lisette and my step-daughter Claire. Special thanks are due to Professor Alan Torrance, Dr Peter Clark (Head of the School of Philosophical and Anthropological Studies), Professor Sarah Broadie, and Professor John Haldane. I wish also to thank the audiences at the lectures for their insightful comments and questions, many of which I have responded to (however inadequately) in this book. These responses are to be found in the endnotes; in a few cases, they have taken the form of revisions of the text of the lectures. Finally, I thank the two readers to whom the Oxford University Press sent a draft of the manuscript of this book. I have tried to meet some of their concerns about particular passages (and I have responded to some of their more general comments and suggestions) in the notes and in the text.

I have not, in turning the text of the lectures into a book, tried to make it anything other than what it was: a text written to be read aloud to an audience. (With this qualification: in the process of revision, some of the "lectures" have become too long actually to be read in the hour that academic tradition allots to a lecture.) Many passages in the text of the lectures have been extensively rewritten, but all the revisions are ones I would have made before the lectures were delivered—if only I had been thinking more clearly at the time.

Most of the material in this book that was not in the original lectures is in the endnotes. The lectures were written for a general audience (as opposed to an audience of philosophers). A few of the notes are simply thoughts that could not be fitted into the text without "breaking the flow". Most of the others (citations of books and articles aside) are for philosophers. I advise readers of the book who are not philosophers to ignore the notes (unless, perhaps, they see a footnote cue attached to a passage in which something I've said seems to them to face an obvious objection; they *may* find their concern addressed in the note).

I will not summarize the content of the lectures here. The Detailed Contents contains a summary of each of the lectures, and the first lecture gives a general overview of their content.

Citations are given in "minimal" form in the notes (e.g. Adams and Adams, *The Problem of Evil*). For "full" citations, see Works Cited. Quotations from the Psalms are taken from the Book of Common Prayer. Other biblical quotations are from the Authorized (King James) Version unless otherwise specified.

PETER VAN INWAGEN

South Bend, Indiana
August 2005

Outline Contents

Detailed Contents

agnostics". If—given world enough and time—the proponent of the argument is unable to use the argument to convince the audience that they should accept its conclusion, the argument is a failure.

LECTURE IV. THE GLOBAL ARGUMENT FROM EVIL

The global argument from evil proceeds from a premise about the totality of the evil (primarily the suffering) that actually exists. Having examined and refuted the popular contention that there is something morally objectionable about treating the argument from evil as "just one more philosophical argument", I imagine this argument presented to an audience of ideal agnostics, and the beginnings of an exchange between Atheist, an idealized proponent of the argument, and Theist, an idealized critic of the argument. The idea of a "defense" is introduced: that is, the idea of a story that contains both God and all the evils that actually exist, a story that is put forward not as true but as "true for all anyone knows". I represent Theist as employing a version of the "free-will defense", a story according to which the evils of the world result from the abuse of free will by created beings.

LECTURE V. THE GLOBAL ARGUMENT CONTINUED

I begin with an examination of three philosophical theses about free will, each of which would, if it were true, refute or raise difficulties for Theist's attempt to reply to the argument from evil by employing the free-will defense: that free will is compatible with determinism; that an omniscient being would know what anyone would freely do in any counterfactual circumstances; that free will is incompatible with divine foreknowledge. Having shown how Theist can show that these theses are doubtful (Theist's use of the free-will defense does not require him to refute the theses), I pass on to a consideration of one of the sharpest arrows in Atheist's quiver, "natural evil"—that is, suffering due to natural events that are not caused by acts of human will, free or unfree. I represent Theist as employing a version of the free-will defense that supposes a primordial separation of our remote ancestors from God, and as defending the conclusion that, according to this story, the suffering of human beings that is caused proximately by, e.g., floods and earthquakes, can also be remotely caused by the abuse of free will.

I invite my audience to consider carefully the question whether "ideal agnostics" would indeed react to this story by saying, "That story is true for all we know".

LECTURE VI. THE LOCAL ARGUMENT FROM EVIL

Local arguments from evil proceed not from a premise about "all the evils of the world", but from a premise about a single horrible event. They take the form, "If there were a God, *that* would not have happened". (There are, of course, vastly many events on which such an argument could be based. Because, the "logic" of every such argument is the same, however, I gather all of them together under the rubric "the local argument from evil".) I defend the conclusion that even if Theist's arguments in the two previous lectures are indisputably correct, they do not refute the local argument, which is really an argument of a quite different kind. But I go on to say that if Theist's response to the global argument is accepted, it provides materials from which a reply to the local argument can be constructed. This reply, oddly enough, turns on considerations of vagueness much like those considered in philosophical discussions of the sorites paradox.

LECTURE VII. THE SUFFERINGS OF BEASTS

Since there were non-rational but sentient organisms long before there were human beings, the free-will defense cannot account for the sufferings of those organisms. (At one time, it might have been possible to say that the sufferings of beasts were due entirely to a corruption of nature that was consequent on our first ancestors' separating themselves from God. It is obviously no longer possible.) I present a defense (in no way related to the free-will defense) that purports to account for the sufferings of pre-human beasts and all the more recent sufferings of beasts that cannot be ascribed to the abuse of free will by human beings. I finally consider some problems that confront anyone who (as I have done) employs both this second defense and the free-will defense.

LECTURE VIII. THE HIDDENNESS OF GOD

The problem of evil can sometimes seem to be a special case of a more general problem, the seeming absence of God from the world, the conviction that some people sometimes feel that, if there is a God at all, he is "hidden". In this lecture, I raise the question: What does it mean, what could it mean, to say that God is hidden? The answer to this question, as I see it, turns on an understanding of the divine attribute of omnipresence. Consideration of the implications of the omnipresence of God shows that there can be only one sense in which God is "hidden": he does not present human beings with (or at least presents very few of them with) unmistakable evidence of his existence in the form of "signs and wonders". The fact that God does not present all human beings with such evidence suggests an argument for the non-existence of God that is of the same form as the global argument from evil: "If there were a God, he would present all human beings with unmistakable evidence of his existence in the form of signs and wonders. And yet no such evidence exists. There is, therefore, no God." I present a response to this argument that is parallel to my response to the global argument from evil in Lectures 4 and 5.

Lecture 1

The Problem of Evil and the Argument from Evil

Like most Gifford lecturers, I have spent some time with Lord Gifford's will and with past Gifford Lectures. The topic of lectures supported by Lord Gifford's bequest was to be:

Natural Theology in the widest sense of that term, in other words, 'The Knowledge of God, the Infinite, the All, the First and Only Cause, the One and Sole Substance, the Sole Being, the Sole Reality, and the Sole Existence, the Knowledge of His Nature and Attributes, the Knowledge of the Relations which men and the whole universe bear to Him, the Knowledge of the Nature and Foundation of Ethics or Morals, and of all Obligations and Duties thence arising'.[1]

Moreover . . .

I wish the lecturers to treat their subject as a strictly natural science, the greatest of all possible sciences, indeed, in one sense, the only science, that of Infinite Being, without reference to or reliance upon any supposed special exceptional or so-called miraculous revelation. I wish it considered just as astronomy or chemistry is.[2]

I am not unusual among Gifford lecturers in that I find myself unable to meet these terms. I cannot meet them because I do not think that natural theology exists; not, at any rate, if natural theology is understood as a science that draws conclusions about an infinite being—a perfect substance, a first and only cause of all things—from the data of the senses, and draws these conclusions with the same degree of assurance as that with which natural science draws conclusions about red dwarf stars and photosynthesis from the data of the senses. I do not have, as Kant thought he had, general, theoretical reasons for thinking that natural theology, so defined, is impossible. It's just that I don't think I've ever seen it done successfully—and I know that *I* don't know how to do it. Having had a standard philosophical education, I have of course seen lots of arguments that, if they were as compelling as arguments in the natural sciences sometimes manage to be, would establish natural theology as a going concern. But, having examined these arguments individually, having considered each on its own merits, I have to say that I find that none of them lends the kind of support to its conclusion that the arguments of astronomers and chemists sometimes—frequently, in fact—lend to their conclusions. And this, I would say, is no more than a special case of a rather depressing general truth about which I shall have something to say in the third lecture: no philosophical argument that has ever been devised for any substantive thesis is capable of lending the same sort of support to its conclusion that scientific arguments often lend to theirs. (Natural theology, whatever else it may be, is a part of philosophy.)

What, then, am I to talk about if these lectures are not simply to flout the terms laid down in Lord Gifford's will? I might talk about the arguments I have alluded to (the ontological argument, say, or the cosmological argument) and try to say what I think their strengths and weaknesses are (for I do think they have strengths as well as weaknesses). If I were to do that, I should be as faithful to Lord Gifford's conditions as most Gifford lecturers have managed to be. I have decided, however, to try something else. I am going to discuss the argument from evil, the most important argument for the non-existence of that Being whose existence and attributes are said to be the province of natural theology. My general topic is therefore what might be called (and has been called—I believe the term was invented by Alvin Plantinga) natural atheology. I shall not speak as a practitioner of natural atheology, however, but as one of its critics. Here is a first approximation to a statement of my conclusion: the argument from evil is a failure. I call this a first approximation because there are many things one could mean by saying that an argument is a failure. What *I* mean by saying that an argument is a failure is so complex that I have reserved a whole lecture (the third) for the task of spelling it out.

As a first approximation to a statement of the *method* of these lectures, I could say that I intend to use only the resources of natural reason, to say nothing that presupposes any special revelation. Thus, I do not think it is stretching the truth to say that the topic of these lectures belongs to natural theology, although not natural theology in Lord Gifford's narrow sense. I will not try to establish any substantive conclusion about God; my only object is to evaluate a certain argument for the non-existence of God, and, of course, a being may well not exist even if a certain argument for its non-existence is the most abject failure imaginable. It is because I do not intend to establish any conclusion about God that I cannot claim that these lectures belong to natural theology in Lord Gifford's sense. I cannot, moreover, claim that my arguments constitute a contribution, however modest or indirect, to a *science* of natural theology. My attempt to show that the argument from evil is a failure does not lend—I do not claim that it lends—the kind of warrant to this thesis that, say, a mathematician's demonstration of an irremediable error in a supposed proof lends to the thesis that proof is a failure.

There are, however, aspects of these lectures that cannot be described as natural theology even in my weaker sense of the term. I shall at several points raise the question how what I say about the argument from evil looks from a Christian perspective. In the course of discussing the argument from evil, I shall tell various just-so stories about the coexistence of God and evil. And I shall later raise the question: What is the relation of these just-so stories to the Christian story? Is one of them perhaps identical with what Christianity says about evil? Are various of them entailed by what Christianity says about evil—are they abstractions from the Christian account of evil? Are some of them suggested but not strictly entailed by the Christian account of evil? Is any of them even consistent with the Christian account? (I do not mean to suggest by the way I have worded these questions that there is such a thing as *the* Christian account of evil; whether there is, is a part of what is being asked.) Since these just-so stories function essentially as proposed counterexamples to the validity of an argument, there is no reason for me to be embarrassed if it turns out that some, or even all, of them are inconsistent with Christian doctrine. (Jean Buridan once presented a counterexample to a certain rule of modal inference, a counterexample that incorporated the thesis that God never creates anything. It would hardly have been to the point to remind him that this thesis was inconsistent with the Nicene Creed.[3]) Still, the question of the relation of my just-so stories to the Christian story, to the Christian narrative of salvation history, is an interesting question, and I mean to address it. My present point is that when I am addressing it I shall in no sense be engaged in natural theology.

This is, however, a relatively minor point, for what I say about Christianity and the stories I shall tell is in the nature of a digression. Here is a more important point. In this lecture, I am going to say something about the relation between philosophical discussions of the argument from evil (like those I shall be engaged in) and the topic whose name is the title of these lectures: the problem of evil. And this discussion, I think, belongs more to theology in the narrow doctrinal sense than to natural theology. To this theological topic I now turn.

The word 'evil' when it occurs in phrases like 'the argument from evil' or 'the problem of evil' means 'bad things'. What, then, is the problem of evil; what is the problem of bad things? It is remarkably hard to say. Philosophers—analytical philosophers at any rate—who say that they are writing something on the problem of evil generally mean that they are writing about the argument from evil. (There are two anthologies of work on the argument from evil, both widely used as textbooks by analytical philosophers of religion. They are called *The Problem of Evil* and *The Problem of Evil: Selected Readings.*[4]) For philosophers, the problem of evil seems to be mainly the problem of evaluating the argument from evil; or perhaps one could say that philosophers see the problem of evil as a philosophical problem that confronts theists, a problem summed up in this question: How can you continue to believe in God in the face of the argument from evil?, or How would you reply to the argument from evil? A philosopher might even offer something like this as a *definition* of 'the problem of evil'. If so, the definition would be too narrow to account for the way most people use the phrase. I suspect that this "philosophical" definition of 'the problem of evil' is too narrow simply because it is a definition; for a definition, in the nature of the case, gives a definite sense to a term, and, in my view, the phrase 'the problem of evil' has no definite sense. If so, any definition of 'the problem of evil' is going to misrepresent its meaning.[5]

I think the reason is this: there are really a lot of different problems, problems intimately related to one another but nevertheless importantly different from one another, that have been lumped together under the heading 'the problem of evil'. The phrase is used to refer to this family of problems collectively. (We may call them a family since their association is no accident: they are, as I say, intimately related to one another.) Any attempt to give a precise sense to the term 'the problem of evil', any attempt to identify it with any "single, reasonably well-defined" philosophical or theological problem, or any single, reasonably well-defined problem of any sort, runs afoul of this fact.

But what I have said is too abstract to convey much. Let me try to say something about the way I conceive the membership of this family of problems. The family may be divided into two sub-families: the practical and the theoretical. By practical problems of evil I do not mean problems about how to respond to evil when we encounter it in our lives, or at any rate I mean only a very small minority of the problems that satisfy this description. I mean problems that confront theists when they encounter evil; and by "encounter evil", I mean primarily "encounter some particular evil".[6] By "problems that confront theists" I mean problems about how their beliefs about, their attitudes concerning, and their actions directed towards, God are going to be affected by their encounter with evil. Practical problems of evil may be further divided into personal and pastoral problems. A personal problem arises typically when one, or someone whom one is close to, suffers some terrible misfortune; or, less typically, when one suddenly learns of some terrible event in the public sphere that does not directly affect one but nevertheless engages one's general human sympathies. (The two most historically salient cases of this are the reactions to the Lisbon earthquake and the Holocaust by contemporaries or near-contemporaries of these events who were not directly affected by them.) Pastoral problems are the problems that confront those who, in virtue of their clerical office or of some other relation to a person, regard themselves as responsible for the spiritual welfare of that person when the person encounters evil in the way I have just described. Personal problems of evil raise questions like these: What shall I believe about God, can I continue to love and trust God, how shall I act in relation to God, in the face of this thing that has happened? Pastoral problems of evil raise the question: What spiritual guidance shall I give to someone for whom some terrible thing has raised practical questions about his relationship with God?

Further distinctions are possible within these categories. One might, for example, as the above discussion suggests, divide personal problems into those that arise out of the person's own misfortune (this was Job's case) and those that arise out of misfortunes of others. (Even for the most altruistic person, problems of these two kinds may have quite different characters.) But let us turn to theoretical problems.

I would divide theoretical problems of evil into the apologetic and the doctrinal. Doctrinal problems are problems faced by theologians: What shall the Christian—or Jewish or Muslim—teaching on evil be? What views on the origin and place of evil in the world are permissible views for Christians—or for Jews or for Muslims? Doctrinal problems are problems that are created by the fact that almost all theists subscribe to some well-worked-out and comprehensive theology that goes far beyond the assertion of the existence of an all-powerful and beneficent Creator. Attempts by theists to account for the evils of the world must take place within the constraints provided by the larger theologies they subscribe to. It is in connection with the doctrinal problems that "theodicies", properly so called, arise. A theodicy—the word was invented by Leibniz; it is put together from the Greek words for 'God' and 'justice'—is an attempt to "justify the ways of God to men". That is, a theodicy is an attempt to state the real truth of the matter, or a large and significant part of it, about why a just God allows evil to exist, evil that is, at least apparently, not distributed according to desert. A theodicy is not simply an attempt to meet the charge that God's ways are unjust: it is an attempt to *exhibit* the justice of his ways. But a doctrinal response to evil need not take the form of a theodicy. I speak under correction, but I believe that no important Christian church or denomination has ever endorsed a theodicy. Nor, as far as I know, has any important Christian church or denomination forbidden its members to speculate about theodicy—although every important Christian church and denomination has, in effect if not in just these words, insisted that any theodicy must satisfy certain conditions (it must not, for example, deny the sovereignty of God; it must not affirm that there is an inherent tendency to evil in matter).

Apologetic problems arise in two situations: when the fact of evil is used as the basis for an "external" intellectual attack on theism by its enemies; when theists themselves, without prompting from the enemies of theism, find themselves troubled by the question whether an omnipotent and loving Creator would indeed allow the existence of evil.[7] It is the apologetic problem that is most closely connected with the argument from evil. The apologetic problem is, in fact, the problem of what to say in response to the argument from evil. It is, an any rate, that problem as it confronts those who, for one reason or another, regard themselves as responsible for the defense of theism or of Christianity or of some other theistic religion. The ordinary believer, the Christian on the Clapham omnibus, who is asked how he can continue to believe in God in the face of all the evils of the world, may well be content to say something like, "Well, what to say about things like that is a question for the experts. I just have to assume that there's some good reason for all the evils of the world and that no doubt we'll all understand some day". But, of course, even if this response is allowable on the Clapham omnibus, it's not one that can be made in the St Andrews lecture-room.

The construction of a theodicy is not demanded of a philosopher or theologian who is concerned with apologetic problems. If apologists for theism or for some theistic religion think they know what the real truth about the existence of evil is, they may of course appeal to this supposed truth in their attempts to expose what they regard as the weaknesses of the argument from evil. But apologists need not believe that they know, or that any human being knows, the real truth about God and evil. The apologist is, after all, in a position analogous to that of a counsel for the defense who is trying to create "reasonable doubt" as regards the defendant's guilt in the minds of jurors. (The apologist is trying to create reasonable doubt about whether the argument from evil is sound.) And lawyers can raise reasonable doubts by presenting to juries stories that entail their clients' innocence and account for the prosecution's evidence without maintaining, without claiming themselves to believe, that those stories are true.[8]

Typically, apologists dealing with the argument from evil present what are called "defenses". A defense is not necessarily different from a theodicy in content. Indeed, a defense and a theodicy may well be verbally identical. Each is, formally speaking, a story according to which both God and evil exist. The difference between a defense and a theodicy lies not in their content but in their purposes. A theodicy is a story that is told as the real truth of the matter; a defense is a story that, according to the teller, may or may not be true, but which, the teller maintains, has some desirable feature that does not entail truth—perhaps (depending on the context) logical consistency or epistemic possibility (truth-for-all-anyone-knows).

Defenses in this sense are common enough in courts of law, historical writing, and science. Here is a scientific example. Someone alleges that the human eye is too complex to have been a product of the interplay of random mutation and natural selection. Professor Hawkins, an apologist for the Darwinian theory of evolution, tells a story according to which the human eye, or the eyes of the remote ancestors of human beings, did come about as a result of the combined operation of these two factors. She hopes her audience will react to her story by saying something like, "That sounds like it would work. The eye might well have precisely the evolutionary history related in Hawkins's story." Hawkins does not present her story as an account of the actual course of evolution, and she does not take it to constitute a proof that the human eye *is* a product of the interplay of random mutation and natural selection. Her story is intended simply to refute an argument for the falsity of the Darwinian theory of evolution: to wit, the argument that the Darwinian theory is false because it is inconsistent with an observed fact, the existence of the human eye.

If the apologetic problem is the problem of what response to make to the argument from evil, there is not really just one apologetic problem, owing to the fact that there is not really just one argument from evil. And, of course, different arguments for the same conclusion may call for different responses. Let us look at the different forms that an argument from evil might take.

Many philosophers distinguish between the "logical" argument from evil (on the one hand) and the "evidential" or "inductive" or "epistemic" or "probabilistic" argument from evil (on the other). The former attempts to show that the existence of evil is logically inconsistent with the existence of God. The latter attempts to show that the existence of evil is strong, even compelling, evidence for the non-existence of God, or that anyone who is aware of the existence of evil should assign a very low probability to the existence of God. But this is not a distinction I find useful—I mean the distinction between logical and evidential versions of the argument from evil—and I am not going to bother with it. A much more important distinction, to my mind, is the distinction between what I shall call the *global* argument from evil and various *local* arguments from evil. The premise of the global argument from evil is that the world contains evil, or perhaps that the world contains a vast amount of truly horrible evil. Its other premise is (or its other premises jointly entail) that a benevolent and all-powerful God would not allow the existence of evil—or a vast amount of truly horrible evil. Local arguments from evil are arguments that appeal to *particular* evils—the Holocaust maybe, or the death of a fawn, unobserved by any human being, in a forest fire—and proceed by contending that a benevolent and omnipotent God would not have allowed that particular evil to occur. In my view, local arguments from evil are not simply presentations of the global argument from evil that make use of a certain rhetorical device (that is, the use of a particular case to make a general point); they are sufficiently different from the global argument that even if one had an effective reply to the global argument, one would not necessarily—one would not *thereby*—have an effective reply to just any local argument from evil. The problem of how to reply to local arguments from evil is therefore at least potentially distinct from the problem of how to reply to the global argument from evil. And this is the case (I contend) even if there really is something that can be called *the* problem of how to reply to local arguments from evil. It is not immediately evident that there is any such problem, for, even if there is a God and, for every particular evil, God has a good reason for allowing that evil to exist, it does not follow that there is some general formula that would yield, for each particular evil, the reason why God permits the existence of that evil when the essential features of that evil are plugged into the general formula. But suppose there is such a formula. My present point is that even if such a formula exists, an explanation, a *correct* explanation, of the fact that God permits the existence of a vast amount of truly horrible evil, could not be expected to yield a statement of that formula—or any conclusion concerning any particular evil. One might, I contend, know or think one knew why God allowed the existence of vast amounts of evil in the world he had created and have no idea at all why he permitted the Holocaust—or any other particular evil. The following is to my mind a logically consistent position: the fact that there is a vast amount of truly horrible evil does not show that there is no God, but the Holocaust does show that there is no God and would have sufficed to show this even if there were no other evils. My point is a logical one and does not depend on the perhaps unique enormity of the Holocaust. I would make the same point in relation to "Rowe's fawn", the fawn that dies a horrible and prolonged death in a forest fire and whose fate never impinges on any human consciousness: even if God has a perfectly good reason for permitting the existence of a vast amount of truly horrible evil, it does not follow that he has or could have a good reason for permitting that particular fawn to suffer the way it did. In these lectures, therefore, I will regard the global argument from evil, on the one hand, and the many and various local arguments from evil, on the other, as presenting intellectual challenges to belief in God that must be considered separately.

Other distinctions could be made as regards arguments from evil. There is, for example, the well-known distinction between "moral evil" and "physical" or "natural" evil, which are commonly supposed to present distinct challenges to the defender of theism. There is the problem of animal suffering (that is, the problem of the sufferings of non-human animals) which is commonly regarded as a different problem from the problem of human suffering. I will address these and other distinctions at various points in these lectures. My purpose in these remarks has been to display some of the many different things that might be meant by "the argument from evil", and to underscore the fact (I say it is a fact) that they are indeed different things. Having said these things, having said that there are many arguments from evil and, in consequence, many apologetic problems of evil, I serve notice that I'm very often going to ignore what I have said and, with no better excuse than a desire to keep the structure of my sentences simple, speak of "the argument from evil" and "the problem of evil". When I do this, what I say could always be easily enough revised to accommodate my official position. My primary focus in these lectures will be on what I have called the apologetic problem. I am going to attempt to evaluate the argument from evil and to present my reasons for considering this argument a failure (in a sense of failure I shall explain in due course).[9] What, then, is the relationship of my discussion of the apologetic problem to the problem of evil in its other forms—to personal problems of evil, or pastoral problems of evil? The answer is that the many problems of evil, for all they are distinct, do form a family and are intimately related to one another. (They are, I would say, separable into categories like those I have proposed only by a severe act of intellectual abstraction. In practice, in concrete cases, they run into one another; they so to speak raise one another.) It is, fortunately, true that anything of value that is said in response to any of these problems is very likely to have implications, and by no means trivial ones, for what can be said in response to the others. I therefore contend that what I shall say on the question as to whether the evils of the world provide any sort of cogent argument for the non-existence of God will have ramifications for what I, or someone else who accepts what I say, should say in response to other problems that evil raises for believers.

I will not attempt to say any of these other things myself. For one thing, I am, by my nature, the wrong person to say them. If a grieving mother whose child had just died of leukemia were to say to me, "How could God do this?", my first inclination would be to answer her by saying, "But you already knew that the children of lots of other mothers have died of leukemia. You were willing to say that he must have had some good reason in those cases. Surely you see that it's just irrational to have a different response when it's your own child who dies of leukemia?" Now I see as clearly as you do that this would be an abysmally stupid and cruel thing to say, and even I wouldn't in fact say it. I should, however, have to bite back an impulse to say it, and that's why I'm the wrong person to respond to that question under those circumstances. And if what I'd be inclined to say would be a stupid and cruel thing to say in the circumstances I've imagined, it would be equally stupid and cruel to respond to the mother's question with some sort of just-so story about why a loving and all-powerful God might allow such things to happen, even given that this just-so story would, in another context, constitute a brilliant refutation of the argument from evil.[10] Nevertheless, or so I think, there is an important connection between theoretical discussions of the argument from evil and the real sorrows, the real despair, that attend life in this world. Perhaps an example will show something about why this is so.

One component of the just-so story which will be the core of my reply to the argument from evil is this: Many of the horrible things that happen in the course of human life have no explanation whatever; they just happen, and, apart from considerations of efficient causation, there is no answer to the question why they happen; they are not a part of God's plan for the world; they have no meaning. I have published a version of this just-so story,[11] and I have had the following response from a clergyman, Dr Stephen Bilynskyj (I quote, with his permission, a part of a letter he sent me after he had read what I had written):

As a pastor, I believe that some sort of view of providence which allows for genuine chance is essential in counseling those facing what I often call the "practical problem of evil". A grieving person needs to be able to trust in God's direction in her life and the world, without having to make God directly responsible for every event that occurs. The message of the Gospel is not, I believe, that everything that occurs has some purpose. Rather, it is that God's power is able to use and transform any event through the grace of Jesus Christ. Thus a person may cease a fruitless search for reasons for what happens, and seek the strength that God offers to live with what happens. Such an approach is very different from simply assuming, fideistically, that there must be reasons for every event, but we are incapable of knowing them.[12]

The relevance of a theoretical discussion of the argument from evil to a pastoral problem of evil is, or can be, this: it may provide materials the pastor can make use of. It is asking too much, it is asking the wrong thing entirely, of a philosopher's or theologian's response to the argument from evil, to ask that it be suitable reading for a mother who has lost a child. But if one cannot ask, one can at any rate hope, that it will be suitable reading for a pastor whose duty it is to minister to people in situations like hers. And that hope, in my experience, can sometimes be fulfilled.

I will not, in these lectures, try to say anything to bring that hope to fulfillment. It is not, in my view, advisable to try to do that sort of thing. If I were to try to say something that could be "immediately" useful to ordinary believers to whom some terrible thing had happened or to the pastors who ministered to them, I should almost certainly fall between two stools: I should neither give the argument from evil its intellectual due nor say anything that would be of any aid to the grieving Christian. The task I propose for myself is a purely intellectual one. I am going to do the only thing having to do with the problem of evil that I am not manifestly unqualified to do. I am going to try to show that the argument from evil is a failure.

I now turn to the topic of evil. I have said that in the phrases 'the problem of evil' and 'the argument from evil', the word 'evil' means simply 'bad things'. And this is correct. That is what the word does mean in those phrases. But why *that* word? Does the word 'evil' not suggest a much narrower idea? (Consider the familiar phrases 'the evil empire' and 'the axis of evil'.) Does the word not bring to mind Sauron and his minions or at any rate Heinrich Himmler and Pol Pot? Mr Gore Vidal has gone so far as to suggest that the idea that there *is* such a thing as evil is a Christian invention, that evil is, like sin, an illusory bugbear that the Church has foisted on a credulous humanity. Whatever plausibility his thesis may have in a world that has just got through the twentieth century, it was, surely, not Vidal's intention to suggest that the idea that bad things happen was an invention of St Paul and the Fathers of the Church. It is evident that one meaning of 'evil' is something like 'the extreme reaches of moral depravity', especially those parts of the extreme reaches of moral depravity that feature delight in systematic cruelty and depraved indifference to the suffering consequent on one's acts. In this sense of the word 'evil', it is reserved for things like the death camps, a government's decision to develop a weapons-grade strain of the Ebola virus, or the production of child snuff-porn. The word is certainly to be understood in this sense in Hannah Arendt's well-known phrases "radical evil" and "the banality of evil".

That the word 'evil' has that meaning is clear, but any dictionary of quotations bears witness to another meaning of the word: "a necessary evil", "the lesser of two evils", "the evil men do", "sufficient unto the day is the evil thereof". That is to say, the meaning that 'evil' has in the phrase 'the problem of evil' is one of its ordinary meanings. "An evil" in this sense of the word is "a bad thing", and the mass term bears the same simple, compositional relation to the count-noun that 'fruit' and 'fire' bear to 'a fruit' and 'a fire'. 'The problem of evil' means no more than this: 'the problem that the real existence of bad things raises for theists'.

That the problem of evil is just exactly the problem that the real existence of bad things raises for theists is a simple enough point. But it has been neglected or denied by various people. The late J. L. Mackie, in his classic presentation of the argument from evil, mentioned one rather simple-minded instance of this:

The problem of evil, in the sense in which I shall be using the phrase, is a problem only for someone who believes that there is a God who is both omnipotent and wholly good. . . . [This point is] obvious; I mention [it] only because [it is] sometimes ignored by theologians, who sometimes parry a statement of the problem [by saying] "Well, can you solve the problem yourself?"[13]

If what Mackie says is true, there are, or once were, theologians who accept (or have accepted) the following thesis:

There is a certain philosophical or theological problem, the problem of evil, that confronts theists and atheists alike. When theists confront the problem, they confront it in this form: How can evil exist if God is good? But the very same problem confronts atheists, albeit in another form.

These theologians, whoever they may be, are certainly confused. The "general" problem they appeal to simply does not exist. For what could it be? It could not be the problem of accounting for the existence of evil. For an atheist, the question "Why do bad things happen?" is so easy to answer that it does not deserve to be called a problem. And there is this point: even if atheists *were* at a loss to explain the existence of bad things, it's hard to see why this inability should embarrass them qua atheists, for the existence of bad things has never been supposed by anyone to be incompatible with atheism. No atheist has a good account of why the expansion of the universe is speeding up, but that's not a fact that should embarrass an atheist qua atheist, since no one supposes that the speeding up of the expansion of the universe is incompatible with atheism. The theist's position with respect to explaining the existence of evil is not at all like that, for many people think that the existence of bad things is incompatible with theism, and there is a well-known argument, an argument that theists themselves say must be answered, for that conclusion.

One source of the confusion exhibited by Mackie's theologians is no doubt the ambiguity of the word 'evil', which, as we have seen, has at least two meanings: 'bad things' and 'the extreme reaches of moral depravity'. Let me use Arendt's term "radical evil" to express the latter meaning unambiguously. It may well be that there is a problem of some sort—philosophical, theological, psychological, anthropological—concerning radical evil, and that this problem faces both theists and atheists. Suppose we distinguish radical evil and "ordinary" evil. (Ordinary evil comprises such diverse items as a twisted ankle, the Lisbon earthquake, and Tamerlane's building a hill of his enemies' skulls.) It may be that although atheists have no trouble accounting for the existence of ordinary evil, they cannot easily account for the existence of radical evil. Since I am saying "it may be", since I have done no more than concede this point for the sake of the argument, I need defend neither the thesis that the distinction between radical evil and ordinary evil is real and important nor the thesis that the existence of radical evil (unlike the existence of ordinary evil) poses some sort of problem for atheists.[14] There may well be people who say that there is no important moral distinction to be drawn between the Holocaust and, say, the Roman obliteration of Carthage following the Third Punic War. And there may well be people who say that, although there is indeed a qualitative moral difference between the two events, atheists can nevertheless as easily account for the existence of the one as the other. I am simply examining, hypothetically, the consequences of supposing, first, that the distinction can be made and is important, and, secondly, that accounting for the existence of radical evil presents atheists with a prima facie difficulty. If these two suppositions are right, a certain problem about evil, the problem of accounting for the existence of radical evil, confronts both the theist and the atheist. My point is this: If there is indeed a "problem of radical evil", it has little to do with the problem of evil. Not nothing, maybe, but not a great deal either.[15] There is, nevertheless, an obvious terminological connection between the two problems. One of the meanings of the word 'evil' is 'radical evil'—and this meaning is not merely *one* of its meanings; it has been the word's primary meaning for several centuries. If the phrase 'the problem of evil' weren't already a name for a certain ancient philosophical or theological problem about a benevolent and omnipotent Creator and a creation that contains an ample supply of very bad things, it would be an excellent name for a problem we must today, on pain of elementary confusion, call by some other name—such as 'the problem of radical evil'. I find it plausible to suppose that the ambiguity of the word 'evil' has something to do with the confused belief of Mackie's theologians that something called "the problem of evil" confronts both theists and atheists.

I have called Mackie's theologians 'simple-minded'. I called them that because I judged that their confusion was a verbal confusion and that they had fallen into it because they were not thinking clearly or not thinking at all. But they are not alone in their belief that there is an overarching problem of evil. (I will say that people who accept the thesis that there is a problem properly called 'the problem of evil' that confronts both theists and atheists believe in an "overarching problem of evil".) They have been joined by the philosopher Susan Neiman, who has defended this view in her book *Evil in Modern Thought*. (Neiman thinks of what she does as philosophy. I'd prefer to call it European intellectual history. But then I have a very narrow conception of philosophy.) In my view, Neiman is, like Mackie's theologians, confused. But I would by no means describe her confusion as 'simple-minded'. My preferred description would be 'too clever by half'. Neiman has not confused a problem that essentially involves God with some other problem that has no essential connection with God. Her view is, rather, that the late eighteenth-century theists who strove to reconcile the goodness of God with the occurrence of the Lisbon earthquake and the recent, mostly European, philosophers who see the Holocaust and other twentieth-century horrors as posing a fundamental philosophical problem are confronting the same problem, although, because of their vastly different historical situations, it assumes very different forms for these two groups of thinkers. (My reference to these two groups of thinkers should not be taken to imply that Neiman thinks that they and no other writers have confronted what she calls the problem of evil. Understanding the responses of various philosophers to the overarching problem of evil, she believes, is a key that opens a doorway through which the whole history of modern philosophy can be viewed from a novel perspective.) Her belief in an overarching problem of evil leads her to make remarks like this one:

Contemporary analytic discussion of the problem of evil... remains squarely confined to the marginalized field of the philosophy of religion. Thus historical discussion, where it does occur, is focused largely on Leibniz and Hume, whose treatment of the problem of evil remained within traditional religious discourse. (p. 290)

But what is the overarching problem of evil that Hume and Leibniz and Nietzsche and Levinas confront (each from within his own historical perspective)? I do not find her attempts to state and explain this problem easy to understand, but the idea is something like this (the words are mine):

Evil threatens meaning. Evil threatens our ability to regard the world in which we find ourselves as comprehensible. The Lisbon earthquake presented late eighteenth-century Christians with an intractable problem regarding the meaning of existence, and the death camps have had a comparable or analogous effect on post-religious thinkers. The problem of evil is the problem of how to find meaning in a world in which everything is touched by evil.

I will say nothing of Neiman's larger project, her project of studying various responses to "the problem of evil" with a view to providing a new understanding of the history of modern philosophy. I will speak only of her thesis that there is an overarching problem of evil. Her arguments for this conclusion strike me, if I may risk repeating the phrase, as too clever by half. In my view, they are no more than an illustration of the fact that one will generally find that any two things have common features if one ascends to a high enough level of abstraction.[16] (As David Berlinski once said, commenting on another application of this method, "Yes, and what a man does when he jumps over a ditch and what Canada geese do when they migrate are very much the same thing. In each case, an organism's feet leave the earth, it moves through the air for a certain distance, and, finally, its feet once more make contact with the earth."[17])

I am only a simple-minded analytical philosopher. (Not, I hope, as simple-minded as Mackie's theologians, but simple-minded enough.) As I see matters, the problem of evil is what it has always been, a problem about God and evil. There is no larger, overarching problem of evil that manifests itself as a theological problem in one historical period and as a problem belonging to post-religious thought in another.[18] I don't know how to argue for this conclusion, because I wouldn't know how enter into anything I would call an argument with someone who would even consider denying it. It is evident to me that any person who would say the sorts of things Neiman says has so different a mind from mine that if that person and I attempted, each with the best will in the world, to initiate a conversation about whether there was an overarching problem of evil, the only result would be two people talking past each other. What I call 'the problem of evil' essentially involves God, and any problem that someone else calls the 'problem of evil' is, if it does not involve God, so remote from "my" problem that the two problems can have very little in common. (Not nothing, maybe, but very little.) If you insist on my saying something in defense of this thesis, I could quote some words that Newman used in a rather different connection: my thesis is true "for the plain reason that one idea is not another idea".

Or, to quote another cleric, "Everything is what it is, and not another thing."[19] It has been said that the greatest benefit Oxford confers on her sons and daughters is that they are not afraid of the obvious. I seem to enjoy the benefit without the bother of the degree. It is just *obvious* that Neiman's attempt to identify an overarching problem of evil that is confronted in one way by Leibniz's *Theodicy* and in another by *Jenseits von Gut und Böse* fails, and must fail, because there is no such problem.[20]

The problem of evil is a problem about God and about the evils, both ordinary and radical, that are such a salient feature of, as I believe, the world he has made. In these lectures I will discuss this problem. In the next lecture, I will discuss this God whose non-existence the argument from evil is supposed to prove.

Lecture 2

The Idea of God

I said that in this lecture I would "discuss this God whose non-existence the argument from evil is supposed to prove". My purpose in this lecture is to say what a being would have to be like to be God, to count as God, to have the attributes, qualities, properties, characteristics, or features that are the components of the concept of God. But can this be done in any principled way? Do people who say they believe in God not disagree about his attributes? Who's to say what features God is supposed to have? I will respond to these questions with a proposal, a proposal I do not think is arbitrary. It is this: the list of properties that should be included in the concept of God are just those properties ascribed to God in common by Jews, Christians, and Muslims—the properties that adherents of these religions would all agree belong to God.[1]

Having said this, I now qualify it. If we obtain a list of properties by the method I have proposed, the list will contain some properties that are thought to belong to God only contingently or accidentally: the property of having spoken to Abraham, for example. Let us therefore restrict our list to properties that Jews, Christians, and Muslims will agree would have been properties of God no matter what—that belong to God independently of the contingencies of history, independently, indeed, of whether there is such a thing as history, independently of the existence of a created world, independently of any contingent matter of fact. Thus our list of properties, the defining properties of the concept of God, will be a list of his essential properties—although, of course, it is not meant to be a *complete* list of his essential properties.

Now a further qualification. By "Jews, Christians, and Muslims", I mean those Jews, Christians, and Muslims who have attained to a high level of philosophical and theological reflection; for some of the properties in the list I shall propose will be ones that most ordinary believers will not have so much as heard of. (I do not take seriously the idea that "the God of the philosophers", the bearer of the attributes in my list, is not the God of the Bible or the God of the ordinary believer. This idea is no more plausible than the idea—Eddington's—that "the table of the physicists" is not the table of the home-furnishings catalogue or the table of the ordinary householder.)

And I think I must add one more qualification: by 'Jews, Christians, and Muslims', I mean 'Jews, Christians, and Muslims who lived before the twentieth century'. If you are puzzled by this qualification, I invite you to examine two quotations from the writings of a theologian of considerable reputation, the sometime occupant of a chair of theology in the Divinity School of a great university. As a matter of deliberate policy, I will not identify him. I assure you, however, that he is real and that the quotations are exact:

To regard God as some kind of describable or knowable object over against us would be at once a degradation of God and a serious category error.

It is a mistake, therefore, to regard qualities attributed to God (e.g., aseity, holiness, omnipotence, omniscience, providence, love, self-revelation) as though they were features of . . . a particular being.

These words mean almost nothing. Insofar as they mean anything, they mean 'There is no God'.[2] It is precisely because a significant proportion of the theologians of the last 100 years would not have agreed with this judgment that I exclude any reference to them from my criterion. I therefore propose that we find the properties to be included in our definition of God by asking what properties Jewish, Christian, and Muslim philosophers and theologians in the year 1900 or earlier would have agreed were essential properties of God. (This, at any rate, was my first inclination. But Richard Swinburne has pointed out to me that theologians said some pretty odd things about God in the nineteenth century, too, and on reflection I had to agree with him. Maybe we should push the date back to 1800, just to be on the safe side. And I suppose I should apologize to the Muslims for including them, quite unnecessarily really, in my historical adjustment. There are serious charges that can justly be brought against some twentieth-century Muslim theology, but the charge of proposing a meaning for the word 'God' that enables atheists who occupy chairs of theology to talk as if they were theists is not one of them.)

I shall first present the list that I contend can be so derived and discuss each item in it individually. Then I shall make some remarks about the list as a whole. These remarks will address two questions: first, is the list just a "laundry list", a jumble of historical accidents, or is there some unifying principle that accounts for the fact that the list contains the particular items it does and no others?; secondly, to what degree, if any, is the list (and the accounts I shall give of each of its members) as we might say open to negotiation? The list that can be obtained by the method I propose is a rich one. In my view, it contains the following properties. God is, first,

—a person.

By a person, I mean a being who may be, in the most straightforward and literal sense, *addressed*—a being whom one may call 'thou'. (Of course a non-person like a flower in the crannied wall or an urn or a city may be addressed in a non-straightforward and non-literal sense. When we do that, we call it personification.) In saying this, I do not mean to be offering an analysis of the concept of a person—whatever exactly 'analysis' may mean. I mean only to fix the concept of a person, to make it plain which of our available concepts I am using the word to express, rather as one might say: By 'knowledge' I shall mean propositional knowledge rather than knowledge by acquaintance; and *not* as one might say, By 'knowledge' I shall mean undefeated justified true belief. If I were to venture a guess as to how the concept of a person should be analyzed, I should say something very lengthy that would like start this: a person is a conscious being having beliefs and desires and values, capable of abstract thought . . . and so on. But I should regard any such analysis of 'person' as provisional, as liable to require revision in just the way 'Knowledge is justified true belief' turned out to require revision. Nothing in this lecture or the remaining lectures in this series is going to turn on any particular analysis of personhood. I include this attribute in my list (and it is really redundant, for most of the attributes in the list could belong only to a person) simply to make it plain that I regard it as part of the concept of God—as do all Jews, Christians, and Muslims—that he cannot possibly be thought of as *im*personal, like Brahman or the Tao or the Absolute Idea or the Dialectic of History or, to descend to a rather more popular level, the Force.

Some of my theologically sophisticated colleagues in the Notre Dame Philosophy Department regard the idea that God is a person as rather crude, as perhaps even wrong. And I'm not talking about disguised atheists, like the theologian I quoted a moment ago—I'm talking about pious, perfectly orthodox Thomists (or at least people with a pretty high blood-Thomism level). But I've never been able to understand why.

They themselves address God daily in prayer, so they must consider him a person in my sense. I suspect that they bear allegiance to some analysis of personhood that I would reject.

Someone may want to ask me how I can consider God a person when, as a Christian, I'm bound to agree that "there is one Person of the Father, another of the Son, and another of the Holy Ghost". Sophisticated theologians will smile when they hear this question, and tell the questioner that 'Person' is a technical term in Trinitarian theology and does not mean what it means in everyday life; they will go on to say that it's doubtless in the everyday sense of the word that van Inwagen is saying that God is a person—not that they will approve of my applying to God everyday terms that apply to human beings, but they will offer me this escape from straightforward contradiction. I won't take the proposed escape route, though. In my view, 'Person' in Trinitarian theology means just exactly what I mean by it—a being who can be addressed, a 'Thou'—and it is they who are confused. As to the "one God, three Persons" question—ah, well, that is, as they say, beyond the scope of these lectures.[3]

Before leaving the topic of the personhood of God, I should say a word about sex—not sex as the vulgar use the word, not sexual intercourse, but sexual dimorphism—what people are increasingly of late, and to my extreme annoyance, coming to call 'gender'. We haven't yet officially said this, but, as everyone knows, God does not occupy space, so he can't have a physical structure; but to have a sex, to be male or female, is, among other things, to have a physical structure. God, therefore, does not have a sex. It is literally false that he is male, and literally false that he is female. My point in raising the issue is simply to address this question: What about this pronoun 'he' that I've been using? This problem is raised not by any feature of God's nature, but by the English language, in which the only third-person-singular pronouns are 'he', 'she', and 'it'. We cannot call God 'it', for that pronoun is reserved for non-persons—like the Dialectic of History or the Force. It would be nice if English had a sex-neutral third-person-singular pronoun that applied to persons, but it doesn't. (Many languages do.) English does have sex-neutral pronouns that apply to persons—'they', for example—and in fact has a good many sex-neutral pronouns that apply *only* to persons, such as 'one' and 'someone' and 'who', but it lacks third-person-singular pronouns having these desirable features. (Some of our more enlightened contemporaries have proposed a system of "divine pronouns", but I can't quite bring myself to say things like,

"God was in Christ reconciling the world unto Godself".) The only real possibilities are to call God 'he' or 'she', and both pronouns raise serious problems. Calling God 'he', when all is said and done, really does carry the implication that God is male. This is both false and reinforces historical prejudices. Calling God 'she', of course, carries the implication that God is female. This implication does not reinforce historical prejudices, but (besides being false) it raises *this* difficulty: the masculine gender is a kind of default setting in the machinery of English grammar—I believe that you express this idea in linguistics-speak by saying 'In English, "masculine" is a marked gender', but I may have got 'marked' backwards. However you say it, the reality is this: when you're speaking English, use of the feminine gender in cases in which there's no basis for it in the nature of the thing you're talking about always calls attention to itself, and use of the masculine gender sometimes does not, not if the thing is a person. English is thus an inherently sexist language, but, unfortunately, that fact can't be changed by fiat or good intentions or an act of will. Well, not all problems have solutions. I'm going to call God 'he', but if someone else wants to call him 'she', I don't mind.

Let this suffice for an account of the attribute "person". I now turn to some more familiar items in the list of the defining properties of God. The first is familiar indeed. God is

—omnipotent (or all-powerful or almighty).

This notion is often explained by saying that an omnipotent being can do anything that is logically possible. I have two unrelated difficulties with this definition. The first is controversial; perhaps I alone find it a difficulty, but I can't ignore it on that ground. It is this. I don't understand the idea of logical possibility. I understand (and believe in) ground-floor or absolute or metaphysical possibility, but, as far as I can see, to say that a thing is logically possible is to say something with no meaning. I don't deny that the concept of logical *impossibility* is meaningful: something is logically impossible if it is impossible *simpliciter*, absolutely or metaphysically impossible, and if its impossibility can be demonstrated using only the resources of logic. But what is logical *possibility?* It would *seem* that a thing is supposed to be logically possible if it is not logically impossible. But this is very puzzling. Why should the fact that a thing can't be shown to be impossible using only the very limited resources that logic provides show that it is in any sense *possible?* A strictly Euclidean procedure for trisecting the angle is impossible. It is as impossible as a thing can be. In no possible world does such a procedure exist. But logic alone does not suffice to establish its impossibility, and, if the logically possible comprises everything that is not logically impossible, it is therefore "logically possible". That is to say, logical possibility is not a species of possibility. I must not spend any more time on this hobby horse of mine.[4] Suppose it is granted that my scruples in the matter of logical possibility are well-founded. Might we not accommodate them simply by saying that omnipotence is the power to do anything that is *metaphysically* possible? We might indeed. But if we did, we should still face the second of the two difficulties I mentioned, and that difficulty is not at all controversial. It is this: most theists contend that there are metaphysically possible acts that God is unable to perform. Two well-known examples are lying and promise breaking. Unlike trisecting the angle, lying and promise breaking are certainly metaphysically possible things. (I don't know about you, but I've actually seen them done.) But, it's commonly said, God is unable to do either of these things because, although *someone's* doing them is metaphysically possible, *his* doing them is metaphysically impossible. Let's suppose that the philosophers and theologians who say that it is metaphysically impossible for God to lie and to break his promises are right. Does it follow from their thesis that God is not omnipotent? According to the proposed definition, yes. But the way the case has been described immediately suggests another definition, a definition one frequently sees in works of philosophical theology, a definition designed to meet exactly the difficulty we have been considering: to say that God is omnipotent means that he can do anything such that *his doing that thing* is metaphysically possible.

This definition meets the two difficulties I have mentioned, but it has problems of its own. The most important of them is this: it doesn't tell us what God can do. Another way to put essentially the same point would be to say that, at least as far as any human being is able to judge, there might be two beings each of which was able to do everything it was metaphysically possible for *it* to do and which were yet such that one of them was vastly more powerful than the other. Suppose, for example, that God exists, that he is able to do everything that it is metaphysically possible for him to do, and that among the things that it is metaphysically possible for him to do is to create things *ex nihilo*. Suppose further that God creates a being, Demiourgos, who, although he is very powerful by human standards, is unable to do many of the things God can do. He is, for example, unable to create things *ex nihilo*.

And Demiourgos is *essentially* incapable of *creatio ex nihilo*: even God couldn't confer that power on him, for, of metaphysical necessity, Demiourgos lacks the power to create things from nothing. And so it is for every power that Demiourgos lacks: he lacks it of metaphysical necessity. (In this he is unlike us human beings: all of us have inabilities that are metaphysical accidents. For example, although I am unable to play the oboe, I'd be able to play the oboe if the course of my life had been different; almost everyone is unable to speak Navaho, but no one is *essentially* unable to speak Navaho; every blind man is sighted in other possible worlds.) But then, if to be omnipotent is to be able to do anything it is metaphysically possible for *one* to do, Demiourgos is omnipotent. Now that seems an odd result when you compare Demiourgos with God, who is able to do so much more than he. And it demonstrates—you'll see this if you think about the question for a moment—that the proposed definition of omnipotence doesn't tell us what an omnipotent being is able to do.[5] This is an important point to keep in mind in a discussion of the argument from evil. Consider this imaginary exchange. A theist responds to the argument from evil by saying that, although the evils of the world grieve God deeply, he was from the foundation of the world unable to prevent, and is now unable to remove, any of the evils that are such a salient feature of that world. "But I thought God was supposed to be omnipotent." "Oh, he is. It is, you see, metaphysically impossible for him to create a world that doesn't contain bad things, and it's metaphysically impossible for him to interfere in any way in the workings of a world once he has created it. But he *is* able to do everything it is metaphysically possible for him to do—so, he's omnipotent."

It would be a very interesting project to try to provide a satisfactory definition of omnipotence. (In his essay "Omnipotence", Professor Geach has defended the conclusion that any such project must fail, and that Christians should give up trying to make philosophical sense of the notion of a God who can do everything. Christians, according to Geach, should rather say that God is almighty: that is, God is, of necessity, the only source of power in every being besides himself. Whatever the merits of this suggestion, I must point out that the statement "God is almighty", understood in Geach's way, tells us nothing about what God is able to do. A being who was able to create only pebbles, for example, could, if we set the case up carefully, be 'almighty' in Geach's sense. And so could a being who was unable to prevent, and is now unable to remove, the evils of the world.) I'm not going to attempt a definition of omnipotence. It is a difficult problem, and a useful discussion of it would lead us deep into the forbidding territory of technical metaphysics. I will suppose in these lectures that we have some sort of pre-analytic grasp of the notion of omnipotence, and I will justify employing this concept in the absence of an adequate definition of it by pointing out that not having at my disposal an adequate definition of omnipotence does not make my task, the task of trying to show that the argument from evil is a failure, any easier. It is, after all, philosophers who *employ* the argument from evil, and not their critics, who make assertions about what God is able to do or would be able to do if he existed. The *critics'* statements about God's abilities are always denials: the critics, insofar as they say anything about God's abilities, are always concerned to deny that God can do some of the things that various premises of the argument imply he can do. In my discussion of the argument from evil, I'll always simply accept any statement that starts 'God can ...' or 'God could have ...'—*unless* the thing God is said to be able to do implies a metaphysical impossibility. (After all—*pace Cartesii*—whatever 'omnipotent' may properly mean, the proposition that God cannot do X is consistent with the proposition that God is omnipotent if X is metaphysically impossible.) And, of course, I don't propose simply to assert that some act that God is alleged to be able to perform involves a metaphysical impossibility; I propose to present arguments for any such statement.

Aquinas, in the famous discussion of omnipotence that I quoted in note 5, says that "whatever implies a contradiction does not fall within the scope of divine omnipotence", and I have been more or less following his lead. (More or less, but closer to less than to more: the notion of metaphysical impossibility is richer than the notion "implies a contradiction".) There is, of course, another, stronger conception of omnipotence, whose most famous advocate is Descartes. According to this conception, God is able to do *anything*, including (Descartes tells us) creating two mountains that touch at their bases and have no valley between them.[6] I shall not discuss this "strong" conception of omnipotence, which seems to me to be pretty obviously incoherent—incoherent because ability (the concept that is expressed by sentences of the form '*x* is able to do *y*') is no more and no less than the power to choose among *possible* states of affairs, to determine which of various incompatible possible states of affairs are to be actual. But I will make a promise. Our interest in the attribute of omnipotence in these lectures has to do only with the role it plays in the argument from

evil. When we finally get round to discussing the argument from evil,
I shall show that the argument is not even faintly plausible if God is
omnipotent in the "strong", or "Cartesian", sense. (When we see *why*
this is the case, we shall probably regard the fact that the argument
from evil can be answered in this way if God is omnipotent in the
Cartesian sense as just one more absurd consequence of understanding
omnipotence in that sense.) I turn now to the next "divine attribute" in
our list. God is

—omniscient (all-knowing).

Here is the standard definition of omniscience: A being is omniscient
if and only if that being knows the truth-value of every proposition.
And here is a second definition, one I like rather better for a number
of reasons. A being is omniscient if, for every proposition, that being
believes either that proposition or its denial, and it is metaphysically
impossible for that being to have false beliefs.[7] The second definition
makes a stronger claim on behalf of an omniscient being than the first,
but it is a claim that theists would be willing to accept on God's behalf.[8]

The existence of an omniscient being raises a famous philosophical
problem: if there is an omniscient being, that being either knows that
when I am put to the test tomorrow I shall lie or knows that when I
am put to the test tomorrow I shall tell the truth. How, then, can I
have a free choice between lying and telling the truth? (Or, in terms of
the second definition: If there is an omniscient being, that being either
believes that when I am put to the test tomorrow I shall lie or believes
that when I am put to the test tomorrow I shall tell the truth; and it
is metaphysically impossible for this being to have false beliefs. How,
then, can I have a free choice between lying and telling the truth?)
I defer discussion of this problem to the fifth lecture, where it will
arise naturally. (It will arise in connection with the famous reply to the
argument from evil called the free-will defense—for whatever virtues or
defects the free-will defense may have, it obviously isn't going to work
if human beings do not have free will.)

In addition to being omnipotent and omniscient, God is said to be

—morally perfect (perfectly good).

That is to say, God has no moral defect whatever. It follows that he is in
no way a subject of possible moral criticism. If someone says something

of the form, 'God did *x* and it was wrong of God to do *x*', that person must be mistaken: either God did not in fact do *x*, or it was not wrong of God to do *x*. (Of course, because God is very different from human beings and stands in very different relations to created things from those human beings stand in, what would be a moral defect in, or a wrong act if performed by, a human being is not automatically a defect in, or a wrong act if performed by, God. Suppose, for example, that a human being inflicts pain on others—without consulting them—to produce what is, in his judgment, a greater good. Many of us would regard this as morally wrong, even if the person happens to be factually right about the long-term consequences of the pain he inflicts. Let us suppose that this moral judgment is correct. My point is that it does not *follow* from the correctness of this judgment that it would be wrong of *God* to inflict pain on human beings—or angels or beasts—without their consent to produce some greater good. That's as may be; such judgments need to be examined individually and with care, taking into account both the ways in which God is similar to human beings and the ways in which God is different from human beings.)

Next, God is

—**eternal.**

This attribute is very frequently mentioned in songs of praise and in liturgy; that God has this attribute seems to be emotionally very important to believers—probably because of our sorrow over the impermanence of human things. Here is a bit of Psalm 90 (churchgoers, besides, I hope, being familiar with the psalm itself, will know its metrical paraphrase by Isaac Watts, the hymn that starts "O God our help in ages past"):

[2]Before the mountains were brought forth, or ever the earth and the world were made, thou art God from everlasting, and world without end. ... [4]For a thousand years in thy sight are but as yesterday, seeing that is past as a watch in the night.

It is well known that theists have understood God's eternity in two ways: He has always existed and always will exist; he is outside time altogether. I shall briefly touch on these rival conceptions of eternity when we discuss free will and divine foreknowledge in connection with the free-will defense. A closely related attribute is this: God is

—immutable.

That is, his attributes and other important properties do not and cannot change—in the words of Watts's hymn he is "to endless years the same". Of course, if God is in time, and if he's aware of the changing world, as he must be, some of his properties, in the broadest sense of 'property', the "Cambridge" sense, are going to have to change with the passage of time: in 45 BC, he knew that Julius Caesar was alive, and in 43 BC he no longer had this property. But, to speak the language of metaphysics, his *intrinsic* or *non-relational* properties do not and cannot change with time: *we* get old and grey and become more (or less) wise; in middle age, our youthful idealism is replaced by cynicism, or our youthful improvidence gives way to prudence; we turn from belief to unbelief, or the other way round; nothing in God's nature corresponds to the mutability that characterizes human existence and the existence of all things present to the senses. (What about such texts as "And it repented God that he had made man"? Well, my topic is not biblical hermeneutics.)

One of the divine attributes is the spatial analogue of eternity: God is

—omnipresent.

To say that God is omnipresent is, obviously, to say that God is everywhere:

Am I a God at hand, saith the Lord, and not a God afar off?

Can any hide himself in secret places that I shall not see him? saith the LORD. Do I not fill heaven and earth? (Jer. 23: 23–4)

It was presumably texts like this one that prompted Haeckel's description of the Judeo-Christian God as a "gaseous vertebrate". There are some serious philosophical questions in the neighborhood of Haeckel's joke: In what manner does God "fill" heaven and earth—does he do this in the manner of an all-pervasive fluid, like the aether of nineteenth-century physics? In what sense is God "everywhere"? I will not address these important questions at this point. The attribute *omnipresence* will figure in our discussion of the question (at least this is how some have framed it), "Why does God hide himself from us?—Why is he a *Deus absconditus*?" It will suit my expository purposes better if we put off discussing omnipresence till we address this question in the final lecture.

Here I will remark only that whatever omnipresence may come to, it is obviously incompatible with God's having any sort of spatial or physical structure (and hence with his being either male or female).

And what is *our* relation to this omnipotent, omniscient, eternal, immutable, omnipresent being? He is, of course, our creator and we, like the heavens and everything else besides himself, are the work of his fingers:

In the beginning, God created the heaven and the earth. And the earth was without form, and void. And the Spirit of God moved upon the face of the waters. And God said, Let there be light: and there was light. (Gen. 1: 1–3)

For thus says the LORD, who created the heavens (he is God!), who formed the earth and made it (he established it; he did not create it a chaos, he formed it to be inhabited!) (Isa. 45: 18, RSV)

I believe in one God, the Father Almighty, maker of heaven and earth, and of all things visible and invisible. (The Nicene Creed, The Book of Common Prayer)

To say that God is the creator of all things besides himself is not to say that he formed them out of some pre-existent stuff, like the cosmic craftsman of the *Timaeus*. If there is a God, then there never was a chaos of prime matter that existed independently of his power and his will, waiting through an eternity of years for him to impress form on it. This could not be, for, if there is a God, nothing does or could exist independently of his will or independently of his creative power. God creates things from the ground up, ontologically speaking. His creation is, as they say, *ex nihilo*. And even he, in his omnipotence, is not capable of bringing a thing into existence and then leaving it entirely to its own devices, for a thing that exists, even for an instant, independently of God's creative power is as impossible as a gaseous vertebrate or an invisible object that casts a shadow. This fact—I mean this conceptual fact—is sometimes emphasized by saying that God is not only the creator of everything but the *sustainer* of everything as well; but this is only for emphasis, for *sustainer* is included in the meaning of *creator*—at least in theological contexts.

Having said this, we must face a minor logical problem created by our criterion for membership in the list of divine attributes; for we said, among other things, that an attribute was to be included in this list only if it was an *essential* attribute of God. And being a creator is, according to the Abrahamic religions, one of God's accidents: it is a property he lacks in certain perfectly good—but, fortunately for us, non-actual—possible worlds: those in which he never creates anything. Jews, Christians, and Muslims insist that whether God creates a world—that is, whether he creates *anything*—is a matter of his free choice. Nothing in his nature compels him to create. He is not, for example, compelled to create by his moral perfection, for it is not better that there should be created things than that there should be no created things. It could not be better, for all goods are already contained—full and perfect and complete—in God. (In the matter of his free will, he does not have a free choice between good and evil, as we imperfect beings do, but he does have a free choice between various alternative goods, and *there being created things* and *there being no created things* is one of the pairs of alternative goods between which he has a choice.) But if being a creator is an accidental property of God, then, by our criterion it cannot occur in the list of divine attributes. The solution to this problem is simply to say that the following is the relevant attribute: God is

—the creator of such things other than God as there may be.

God has this property vacuously, as philosophers say, in those possible worlds in which he exists and creates nothing, and non-vacuously in all other worlds in which he exists; but he has it in every world in which he exists, and it is therefore one of his essential properties.

I have just used the phrase 'in those possible worlds in which he exists'; but are there any possible worlds in which he does not exist? His possession of the next attribute in our list implies that there are none: God is

—necessary.

That is, he exists in all possible worlds; he would exist *no matter what*. Thirty or forty years ago, many philosophers denied that the concept of a necessary being made any sense. It is easy to refute them. Consider *me*. I might not have existed; I am, therefore, in the language of metaphysics, a contingent being. And, surely, if the concept of a contingent being makes sense, the concept of a non-contingent being makes sense. If a concept is intelligible, then the concept of a thing that does not fall under that concept is at least *prima facie* intelligible. (I say "at least *prima facie* intelligible", for Russell's Paradox threatens the general thesis. But Russellian scruples hardly seem relevant to the present case. The thesis 'If the concept of a contingent being is intelligible, the concept of a non-contingent being is intelligible' seems no more implausible than the thesis 'If the concept of a thinking being is intelligible, the concept of a non-thinking being is intelligible'.) Of course, from the fact that a concept makes sense, it does not follow that it is the concept of a possible thing, that it is metaphysically possible for anything to fall under it. The concept of a method for trisecting any angle using only a stylus, straightedge, and pair of compasses makes sense, but it is an impossible concept. It may well be that the concept of a necessary being is an impossible concept. The question whether this is so falls outside the scope of these lectures.[9] We should note that if God is, of conceptual necessity, a necessary being, then the old taunt, "But then who created God?", is conceptually defective; one might as well ask who created the natural numbers. (Kronecker's famous aphorism, according to which God created the natural numbers, cannot be regarded as a serious contribution to the metaphysics of creation.)

The final item in our list of divine attributes is this: God is

—unique (and *necessarily* so).

That is, he is the only being who possesses the properties in our list in any possible world. This is, as philosophers say, a modal statement *de re*, or, equivalently, a statement that involves "identity across possible worlds". But that's all right, I suppose. The concept of God (to put everything together) is the concept of a being who exists in every possible world, who has the attributes in our list in every possible world, and who is the only omnipotent, omniscient, eternal, immutable, omnipresent, necessary creator who exists in any possible world.

I suppose someone might object to my saying this on the ground that it is a gross anachronism for me to use the language of possible worlds to describe the attributes that have historically been ascribed to God in the Abrahamic religions. I dispute the charge. To speak in terms of possible worlds is—*I* say—simply to a use a slightly refined version of the modal idioms we use in everyday life; and this is what philosophers and theologians who use modal concepts like contingency and necessity and essence and accident have always done. I use a refinement of ordinary modal idiom that is not quite the refinement of ordinary modal idiom that, say, Duns Scotus used, but it is a refinement of the same idiom, and his way of talking and mine are intertranslatable because they grow from the same root and have in fact not grown very far away from each other. I do not deny that in saying this I say something controversial (it would certainly be controverted by one or two of my departmental colleagues at Notre Dame); my only purpose is to make it clear what my controversial reply to the charge of anachronism is. It would be beyond the scope of these lectures to defend it.

I now turn to two questions I promised an answer to at the beginning of this lecture. The first is this: Is there some principle or general idea that binds together the attributes in the list I have given? (Note, by the way, that it is, as I promised it would be, a very *rich* list.) Is the list—I asked rhetorically—just a "laundry list"? Is it anything more than a jumble of historical accidents? The answer is that it is not a mere jumble. It represents an attempt by many thinkers—not, I would suppose, for the most part a conscious attempt—to provide some specific content to the Anselmian notion of a greatest possible being, a something a greater than which cannot be conceived, *aliquid quo nihil maius cogitari possit.* If an argument for this thesis is wanted, I ask you simply to see whether you can think of some attribute that could be added to the list that would make a being who possessed the attributes in the expanded list greater than a being who possessed only the attributes in the original list. And I ask you to consider whether there is some attribute in the list that could be removed without diminishing the degree of greatness represented by the list. It seems obvious that a greatest possible being must be omnipotent—at least supposing omnipotence to be a possible property. A being who is capable of, say, creation *ex nihilo* is—all other things being equal—greater than a being whose powers do not extend to creation *ex nihilo.* A necessarily existent being, a being who would exist in every possible circumstance, is greater—all other things being equal—than a contingent being, a being who could fail to exist. And so on, it seems to me, for each of the attributes in the list. And what could be added to the list that would make for "greater greatness"? Nothing that I can see. In saying this, I do not mean to imply that our list contains all the properties of God that are relevant to the degree of greatness he enjoys. No doubt there are "great-making" properties of God that no human being—perhaps no angel, perhaps no *possible* created being—could form the dimmest conception of. I do claim that the list can plausibly be said to contain all the great-making properties that human beings can form a conception of. My definition of 'God', like any definition, does not claim to be a list of all the important properties, even all the important *essential* properties, of a thing that falls under the concept whose content it exhibits. If I define a 'cat' as a small, lithe, furry quadruped of the genus *Felis*, I do not pretend that my definition is an enumeration of all the essential properties of cats; and if I did, I should obviously be wrong, since, for example, every cat has essentially the property of having a carbon-based body chemistry, and my definition says nothing about that.

The second question is this: To what extent is the list at all "flexible"? To what extent can someone who calls himself a theist modify the list (or modify the definitions and explanations I have given of the items in the list) and still *rightly* call himself a theist? I think there is some flexibility in what I have said, but not much, and that the line between "having a different conception of God from the one expressed by the list" and "using the name 'God' for a being who is not properly so-called" can be drawn in a principled way. Let me give examples of proposed alterations to the list of divine attributes—ones that have been actually proposed, although I name no names so as not to have to take responsibility for getting a particular author right when my only interest is in finding cases that illustrate a point—that fall on both sides of the line.

(1) The property of existing necessarily is an impossible property. Therefore, we should, in Whitehead's words, be paying God an ill-judged metaphysical compliment if we ascribed it to him. Let us replace 'exists necessarily' with 'exists *a se*'. A being exists necessarily just in the case that it exists in all possible worlds—and a necessary being is therefore impossible, for, as Hume pointed out, we can easily conceive of there being nothing. The reality of a being whose existence is *a se*, however, is consistent with the possibility of there being nothing at all.

(2) If God is omnipotent, the problem of evil is intractable. Let us therefore understand God's powers as being severely limited.

In my view, the theist who proposes the first of these alterations does succeed in saying that God does not, as others have supposed, exist necessarily. I think he's wrong—for I don't think that necessary existence is impossible—but I don't think that what he's saying is conceptually defective. It is otherwise with the second case. In the words of J. L. Austin's inarticulate judge, the man isn't on the thing at all. I say that someone who says that God is a being of "severely limited powers" refers to nothing at all—even on the assumption that there is a God. No being of severely limited powers could be God, could fall under the concept properly expressed by the word 'God'; not even if that being was the greatest being who in fact existed and had created the heavens and the earth and all things besides himself.

Now why do I draw the line in such a way that the person in my first example is using the concept 'God' properly and the second isn't? The reason is simply that the person in my first example is, so to speak, loyal to the idea of God as the greatest possible being, and the person in my second example isn't. Contrast the denial of omnipotence to God in the second example with the case of a theist who, impressed by the Paradox of the Stone—"Can God make a stone so heavy he can't lift it?"—decides that omnipotence is an impossible property. And suppose this theist believes that there is a greatest possible degree of power, which he defines carefully, and to which he gives the name, say, 'demi-omnipotence'. He then replaces 'omnipotence' in the list with 'demi-omnipotence', and leaves all else unchanged. This person, I believe, does succeed in referring to God when he says, "God is not omnipotent but rather demi-omnipotent"—because he, too, is loyal to the idea of God as the greatest possible being. I believe, of course, that his contention that omnipotence is an impossible property is a metaphysical error, and that his contention that this conclusion can be proved by an argument based on the Paradox of the Stone is a logical error. And I believe that the theist who thinks that necessary existence is impossible is metaphysically wrong in thinking this, and logically wrong in thinking that it can be proved by a Humean "conceivability implies possibility" argument. But this is the extent of my disagreement with these people. I don't accuse them of having got the concept of God wrong; they have the concept right—the concept of a unique occupier of the office "is not exceeded in greatness by any possible being". Theists who decide that God is not omnipotent simply because, in their view, the fact of evil is inconsistent with the existence of a good and omnipotent being, and who do not say that an omnipotent being is intrinsically impossible, are paying no attention to the conception of a greatest possible being. Their position, I would say, should be put this way: The fact of evil shows that there is no God; nevertheless the world was created by a benevolent being of vast but limited powers, a being who is immensely greater than all created beings. We who were theists should "transfer" to this being the attitudes and loyalties we formerly and mistakenly directed at the God we thought existed.

Let me sum up my position this way. The concept of God is not, in the strictest sense, the concept formed by conjoining the attributes I have listed. In the strictest sense, the concept of God is the concept of a greatest possible being.[10] The list of attributes I have provided—guided by the question, What features of God do Jews, Christians, and Muslims

agree on?—is an attempt to say what a greatest possible being would
be like. This list is *explained by* the fact that Jewish, Christian, and
Muslim theologians and philosophers agree that the concept of God
is the concept of a greatest possible being (though not all of them
will have had this thought explicitly), and *represents* an attempt to
provide as much specific content as is humanly possible to the very
abstract and general idea "greatest possible being". Alternative lists of
the attributes that would belong to a greatest conceivable being (or
different understandings of various of the attributes in the list from
those I have provided) are possible and do not signal an attempt to
attach a different sense to the word 'God' from its traditional (that is to
say, its proper) sense—provided that is what they really are: attempts
to provide as much content as possible to the abstract and general idea
of a greatest possible being. If two theologians or philosophers present
significantly different lists of divine attributes, this should be because,
and only because, they have different ideas about what is metaphysically
possible, and thus different ideas about what the properties of the
greatest metaphysically possible being would be. (Thus Descartes can
properly accuse me of having made a mistake about metaphysics when I
say that omnipotence in his sense is metaphysically impossible and that I
am, for that reason, not going to include it in my list of divine attributes.
He can accuse me of having made a mistake about the properties of
God. He cannot accuse me of having attached the wrong concept to
the word 'God'. And I am in a formally identical position vis-à-vis
the philosopher who contends that I should replace the attribute of
necessity in my list with aseity.) Or you could put my position this way:
if a list of attributes is to provide an absolutely incontrovertible list of
the properties that belong to the concept of God, it should contain the
single item "is the greatest possible being"; long, traditional lists like the
one I have provided represent attempts, defeasible attempts, to provide
a more or less complete specification of those properties accessible to
human reason that are *entailed by* "is the greatest possible being".

I say "defeasible", but, as things stand, I see little in the way of
serious possibility of defeat. With one small exception, which I shall
mention in a moment, I think there can be no serious objection to
the contention that the attributes in my list are entailed by "is the
greatest possible being". The exception is this: in the fifth lecture, I
am going to contend that the "standard" definition of omniscience,
the definition I gave earlier in the present lecture, needs to be revised,
owing to the fact that, by the terms of that definition, omniscience is

not a possible property if human beings have free will. I am, however, going to treat the two divine attributes most closely connected with the argument from evil—omnipotence and moral perfection—as "non-negotiable" components of the concept of God. (And I will adopt a similarly intransigent attitude in respect of omnipresence, which will figure in our discussion of "divine hiddenness.") That is to say, I shall rule out any attempt to meet the argument from evil that proceeds by attempting to place restrictions on the power of God or attempts in any way to qualify his moral perfection. I shall do this because I regard omnipotence and perfect goodness as just obviously entailed by the idea of a greatest possible being.

I claim now to have spelled out, in just the relevant sense, the content of the concept 'God'—or at least to have made a pretty good start on spelling out this content. (It may be that some will want to add attributes to my list. What about beneficence or benevolence, for example? This property obviously has some sort of connection with moral perfection, but it is not obviously entailed by it. What about freedom?—for, although I have affirmed God's freedom in my discussion of the attribute "creator", 'freedom' is not one of the items in my list of attributes. What about love? Does St John not tell us that God is love? And is love not a plausible candidate for an attribute of an *aliquid quo nihil maius cogitari possit*? I have no objection in principle if someone wants to add properties to my list, provided they are consistent with the ones already there. I shall, of course, want to look carefully at each candidate for admission.) My central concern in these lectures is an argument whose conclusion is that there is no omnipotent and morally perfect being, a conclusion that immediately entails that God does not exist. As I have said several times, my position is that this argument, the argument from evil, is a failure. But what does this mean? What is it for a philosophical argument to be a failure? In the third lecture, I will attempt to answer this question. In Lectures 4–7 I will try to show that the argument from evil is a failure in the sense spelled out in the Lecture 3.

Lecture 3
Philosophical Failure

I have said that my project in these lectures is to defend the conclusion that the argument from evil is a failure. My purpose in the present lecture is to explain what I mean by calling this argument, or any philosophical argument, a failure.

Let us therefore turn to the depressing topic of philosophical failure. I expect most philosophers believe that at least one well-known philosophical argument is a failure. But what do philosophers mean, or what should philosophers mean, by calling a philosophical argument a failure? I begin my attempt to answer this question with an observation about the nature of philosophical arguments. Philosophical arguments are not best thought of as free-floating bits of text—as mathematical proofs can perhaps be thought of. A proper mathematical proof, whatever else it may be, is an argument that should convince anyone who can follow it of the truth of its conclusion. We cannot think of philosophical arguments as being like that. (The idea that we can was gently ridiculed by the late Robert Nozick when he said that as a young man he had thought that the ideal philosophical argument was one with the following property: someone who understood its premises and did not accept its conclusion would *die*.) The idea that there are proofs in philosophy as there are proofs in mathematics is ridiculous, or not far short of it; nevertheless, it is an all but irresistible idea. I have just—I mean I did this when I was sitting in my study writing these words—I have just taken a volume of metaphysics at random from my shelves and opened it at random. I found these two sentences within the span of the two facing pages at which the book fell open:

We do well to postpone as long as possible the admission into our ontology of elements elusive and opaque to the understanding [such as Aristotelian Prime Matter or the Lockean substratum] . . . To avoid such elements, we must deny that in the ontic structure of an individual is to be found any non-qualitative element.

Note the word 'must' here. The author writes as if he or she—never mind who it is—has *established* the conclusion that if one regards the properties of material individuals as universals, one must either accept the existence of "elements elusive or opaque to the understanding" or else accept a bundle theory of the nature of material individuals. If you say that you could produce a much clearer example of a philosopher who believes he has proved something of philosophical interest, I will remind you that I really did find these words on two pages chosen at random (and if you recognize the passage and think I meant to pillory a particular author, I will remind you of the same thing). I mean these words to be an example of something absolutely typical in philosophical writing. We all write this way. We have no other way of writing—not, at least, when we are defending a conclusion. These lectures themselves will provide a fund, a plethora in fact, of examples of the very conception of philosophical argument that I am now attempting to undermine. That conception of philosophical argument is an "all but irresistible idea" because it is inherent in the way we philosophers have learned to write philosophy—not that I have an alternative way of writing philosophy to recommend to you. We are, after all, philosophers. We do not, we flatter ourselves, simply *assert*: we argue. To argue is to put forward reasons for believing things. And what is the point of putting forward reasons for believing things if those reasons are not decisive? That this rhetorical question represents the way we think, or a way we often think, is implied by the way we treat the reasons we present. The reasons we present our readers with when we write do generally seem decisive to us when we are putting them forward—this is shown by the fact that we do not generally immediately qualify our presentations of reasons for accepting philosophical theses with some variant on "But of course these considerations are merely suggestive, not decisive".

But if argument in philosophy does not have the enviable indisputability of mathematical proof, what good is it? Is there even such a thing as success and failure in philosophical argument? If philosophical arguments are not proofs, what can we mean by calling them successes or failures? What can I mean when I say that the argument I am going to examine in these lectures, the argument from evil, is a failure?

Let us consider an example. Suppose someone offers an argument for some philosophical thesis—for the existence of God, it may be, or for the non-existence of universals, or for the impossibility of a private language. Let us say an argument for the existence of God. What would it be for this argument to be a success or a failure? Here is a suggestion I borrow from Alvin Plantinga's book *God and Other Minds.* (I don't mean to imply that Plantinga endorsed this suggestion.) The argument is a success if it starts with premises almost no sane, rational person would doubt, and proceeds by logical steps whose validity almost no sane, rational person would dispute, to the conclusion that God exists. Otherwise, it is a failure. (I say "*almost* no sane, rational person" because of cases like the following. St Thomas's First Way begins with the premise that some things change. And Zeno denies that anything changes. I should not want to say that Thomas's argument was defective, not a success, *simply* because it assumed without argument that change was a real feature of the world. And I should also not want to say that Zeno was insane or irrational.)

Only one thing can be said against this standard of philosophical success: if it were accepted, almost no argument for any substantive philosophical thesis would count as a success. (I say "*substantive* philosophical thesis" because I concede that there are, so to call them, minor philosophical theses—such as the thesis that, whatever knowledge may be, it is *not* simply justified true belief—for which there are arguments that should convert any rational person. I call this thesis minor not because I think that the problem of the analysis of knowledge is unimportant, but precisely because the thesis does not constitute an analysis of knowledge; its message is only that a certain proposed analysis is a failure. Or suppose, as many have supposed, that Gödel's incompleteness results *show, establish* that the formalists were wrong about the nature of mathematics. The thesis that formalism is false may in one way be an important philosophical thesis, but only because a lot of people had thought that formalism was true. It is not a substantive philosophical thesis in the way formalism itself is. I am inclined to think that most philosophical theses for which there is an argument that is a success by the standard we are considering are of this general sort, theses to the effect that a certain analysis does not work, or that some plausible generalization has exceptions, or that some argument turns on a logical fallacy.) If there were an argument, an argument for a substantive philosophical thesis, that was a success by this standard, there would be a substantive philosophical thesis such that every philosopher who rejected it was either uninformed—unaware of the existence of a certain argument—or irrational or mad. Are there any? Well, I used to think that Church's Thesis (a rather recondite thesis in the philosophy of mathematics—it has to do with how to provide a certain important intuitive concept with a mathematically precise definition) could be proved by an argument that was a success by the standard we are considering. Then I discovered that at least one important authority (László Kalmár) had his doubts about the cogency of the argument I had found so impressive and was in fact inclined to think that Church's Thesis was false.[1] Since I was unwilling to suppose that Kalmár was mad or irrational, I changed my mind. "Back to zero," I thought. (And, in any case, Church's Thesis is a best a borderline case of a substantive philosophical thesis.)

The account of philosophical success we have been examining sets the bar too high. I propose to lower it by relativizing success in philosophical argument to context. A few moments ago, I said, "Philosophical arguments are not best thought of as free-floating bits of text". By "free-floating", I meant detached from any context—that is, I meant that a philosophical argument should be evaluated only in relation to the various circumstances in which it might be offered. I will mention two ways in which whether a philosophical argument was a success or a failure might depend on context.

First, whether an argument was counted a success or a failure might depend on the purposes of the philosopher who has offered the argument. Did this philosopher mean, for example, to produce converts to its conclusion? It is not invariably the case that the purpose of a philosopher in offering an argument is the winning of converts. The philosopher may frankly admit that the argument is unlikely to convince very many people to accept its conclusion—and not necessarily because he thinks most people are mad or stupid or "logically challenged" or irrationally attached to some false view of the world. Perhaps he thinks that the conclusion of his argument lies in an area in which it is very difficult to reach any conclusion with certainty—owing, in the words of Xenophanes or someone of that sort, to the obscurity of the matter and the shortness of human life. And yet he may think that the argument is a pretty good one. (This is the attitude *I* try, without any very conspicuous success, to cultivate with respect to arguments I am particularly fond of.) To take a different sort of example, there are philosophers who have devoted a great deal of time and care to arguments for conclusions that almost everyone was going to accept in any case. Arguments for the existence of an external world, for other minds, for the mathematical or physical possibility of one runner's overtaking another . . . . Presumably, the purpose of such philosophers is not to increase the number of people who accept the conclusions of these arguments. (It is not even, necessarily, to provide a rational basis for things that people had hitherto believed without any rational basis. My wife is one of those people who don't quite see the point, evident as it is to us philosophers, of discussions of Zeno's paradoxes, and who has, in consequence, never read Salmon or Grünbaum or any other author on this topic. But I very much doubt whether her belief that it is possible for one runner to overtake another—I'm sure she does believe this, although in fact I've never asked her—is a mere prejudice lacking any rational foundation.)

Now the second sort of consideration I offer in support of the thesis that success in philosophical argument should be thought of as context-relative. Even if a philosopher's purpose in producing an argument is to produce converts to its conclusion, the kind of argument that is best for his or her purposes will depend on various features of the audience to which it is addressed. A trivial example would be this: Thomas's First Way is suitable for presentation to an audience of people who have normal beliefs about the reality of motion in a way in which it would not be suitable for presentation to an audience of Eleatics. The following would seem to be a reasonable principle to adopt as regards the presentation of arguments in philosophy or any other field. Suppose one is presenting an argument for the thesis q to a certain audience, and that p is one of the premises of this argument; if one thinks that p is true, and if it is reasonable for one to suppose that one's audience will agree that p is true, then one need not bother to present an argument for p—not even if one happens to know of a really lovely argument for p, and one is aware that there exist philosophers, philosophers of a school unrepresented in one's audience, who deny p. Few works of political philosophy open with a refutation of solipsism.

Now let me take a step back and ask how these rather abstract reflections are to be applied. How do *I* mean to apply them? What use do I propose to make of the idea that questions about the success of an argument should be raised in a way that takes account of the context in which the argument is presented? One way in which I might apply this idea in these lectures would be for me to ask myself which premises of the argument I propose to examine—the argument from evil—might seem doubtful to *you*, my actual audience. But I really know very little about you, and, even if I did, I should not want to present arguments that were so carefully tailored to your beliefs and preconceptions that they might be effective only in this company—select though it be. I am inclined, rather, to direct my efforts to a more general and abstract goal. Let me try to describe this more general goal. It is something like this: to ask myself which premises of the argument from evil might seem doubtful to the members of an *ideal* audience—an audience composed of people whose nature is suggested by that "ideal observer" to which certain ethical theories appeal. But in trying, in my own mind, to flesh out this idea, I have found it necessary to consider not only an ideal audience but an ideal presentation of an argument to that audience. The concept of an ideal presentation of an argument, I think, is best explained by supposing that argument to be presented within the context of an ideal *debate*.

Let us take a moment to think about what a debate is, for there is more than one way to understand this idea. When philosophers think of a debate—at least this is what my experience of philosophers seems to show—they usually think of two people, generally two philosophers, arguing with each other. On this model, so to call it, of debate, a debate comprises two people who hold opposed positions on some issue each trying to convert the other to his own position—and each trying himself to avoid being converted to the other's position. Thus, a debate about the reality of universals would be of this nature: Norma the nominalist and Ronald the realist carry on an exchange of arguments; Norma's purpose in this exchange is to turn Ronald into a nominalist (and, of course, to prevent Ronald from turning *her* into a realist), and Ronald's purpose is to turn Norma into a realist (and, of course, to prevent Norma from turning *him* into a nominalist). This model of debate suggests a definition of what it is for a philosophical argument to be a success. A successful argument for nominalism would be an argument that a nominalist could use to turn a realist into a nominalist—and a successful argument for realism would be similarly understood. But how are we to understand the generality implied by the phrases "a nominalist" and "a realist"? Perhaps we could make this generality more explicit, and therefore clearer, by saying something like this: A successful argument for nominalism would be an argument that *any* ideal nominalist could use to turn *any* ideal realist into a nominalist. By ideal nominalists, I understand nominalists who satisfy the following two conditions, or something that could be obtained from them by a minimal amount of tinkering and adjustment of detail:

ideal nominalists are of the highest possible intelligence and of the highest degree of philosophical and logical acumen, and they are intellectually honest in this sense: when they are considering an argument for some thesis, they do their best to understand the argument and to evaluate it dispassionately.

ideal nominalists have unlimited time at their disposal and are patient
to a preternatural degree; they are, like General Grant, prepared to fight
it out on this line if it takes all summer, and if their opponents think
it necessary to undertake some lengthy digression into an area whose
relevance to the debate is not immediately evident, they will cooperate.

(Ideal realists, of course, share these features.) A successful argument
for nominalism, I said, would be an argument that any ideal nominalist could use to turn any ideal realist into a nominalist— "could"
in the sense that, given a quiet, comfortable room with a blackboard,
and chalk enough and time, any ideal nominalist, wielding this argument, could eventually turn any ideal realist into a nominalist; in the
end, the erstwhile realist would have to say, "All right, I give up.
The argument is unanswerable. There are no universals." A moment
ago, I examined and rejected the idea that a successful philosophical
argument would be one whose conclusion followed from indubitable
premises by indisputably valid logical steps. Any argument for nominalism that was successful by the terms of that stern criterion would, I
should think, have the power to convert an ideal realist to nominalism. It is an interesting question whether there could be an argument
that would convert any ideal realist to nominalism but which did
not proceed by indisputably valid steps from indubitable premises to
its conclusion. I will not try to answer this question, or the more
general question of which it is an instance, since I am not going to
identify success in philosophical argument with the power infallibly
to convert an ideal opponent of the position being argued for. My
reason for rejecting this identification is the same as my reason for
rejecting the first proposal for understanding philosophical success and
failure. In my view, it is very implausible to suppose that nominalism
or any other important philosophical thesis can be supported by an
argument with that sort of power. I very much doubt whether any
argument, or any set of independent arguments, for any substantive
philosophical conclusion has the power to turn a determined opponent of that conclusion, however rational, into an adherent of that
conclusion.

Of course, I can't speak to the topic of unknown arguments,
arguments unknown to us, the arguments of twenty-fourth-century
philosophy. But I doubt whether any argument so far discovered by
philosophers has the power to convince just any ideally rational and
ideally patient person of the truth of any substantive philosophical

thesis. Although the ideal philosophers and ideal circumstances of the debate I have imagined do not exist, reasonable approximations of them have existed at various times and places, and the recorded results of philosophical debate seem (to me at least) to tell very strongly against the thesis that any argument has this sort of power.

Let me move to another picture of what it is for a philosophical argument to be a success, a suggestion based on another model of debate. Let us not think of a debate as an attempt by two persons with opposed views each to convert the other. Let us think of a debate rather on the forensic model. On this model, two representatives of opposed positions carry on an exchange of arguments before an audience, and their purpose is not to convert *each other* but rather to convert the audience—an audience whose members (in theory) bear no initial allegiance to either position, although they regard the question "Which of these two positions is correct?" as an interesting and important one. This situation, too, we shall consider in an ideal form. We retain the idealization of the two debaters that we set out in describing the first model, and the idealization of the circumstances of debate as well. We proceed to an idealization of the audience.

The audience is composed of what we may call agnostics. That is, they are agnostic as regards the subject-matter of the debate. If the debate is about nominalism and realism (let us continue to use that famous debate as our example), each member of the audience will have no initial opinion about whether there are universals, and no predilection, emotional or otherwise, for nominalism or for realism. As regards a tendency to accept one answer or the other, they will stand to the question whether there are universals as you, no doubt, stand to the question of whether the number of Douglas firs in Canada is odd or even. But that is not the whole story; for you, no doubt, have no desire to have the question whether that number is odd or even settled. My imaginary agnostics are not like that in respect of the question of the existence of universals. They would very much like to come to some sort of reasoned opinion about the existence of universals—in fact, to achieve knowledge on that matter if it were possible. They don't care *which* position, nominalism or realism, they end up accepting, but they very much want to end up accepting one or the other. And, of course, we attribute to them the same unlimited leisure and superhuman patience as we previously ascribed to our ideal nominalist and ideal realist—and the same high intelligence and high degree of logical and philosophical acumen and intellectual honesty.

An argument for nominalism will be counted a success—this is my proposal—if *and only if* an ideal nominalist can use it convert, *eventually* to convert, an audience of ideal agnostics (*sc.* with respect to the existence of universals) to nominalism. And, of course, it is stipulated that the conversion must take place under the following circumstances: an ideal realist is present during the nominalist's attempt to convert the agnostics and will employ every rational means possible, at every stage of the debate, to block the nominalist's attempt at conversion.

A moment's thought will reveal that, at this point in the debate, the nominalist has, formally at least, a more demanding task than the realist. The nominalist must convince the agnostics that the argument—the argument whose effectiveness is being tested—is both valid and sound, and the realist (the counsel for the defense, as it were: realism is in the dock) need only cast doubt on either the validity or the soundness of the argument. Or let us say this: need only cast doubt on the *soundness* of the argument. The question of the argument's validity can be eliminated from the theoretical picture by the application of an obvious fact, to wit, that formal validity is cheap: it can always be purchased at the price of additional premises. Let us therefore imagine that all the arguments we shall examine are formally valid (if they were not valid to start with, they have been made valid by the addition of suitable additional premises), and the debate is entirely about the truth-values of the premises of the argument—or, more likely, about the truth-values of *some* of the premises. Then the job of the nominalist is to convince the agnostics that all the premises of the argument are true, and the realist's job is to convince the jury of agnostics to render a "Scotch verdict"—"not proven"—on one or more of those premises. I mean this criterion of success in philosophical argument to be perfectly general, of course; it is to apply to an argument for any (controversial) philosophical conclusion whatever.

Looking at a "debate" this way has several advantages over looking at a "debate" as an exchange in which two philosophers who hold opposed views try to convert each other. A definition of philosophical success based on the latter model of debate would allow few if any philosophical arguments to count as successes. An argument for a thesis *p* would count as a success only if an ideal debater could accomplish a very difficult task indeed: to turn a determined and committed believer in the denial of *p* into a believer in *p* by presenting him or her with that argument. To revert to the example I have been using, an argument for nominalism would count as a success only if an ideal nominalist could turn an ideal realist into a nominalist by means of that argument. On the account of success I propose, however, a successful argument for nominalism need only have the power to turn people who accept neither nominalism nor realism (and who have no initial predilection for either thesis) into people who accept nominalism—certainly an easier task, a task that it is more plausible to suppose might actually be accomplished. And here is an important and related point: on the model of debate I have endorsed, Norma the nominalist need not worry about whether Ronald the realist will accept her premises. She is perfectly free to employ premises she *knows* Ronald will reject; her only concern is whether the audience of agnostics will accept these premises. Suppose, for example, that she uses the premise, "We can have knowledge only of things that have the power to affect us." It may well be that no realist, certainly no realist who had thought the matter through, would accept that premise. If Norma tried to use this premise in a debate of the first sort, in an attempt to convert Ronald the realist to nominalism, Ronald would very likely say, "Well, of course I don't accept *that*; that just begs the question against my position." But in a debate conceived on the forensic model, Ronald can't make that response, for the simple reason that what *he* thinks is quite irrelevant to the logic of the debate. If Ronald thinks that there is any danger of the agnostics accepting this premise, it will do him no good to tell the audience that of course no realist would accept this principle and that it therefore begs the question against realism. He'll have to get down to the business of convincing the agnostics that they should reject, or at least not accept, this premise.

Mention of "begging the question" brings to mind a closely related concept, the concept of "the burden of proof".[2] Where does the burden of proof lie in a philosophical debate? In a debate of the type we are imagining, the answer is clear—in fact, trivial. The burden of proof lies on the person who's trying to prove something to someone. If Norma is trying to turn agnostics into nominalists, she is the one who is trying to prove something to someone: she's trying to prove to the agnostics that there are no universals, or at least that it's more reasonable than not to believe that there are no universals; that both realism and agnosticism are untenable positions and that nominalism is the only tenable position concerning the existence of universals. Ronald the realist isn't (at this point in the debate) trying to prove anything—or nothing but things like, "My nominalist opponent hasn't established the truth of the third premise of her argument beyond a reasonable doubt." So, trivially, in the case we are imagining, the burden of proof lies on the nominalist.

Of course the judgment would go the other way if Ronald were trying to convert the agnostics to realism, and Norma's only job were to block the attempted conversion. You will see that I have imagined our ideal debate as based on a certain division of labor or, better, a certain principle of dialectical organization. I have not imagined a nominalist and a realist as *simultaneously* attempting to convert the audience to their respective positions. That way dialectical anarchy lies. I am really imagining two debates, or imagining that each side in the debate gets what might be called its innings. When Norma the nominalist is at bat, she tries to convert the agnostics, and Ronald the realist attempts to block the conversion. When the Ronald is at bat, he tries to convert the agnostics, and Norma attempts to block the conversion. But in order to evaluate the success of a particular philosophical argument, we need not consider both innings. The question whether a particular argument for nominalism is a success is settled by how well it performs during the nominalist's innings.

So we have a criterion of philosophical success. An argument for p is a success just in the case that it can be used, under ideal circumstances, to convert an audience of ideal agnostics (agnostics with respect to p) to belief in p—in the presence of an ideal opponent of belief in p. Now this definition is counterfactual in form: it says that an argument is a success if and only if presenting it in certain circumstances would have certain consequences. One might well object to the criterion on the ground that it might be very hard indeed—perhaps impossible—to discover the truth-values of the relevant counterfactual propositions. But that comes down to objecting to a criterion of success in philosophical argument because it has the consequence that it might be very hard, or impossible, to discover whether certain philosophical arguments were successes, and it's hardly evident that having that consequence is a defect in a criterion of philosophical success.

I have to admit that my statement of the criterion raises a lot of questions, some of which at least I cannot evade by pleading limitations of time. Here is one: do I mean my ideal agnostics to be drawn from all times and all cultures—or at least from all times and all cultures consistent with their being agnostics of the relevant sort? No, I mean the agnostics to be drawn from our time and our culture; so limiting the jury pool, of course, relativizes our criterion of philosophical success to our time and our culture, for it is certainly possible that an argument that would have succeeded in, say, convincing an eighteenth-century audience that space was infinite would not succeed with an audience of our contemporaries. A present-day advocate of the possibility of the finitude of space could, for example, point to the fact that many scientists think that it is a real possibility that space is finite (although unbounded), a fact that could not have been appealed to in the eighteenth century. And it is not parochial of us to be specially interested in the question of which philosophical arguments are successes given what we know today, or what is for all practical purposes the same thing, what we think we know today. After all, we know lots of things of philosophical relevance that were not known in the Age of Reason or the Middle Ages or in classical antiquity. And we know that lots of things that people in those times and cultures thought they knew are false—things whose falsity is of great philosophical importance.

Here is another important question that confronts my criterion, a question that confronts it in virtue of my limiting membership in the audience of agnostics to our contemporaries. Might there not be an argument that's an absolutely perfect and compelling argument in the eyes of God, so to speak, but that would not be a success by my criterion because of some misconception universal in our time and culture? (And, of course, the opposite possibility also exists: an argument might convince everyone who shares the misconceptions of the present day, but be an abject failure in the eyes of God.) These possibilities are real, but I insist that the criterion is an interesting and useful one despite their reality. It would be an interesting thing to establish that a certain argument was a success in my sense, even if there were some deeper, Platonic sense, in which it might be a failure.

Here is a third question. Might it not be that there was an argument for *p* that was a success by my proposed criterion and another argument, an argument for the denial of *p*, that was *also* a success? And isn't this possibility an embarrassment for the criterion? Shouldn't a criterion of success in philosophical argument rule out a priori any possibility of there being two arguments, both successes, whose conclusions are logical contradictories? But does this possibility in fact exist? Only, I think, if we suppose that one of the two arguments is unknown to the debaters. There is no contradiction in supposing that there exist, Platonically speaking, two arguments, N an argument for nominalism and R an argument for realism, such that (i) if the nominalist knew of N and the realist did not know of R, the nominalist, wielding N, would be able to convert the agnostics to nominalism, despite the best efforts of the realist to prevent their conversion, *and* (ii) if the realist knew of R and the nominalist did not know of N, the realist, wielding R, would be able to convert the agnostics to realism, despite the best efforts of the nominalist to prevent their conversion. It would seem, however, that the first possibility vanishes if the realist knows of R, and that the second possibility vanishes if the nominalist knows of N. Consider the first case. (We need not also consider the second: what we say about the first will apply equally to the second.) Norma the nominalist presents the agnostics with the argument N, and this would, in the end, be sufficient to convert them to nominalism—if Ronald the realist did not know of R. But suppose that Ronald *does* know of R. Then, it would seem, he does have a way to prevent the agnostics from assenting to the premises of N: he need only present R. If R is an argument that would, in the absence of N, have succeeded in converting the agnostics to realism, it seems that it ought, in the presence of N, to have the power to convince the agnostics that at least one of the premises of N might well be false. (Remember: Ronald's task with respect to N is not to convince the agnostics that at least one of the premises of N *is* false, but only that at least one of its premises *may well be* false. And he need not identify some *particular* premise or premises of N as doubtful; he need only establish that the proposition that *all* the premises of N are true is open to reasonable doubt.) Would there not be, in this case, in Hume's fine phrase, "a mutual destruction of arguments", a destruction that would leave the agnostics agnostics?

I will mention but not discuss one final problem for the criterion of success I have proposed. How can this criterion be applied to philosophical arguments whose conclusions are doubted by no one or almost no one—arguments for the reality of motion, the reliability of induction or sense-perception, or the existence of an external world or other minds? I mention this problem out of vanity, lest you conclude I had not thought of it. I will not discuss it because to do so would take us out of our way, and the argument we shall be considering, the argument from evil, is not of this sort.

We have, then, our criterion of success and failure in philosophical argument. My purpose is to defend the conclusion that the argument from evil is to be judged a failure by the—I think—very liberal terms of this criterion.

Let us therefore imagine a debate. Two ideal characters, whom I shall call Atheist and Theist, are debating before an audience of ideal agnostics—and now we understand by this term agnostics of the common-or-garden variety, people who neither believe that God exists nor believe that God does not exist.[3] But our ideal agnostics are not mere agnostics. They are, so to speak, *neutral* agnostics. When I was using a debate about nominalism and realism as my example of an ideal debate, I said the following about the audience : "they... stand to the question whether there are universals as you, no doubt, stand to the question whether the number of Douglas firs in Canada is odd or even." This sort of neutrality is no consequence of agnosticism *simpliciter*. I am an agnostic in respect of the question whether there are intelligent non-human beings inhabiting a planet within, say, 10,000 light-years of the Earth. That is, I do not believe that such beings exist, and I do not believe that no such beings exist. But here is a belief I *do* have: that the existence of such beings is vastly improbable. (If I were a bookie, and if there were some way to settle the bet, I'd be willing to give anyone who wanted to bet that there were such beings just about any odds I needed to give him to get him to place his bet with me and not some rival bookie.) There is no inconsistency in saying both that one does not believe (does not have the belief) that *p* and that one regards *p* as very, very probable, although the unfortunate currency of the idea of "degrees of belief" has caused some confusion on this point. After all, the proposition that Jill is in Budapest today and the proposition that it's highly probable that Jill is in Budapest today are distinct propositions, neither of which entails the other, and it is possible to accept the latter without accepting the former. I would suppose that most real agnostics, most actual people who do profess and call themselves agnostics, are not *neutral* agnostics. Most agnostics I have discussed these matters with think that it's pretty improbable that there's a God. Their relation to the proposition that God exists is very much like my relation to the proposition that there are intelligent non-human beings inhabiting some planet within 10,000 light-years of the Earth. And this consideration suggests a possible objection to my definition of philosophical success. Call those agnostics who think that it's very improbable that there is a God *weighted* agnostics. An argument for the non-existence of God, the argument from evil for example, might be a failure by my criterion because it lacked the power to transform ideal (and hence neutral) agnostics into atheists. But it might, consistently with that, have the power to transform neutral agnostics into weighted agnostics. If it does, isn't it rather hard on it to call it a failure? In response, I will say only that if you want to revise the definition to take account of this, I don't object. In practice, it will make no real difference. I'm going to try to convince you that the argument from evil has not got the power to transform ideal (and hence neutral) agnostics into atheists. But I should be willing to defend the following conclusion, although I shall not explicitly do so: *if* the considerations I shall present indeed show that the argument from evil is incapable of turning neutral agnostics into atheists, these considerations will also show that the argument from evil is incapable of turning neutral agnostics into weighted agnostics.

To return to the main line of argument, Atheist and Theist are carrying on a debate before an audience of ideal agnostics. The debate is divided into two innings or halves. In one, Atheist attempts to turn the agnostics into atheists like herself. In the other, Theist attempts to turn the agnostics into theists like himself. (I am going to make Atheist a woman and Theist a man. I make my debaters of opposite sexes to make things easier for myself: it will automatically be clear which of them any third-person-singular pronoun refers to. As to the match of sex and doctrine I have chosen—well, I suppose I could get into trouble either way.) In these lectures, we shall be concerned only with one half of the debate, Atheist's attempt to turn the agnostics into atheists. And, of course, I shall be concerned only with her attempt to do so by laying one particular argument, the argument from evil, before the agnostics. Here is a very general, abstract description of the course the debate will take. Atheist opens the debate by laying out the argument from evil. (We shall assume that the argument she presents is formally valid.) Theist then attempts to cast doubt on at least one premise of the argument. (Of course, one way to "cast doubt on" a proposition is to show it to be false, but Theist is not *required* to do that.) And the doubts are to exist in the minds of the agnostics; it is not required of Theist that he in any way weaken *Atheist's* allegiance to the premises he is attempting to cast doubt on. Atheist then presents a rejoinder to this reply; perhaps she finds some flaw in Theist's counterargument (a flaw that the agnostics will be willing to accept as such; it will be a waste of time for her to point to something she sees as a flaw if *they* don't see it as a flaw); perhaps she reformulates her argument in such a way that the reformulated argument escapes Theist's criticism; that's really up to her: she can say anything she likes. When she has done this, Theist replies to the rejoinder to his criticism of the argument. And so it goes—for as long as at least one of the participants still has something to say. In the end, we shall have to ask ourselves what the agnostics will make of all this. How will they respond? Will they become atheists, or will they remain agnostics? If the former, Atheist's argument is a success. If the latter, it is a failure. (What if some of them are converted and some are not? Well, I'll make an idealizing assumption: since the debaters and the audience are ideal representatives of the categories "atheist", "theist", and "agnostic", and because the debate is carried on under ideal conditions, the response of the audience, whatever it may be, will be uniform. The consequences of rejecting this assumption would be an interesting topic for further investigation.) As I have said, I am going to try to convince you that the argument from evil is a failure by this standard.

There are certainly successful arguments, both in everyday life and in the sciences. But are there any successful philosophical arguments? I know of none. (That is, I know of none for any *substantive* philosophical thesis.) I hate to admit this, if only because I should like to think that some of the arguments associated with *my* name are successes. But I have to admit that it's at best highly improbable that they are. It's true that none of them has been tested in an ideal debate like the one I have imagined, but, to expand on a point I made earlier, there are less-than-ideal debates that come close enough to being ideal that the performance of my arguments in these debates is strongly indicative of how they would fare in an ideal debate. I know something of how these debates have gone, and I regard myself as in a position to say that it seems very unlikely that my arguments would succeed in an ideal debate. Take, for example, my arguments for the incompatibility of free will and determinism.[4] These arguments have been tested by being presented to several successive generations of graduate students in various universities. And that test is a real-world approximation to the ideal debate I have imagined. The outcome of this test has been as predictable as it was disappointing: some of the graduate students were convinced by my arguments, and some of them weren't. True, these graduate students were not all initially neutral as regards the question of the compatibility of free will and determinism. And most of the graduate seminars in which the arguments were presented were not "team taught" by a compatibilist and an incompatibilist. But the diverse response of the real-world graduate students to my arguments leads me to suppose that the response of an audience of ideal agnostics to an ideal presentation of these arguments would be uniform: they would *remain*, one and all, agnostics in the matter of the compatibility of free will and determinism. And all philosophical arguments, or at any rate all philosophical arguments that have attracted the attention of the philosophical community, have been tested under circumstances that approximate sufficiently to the circumstances of an ideal debate, that it is reasonable to conclude that they would fail the "ideal debate" test. If any reasonably well-known philosophical argument for a substantive conclusion had the power to covert an unbiased ideal audience to its conclusion (given that it was presented to the audience under ideal conditions), then, to a high probability, assent to the conclusion of that argument would be more widespread among philosophers than assent to any substantive philosophical thesis actually is.[5]

Now if it is indeed true that no philosophical argument for any substantive conclusion is successful in the sense that I have proposed, it immediately follows that the argument from evil is not a success in that sense—given, at any rate, two premises that I don't think anyone would deny: that the argument from evil is a philosophical argument and that the non-existence of God is a substantive philosophical thesis. If we think of what I have just said as an argument for the conclusion that the argument from evil is (in my sense) a failure, I don't think it's a bad argument. But even if it's a good argument, it has an important limitation: it doesn't really tell us anything of philosophical interest about the argument from evil; it doesn't interact with the content of the argument from evil. I might have offered essentially the same argument for the conclusion that the private-language argument or the ontological argument or the analogical argument for the existence of other minds was a failure. It is my project in these lectures to try to convince you that the argument from evil does not have the power to turn ideally rational and serious and attentive and patient neutral agnostics into atheists. And, of course, I mean to do this by actually coming to grips with the argument. Even if it's true (as I believe it is) that no philosophical argument for a substantive conclusion has the power to convert every member of an ideal and initially neutral audience to its conclusion, I don't mean to argue from that premise. I mean to show how Theist can block Atheist's every attempt to turn the audience of agnostics into atheists like herself. I mention my general thesis about the inability of philosophical argument to produce uniformity of belief even among the ideally rational simply because I think it is a plausible thesis, and if you agree with me on this point, your agreement will predispose you to accept a conclusion that I will defend on other grounds.

Let me put the point this way. Lay to one side for a moment the argument from evil and all other arguments for the existence or the non-existence of God. Consider only philosophical arguments for substantive conclusions that do not imply the existence or non-existence of God—non-theological arguments, so to call them. And let us also lay aside those arguments whose conclusions almost everyone would have believed without argument—arguments for the existence of other minds, say, or for the thesis that it is possible for one runner to overtake another. Do you think that any substantive philosophical argument that does not fall into either of these categories is a success by the standard I have proposed? If so, how do you account for the fact that its conclusion is controversial? For controversial it certainly is. Leaving aside those philosophical theses that almost everyone would accept *without argument*, there are no philosophical theses that are both substantive and uncontroversial. If the argument is a success by the terms of my definition, why has it not got the power to produce considerably greater uniformity of opinion among philosophers in the matter of its conclusion than in fact exists? Or if it has got that power, why has this power not been exercised? These questions, I believe, have no good answers. And if they have no good answers, it seems reasonable to believe that no non-theological philosophical argument for a substantive conclusion is a success.

Is it plausible to hold that philosophy can provide a successful argument for the non-existence of God, even though philosophy is unable to provide a successful argument for any other substantive thesis? I have to say that this seems implausible to me. It seems antecedently highly improbable that philosophy, in whose house there have been debated scores (at least) of important questions, should be able to provide a decisive answer to *exactly one* of them. It is implausible to suppose that philosophy should be able to answer the question "Does free will exist?"—but no other substantive philosophical question. It is implausible to suppose that philosophy should be able to answer the question "Are thoughts events in the brain?"—but no other substantive philosophical question. It is implausible to suppose that philosophy should be able to answer the question "Does mathematics treat of an objective reality that exists independently of the physical world?"—but no other substantive philosophical question. One would expect that either philosophy would be able to answer lots of the questions that philosophy has posed, or else it would be able to answer none of them. There is something suspicious about the number one, about uniqueness. It is implausible to suppose that philosophy should be able to answer the question "Does God exist?"—but no other substantive philosophical question. Still, highly implausible things, or things that at one point in the history of thought *seemed* highly implausible, have turned out to be true. It seemed implausible at one point in history to suppose that the solid earth beneath our feet was in rapid motion, but it turned out to be true. Further investigation of this question would require a detailed examination of the available arguments for the non-existence of God—the argument from evil, for example. My hope is that my reflections on the topic of philosophical argument will lead you to the conclusion that it would be a very odd thing if the argument from evil were a success.

Lecture 4

The Global Argument from Evil

By the *global* argument from evil, I understand the following argument (or any argument sufficiently similar to it that the two arguments stand or fall together): We find vast amounts of truly horrendous evil in the world; if there were a God, we should not find vast amounts of horrendous evil in the world; there is, therefore, no God. (The global argument from evil, you will remember, is named by contrast to the many *local* arguments from evil, arguments that proceed from premises concerning some particular evil. It is my position that the global argument from evil and local arguments from evil are best treated separately.)

I will preface my examination of this argument with a defense of the moral propriety of examining it. My preface is by no means shadow-boxing. It is quite common for people to say that to examine the argument from evil (in any of its forms), to treat it as if it were just one more philosophical argument, an argument whose virtues and defects could and should be weighed by impartial reason, is a sign of moral insensitivity—or downright wickedness. One might suppose that no argument was exempt from critical examination. One might suppose that if an argument had sufficient force that it would be intellectually dishonest for the opponents of its conclusion to ignore it (a feature that many ascribe to the argument from evil), it would follow that it would be intellectually dishonest for advocates of its conclusion to forbid the opponents of the conclusion to criticize it. But those people to whom I have alluded assert, and with considerable vehemence, that it is *extremely* insensitive (or extremely wicked) to examine the argument from evil with a critical eye. Here, for example, is a famous passage from John Stuart Mill's *Three Essays on Religion* (pp. 186–7):

We now pass to the moral attributes of the Deity, so far as indicated in the Creation; or (stating the problem in the broadest manner) to the question, what indications Nature gives of the purposes of its author. This question bears a very different aspect to us from what it bears to those teachers of Natural Theology who are incumbered with the necessity of admitting the omnipotence of the Creator. We have not to attempt the impossible problem of reconciling infinite benevolence and justice with infinite power in the Creator of a world such as this. The attempt to do so not only involves absolute contradiction in an intellectual point of view but exhibits to excess the revolting spectacle of a jesuitical defense of moral enormities.

Here is a second example. The following poem occurs in the late Kingsley Amis's novel *The Anti-Death League* (it is the work of one of the characters), and it puts a little flesh on the bones of Mill's abstract Victorian indignation. It contains several specific allusions to just those arguments that Mill describes as jesuitical defenses of moral enormities. Its literary effect depends essentially on putting these arguments, or allusions to them, into the mouth of God:

TO A BABY BORN WITHOUT LIMBS

This is just to show you who's boss around here.
It'll keep you on your toes, so to speak.
Make you put your best foot forward, so to speak,
And give you something to turn your hand to, so to speak.
You can face up to it like a man,
Or snivel and blubber like a baby.
That's up to you. Nothing to do with Me.
If you take it in the right spirit,
You can have a bloody marvelous life,
With the great rewards courage brings,
And the beauty of accepting your LOT.
And think how much good it'll do your Mum and Dad,
And your Grans and Gramps and the rest of the shower,
To be stopped being complacent.
Make sure they baptize you, though,
In case some murdering bastard
Decides to put you away quick,
Which would send you straight to LIMB-O, ha ha ha.
But just a word in your ear, if you've got one.
Mind you, DO take this in the right spirit,
And keep a civil tongue in your head about Me.
Because if you DON´T,
I've got plenty of other stuff up My sleeve,
Such as leukemia and polio,
Which, incidentally, you're welcome to any time,
Whatever spirit you take this in.

I've given you one love-pat, right?
You don't want another.
So watch it, Jack.[1]

The attitude expressed in these two quotations is not confined to avowed enemies of Christianity. The theologian Kenneth Surin, a Christian, contends in his book *Theology and the Problem of Evil* that anyone who attempts to reconcile the goodness and omnipotence of God with such evils as the Holocaust actually undermines his own and others' abilities to oppose those evils and is, therefore, at least in a sense, cooperating with their perpetrators. (At any rate, I think that's what his thesis is. As is the case with a great many twentieth-century academic theologians, Surin writes a kind of prose that seems to an untutored analytical philosopher like me designed to conceal his meaning.)

I am not entirely out of sympathy with writers like Mill, the fictional author of the poem in Amis's novel, and Surin. There *is* one sort of position on God and evil toward which the intellectual scorn of Mill (I'll discuss his moral scorn presently) seems entirely appropriate, and it could plausibly be argued that Surin would be right to say that anyone who defended this position was encouraging indifference to the evils of the world. I have in mind the idea that—in the most strict and literal sense—evil does not exist. Now it might seem surprising that anyone would defend this idea. Consider the following well-known passage from *The Brothers Karamazov*:

"By the way, a Bulgarian I met lately in Moscow . . . told me about the crimes committed by Turks and Circassians in all parts of Bulgaria through fear of a general rising of the Slavs. They burn villages, murder, outrage women and children, they nail their prisoners by the ears to the fences, leave them so till morning, and in the morning they hang them . . . . These Turks took a pleasure in torturing children, too; cutting the unborn child from the mother's womb, and tossing babies up in the air and catching them on the points of their bayonets before their mothers' eyes . . ."[2]

How can anyone listen to stories like this and say that evil does not exist? Well, one sort of answer to this question is provided by the adherents of more than one Eastern religion: the appearance of evil that is all about us is *mere* appearance, illusion, for the simple reason that *all* appearance, everything ordinary people take for sensible reality, is illusion. I will not consider this position. I'll take it for granted that what our senses tell us about the world around us is reasonably accurate. But there have been thinkers who held that evil was an illusion even though the sun and the stars and St Rule's Tower were not. Their idea, if I understand it, is something like this. An event like the Turkish massacres in Bulgaria *would* be an evil if it constituted the entire universe. But, of course, no such event does. The universe as a whole contains no spot or stain of evil, but it looks to us human beings as if it did because we view it from a limited perspective. Perhaps an aesthetic analogy will help us to understand this rather difficult idea. (I found this helpful analogy in a book by the philosopher Wallace Matson;[3] I hasten to add that it does not represent his own point of view.) Many pieces of music that are of extreme beauty and perfection contain short discordant passages that would sound very ugly if they were played all by themselves, outside the musical context in which the composer meant them to occur. (Bach's *Well-Tempered Clavier* is an example.) But these passages are not ugly in their proper musical context; they are not the kind of passage that Rossini was referring to when he said, "Wagner has lovely moments but awful quarters of an hour". Seen, or rather heard, in the context of the whole, they are not only not ugly but are essential elements of the beauty and perfection of that whole. The idea I am deprecating is that the horrors and atrocities of our world are the moral analogues of these discordant passages. The *loci classici* of this idea are Leibniz's *Theodicy* and Pope's *Essay on Man*, particularly the famous lines:

> All nature is but art unknown to thee,
> All chance, direction which thou canst not see;
> All discord, harmony not understood;
> All partial evil, universal good;
> And, spite of pride, in erring reason's spite,
> One truth is clear, Whatever is, is right.[4]

(In the matter of Leibniz, if you want to tell me that I am wrong to imply that his position was the same as Pope's, or anything close to it, I won't fight back. Let's say that by 'Leibniz' I mean Leibniz as he has commonly been understood. Even if this Leibniz is a fiction, he has been an influential one.) I don't see how anyone could accept this position. It seems to me to be wholly fantastic. Do not misunderstand this statement. I wish to distance myself from the vulgar slander that ascribes moral insensibility (or downright wickedness) to Pope—a slander about which I'll have more to say in a moment. For my part, I accuse him only of intellectual error. But the intellectual error is of enormous magnitude—comparable to the intellectual error of, say, the astronomer Percival Lowell, who believed that Mars was covered with canals (of which he drew a detailed map), the work of an ancient and dying civilization. This belief was based on no more than the romantic appeal of the tale of an ancient civilization bravely laboring to stave off the fall of night—with, perhaps, some assistance from optical illusion. Pope's belief that "Whatever is, is right" can have had no more basis than his desire that it be true—with, perhaps, some assistance from Leibniz's *Theodicy*. If we think of soldiers making mothers watch while they throw their babies in the air and catch them on the points of their bayonets, or of the ancient Mesopotamian practice of moloch—of throwing living infants into a furnace as a sacrifice to Baal—or of a child born without limbs, we shall, I hope, find it impossible to say that evil is not real. Bad things really do happen. (Remember that by 'evil' we mean simply 'bad things'.) Anyone who, like Pope, says that we call certain things bad only because we don't see them *sub specie aeternitatis* is in grave error. One might as well say that if we could only observe pain from God's point of view, we'd see that it doesn't hurt.

Now what I am calling a grave (or, to put it another way, an absurd) error must be carefully distinguished from three theses I do not call errors; each of these has sometimes been confused with it.

First, it must be distinguished from the thesis that out of every evil God brings some greater good—or that out of the totality of evil he brings some great good or goods that outweigh that totality. That may or may not be so, but if it is so, it doesn't imply that evil is an illusion. In fact, it implies that evil *isn't* an illusion; for even God can't bring good out of evil if there is no evil.

Secondly, it must be distinguished from a famous thesis of St Augustine's, that evil is not a thing that exists in its own right, but is rather a privation of good. That may or may not be so, but if it is so, it doesn't imply that evil is an illusion. A hole in the seat of your trousers isn't a thing that exists in its own right, but is (so to speak) a privation of cloth. But that doesn't mean that the hole is an illusion. If a hole isn't a real thing but a mere absence, that nice metaphysical point doesn't change the fact that your trousers need mending. To maintain that defects in things are not themselves things isn't to maintain that nothing is really defective.

Thirdly, it must not be confused with the biblical promise that some day God will wipe away every tear. That may or may not be so, but if it is so, it doesn't imply that there aren't tears now, and it doesn't imply that the tears of the present day are shed over illusions—that, if we could only see things as God sees them, we'd see that there was nothing to cry about.

If anyone takes the Leibniz/Pope line on the reality of evil, then, I think, that person deserves some of the scorn that Mill and the other writers I've quoted so eloquently express. I insist, however, that the scorn should be intellectual, rather than moral. In believing that "Whatever is, is right", Pope is guilty of no moral error; but his intellectual error is profound, and not to be imitated. I don't say that intellectual and moral error can't be mixed. Those who deny the reality of the Holocaust, for example, are guilty of both. But I would say that an important part of the cause of their intellectual error was antecedently existing moral defects in themselves; these moral defects have led them to deny empirically ascertainable facts. I don't think that Pope and Leibniz believed that evil was an illusion of perspective because they were particularly bad men (I expect they were no better or worse than most of us, something I certainly shouldn't be willing to say of Holocaust-deniers); I think they simply went badly wrong about how things are. Similar cases abound. Descartes, for example, believed that animals felt no pain. I don't suppose he was guilty of this intellectual error (and it is an intellectual error; someone who thinks that animals feel no pain has gone badly wrong about how things are) because of some moral defect he brought to his theorizing about animals. (That might be true of someone whose livelihood depended on causing pain to animals, and who therefore found it convenient to believe that animals felt no pain.) No, Descartes believed this because he thought he saw a good argument for it. He *should* have seen that if the proposition that animals don't feel pain is the conclusion of a valid argument, at least one of the premises of that argument must be false. Somehow he didn't. But this was not a moral failure—and the same should be said of Pope's and Leibniz's failures to accept the reality of evil.

In any case, the scorn of Mill and the other writers I've quoted is not directed only at those who deny the reality of evil. This scorn is poured on anyone who is unwilling to admit, without further argument, that the evils of this world entail the non-existence of a good and omnipotent God. And when they imply that all such people, all people who are not immediately converted to atheism by the argument from evil in its simplest form, are morally defective, they go too far—they go *far* too far—and I must accuse them of intellectual dishonesty.[5]

Philosophy is *hard*. Thinking clearly for an extended period is hard. It is easier to pour scorn on those who disagree with you than actually to address their arguments. (It was easier for Voltaire to caricature Leibniz's arguments and to mock the caricature than actually to address them. And so he wrote *Candide*.) And of all the kinds of scorn that can be poured on someone's views, moral scorn is the safest and most pleasant (most pleasant to the one doing the pouring). It is the safest kind because, if you want to pour moral scorn on someone's views, you can be sure that everyone who is predisposed to agree with you will believe that you have made an unanswerable point. And you can be sure that any attempt your opponent in debate makes at an answer will be dismissed by a significant proportion of your audience as a "rationalization"—that great contribution of modern depth psychology to intellectual complacency and laziness. Moral scorn is the most *pleasant* kind of scorn to deploy against those who disagree with you because a display of self-righteousness—moral posturing—is a pleasant action whatever the circumstances, and it's nice to have an excuse for it. No one can tell me that Mill wasn't enjoying himself when he wrote the words "exhibits to excess the revolting spectacle of a jesuitical defense of moral enormities". (Perhaps he was enjoying himself so much that his attention was diverted from the question, "What would it be to exhibit a revolting spectacle in moderation?")

To those who avoid having to reply to criticism of the argument from evil by this sort of moral posturing, I can only say, "Come off it". These people are, in point of principle, in exactly the same position as those defenders of law and order who, if you express a suspicion that a man accused of molesting a child may have been framed by the police, tell you with evident disgust that molesting a child is a monstrous crime and that you're defending a child molester.

Having defended the moral propriety of critically examining the argument from evil, I will now do just that. The argument presupposes, and rightly, that two features God is supposed to have are "non-negotiable": that he is omnipotent and that he is morally perfect. As we saw in the second lecture, it isn't easy to say what omnipotence means. My non-negotiable adherence to "God is omnipotent" comes to this: in these lectures, in attempting to answer the argument from evil, I will never contend that God is unable to do a certain thing unless I am prepared to defend the thesis that the thing in question is intrinsically or metaphysically impossible. (And this despite the fact that I believe that there are certain intrinsically possible acts—lying and promise breaking, for example—that the one, the only possible, omnipotent being is unable to perform.) To say that God is morally perfect is to say that he never does anything morally wrong—that he could not possibly do anything morally wrong.[6] Omnipotence and moral perfection are, as I said, non-negotiable components of the idea of God. A being that is the greatest being possible and is less powerful than it might have been (or is less powerful than some other possible being might have been) is a contradiction in terms, and so is a being who is the greatest being possible and sometimes acts wrongly. If the universe was made by an intelligent being, and if that being is less than omnipotent (and if there's no other being who *is* omnipotent), then the atheists are right: God does not exist. If the universe was made by an omnipotent being, and if that being has done even one thing that was morally wrong (and if there isn't another omnipotent being, one who never does anything morally wrong), then the atheists are right: God does not exist. If the Creator of the universe lacked either omnipotence or moral perfection, and if he claimed to be God, he would be either an impostor or confused—an impostor if he claimed to be both omnipotent and morally perfect, and confused if he admitted to being either not omnipotent or not morally perfect and still claimed to be God.

I began this lecture with a simple statement of the global argument from evil. One premise of this argument was: 'If there were a God, we should not find vast amounts of horrendous evil in the world.' But the statement "If there were an omnipotent and morally perfect being, we should not find vast amounts of horrendous evil in the world" might well be false if the all-powerful and morally perfect being were ignorant, and not culpably ignorant, of certain evils. But this is not a difficulty for the proponent of the global argument from evil, for God is, as we have seen, omniscient. The proponent of the simple argument could, in fact, defend his premise by an appeal to far weaker theses about the extent of God's knowledge than 'God is omniscient'. If the evils of the world constitute an effective prima facie case for the conclusion that there is no omnipotent, morally perfect, and omniscient being, they present an equally effective prima facie case for the conclusion that there is no omnipotent and morally perfect being who has even as much knowledge of what goes on in the world as we human beings have. The full panoply of omniscience, so to speak, does not really enter into the initial stages of a presentation and discussion of an argument from evil. Omniscience—omniscience in the full sense of the word—will become important only later, when we come to discuss the free-will defense.

It is time now to turn to our promised ideal debate, the debate between Atheist and Theist before the audience of ideal agnostics.

We are imagining that stage of the debate in which Atheist is trying to convince the agnostics to abandon their agnosticism and become atheists like herself, and, more specifically, that stage in the debate in which she attempts to employ the global argument from evil to that end. She inaugurates this stage of the debate with a statement of the global argument, a slightly more elaborate version of the argument than the one I have given:

God, if he exists, is omniscient, or, at the very least, knows as much as we human beings do. He therefore knows at least about the evils of the world we know about, and we know that the world contains a vast amount of evil. [I am going to assume that neither party to the debate thinks the Leibniz/Pope thesis on evil, the thesis that evil is an illusion of our limited perspective, is worth so much as a passing mention.] Now consider those evils God knows about. Since he's morally perfect, he must desire that these evils not exist—their non-existence must be what he *wants*. And an omnipotent being can achieve or bring about whatever he wants—or at least whatever he wants that is intrinsically possible. And the non-existence of evil, of bad things, is obviously intrinsically possible. So if there were an omnipotent, morally perfect being who knew about the evils we know about—well, they wouldn't have arisen in the first place, for he'd have prevented their occurrence. Or if, for some reason, he didn't do that, he'd certainly remove them the instant they began to exist. But we observe evils, and very long-lasting ones. So we must conclude that God does not exist.

What shall Theist—who grants that the world contains vast amounts of truly horrible evil—say in reply? I think that he should begin with an obvious point about the relations between what one wants, what one can do, and what one will, in the event, do:

I grant that, in some sense of the word, the non-existence of evil must be what a perfectly good being *wants*. But we often don't bring about states of affairs we can bring about and want to bring about. Suppose, for example, that Alice's mother is dying in great pain and that Alice yearns desperately for her mother to die—today and not next week or next month. And suppose it would be easy for Alice to arrange this—she is perhaps a doctor or a nurse and has easy access to pharmaceutical resources that would enable her to achieve this end. Does it follow that she will act on this ability that she has? It is obvious that it does not, for Alice might have *reasons* for not doing what she can do. Two obvious candidates for such reasons are: she thinks it would be morally wrong; she is afraid that her act would be discovered, and that she would be prosecuted for murder. And either of these reasons might be sufficient, in her mind, to outweigh her desire for an immediate end to her mother's sufferings. So it may be that someone has a very strong desire for something and is able to obtain this thing, but does not act on this desire—because he has reasons for not doing so that seem to him to outweigh the desirability of the thing. The conclusion that evil does not exist does not, therefore, follow *logically* from the premises that the non-existence of evil is what God wants and that he is able to bring about the object of his desire—since, for all logic can tell us, God might have reasons for allowing evil to exist that, in his mind, outweigh the desirability of the non-existence of evil.

Theist begins his reply with these words. But he must say a great deal more than this, for, if we gave her her head, Atheist could make pretty good prima facie cases for two conclusions: that a morally perfect Creator would make every effort to prevent the suffering of his creatures, and that the suffering of creatures could not be a necessary means to any end for an omnipotent being. Theist must, therefore, say something about God's reasons for allowing evil, something to make it plausible to believe that there might be such reasons. Before I allow him to do this, however, I will remind you of some terminology I introduced in the first lecture that will help us to understand the general strategy I am going to have him follow in his discussion of God's reasons for allowing evil to exist.

Suppose I believe both in God and in the real existence of evil. Suppose I think I know what God's reasons for allowing evil to exist are, and that I tell them to you. Then I have presented you with a *theodicy*. (Here I use 'theodicy' in Plantinga's sense. Various writers, Richard Swinburne and I among them, have found it useful to use the word in other senses. In these lectures, I will stick with the usage that Plantinga's work has made more or less standard in philosophical discussions of the argument from evil.) If I could present a theodicy, and if the audience to whom I presented it found it convincing, I'd have an effective reply to the argument from evil, at least as regards that particular audience. But suppose that, although I believe in both God and evil, I *don't* claim to know what God's reasons for allowing evil are. Is there any way for someone in my position to reply to the argument from evil? There is. Consider this analogy.

Your friend Clarissa, a single mother, left her two very young children alone in her flat for several hours very late last night. Your Aunt Harriet, a maiden lady of strong moral principles, learns of this and declares that Clarissa is unfit to raise children. You spring to your friend's defense: "Now, Aunt Harriet, don't go jumping to conclusions. There's probably a perfectly good explanation. Maybe Billy or Annie was ill, and she decided to go over to the clinic for help. You know she hasn't got a phone or a car and no one in that neighborhood of hers would come to the door at two o'clock in the morning." If you tell your Aunt Harriet a story like this, you don't claim to know what Clarissa's reasons for leaving her children alone really were. And you're not claiming to have said anything that shows that Clarissa really is a good mother. You're claiming only to show that the fact Aunt Harriet has adduced doesn't prove that she isn't one; what you're trying to establish is that for all you or Aunt Harriet know, she had some good reason for what she did. And you're not trying to establish only that there is some remote possibility that she had a good reason. No counsel for the defense would try to raise doubts in the minds of the members of a jury by pointing out to them that for all they knew the defendant had an identical twin, of whom all record had been lost, and who was the person who had actually committed the crime the defendant was charged with. That may be a possibility—I suppose it *is* a possibility—but it is too remote a possibility to raise real doubts in anyone's mind. What you're trying to convince Aunt Harriet of is that there is, as we say, *a very real possibility* that Clarissa had a good reason for leaving her children alone; and your attempt to convince her of this consists in your presenting her with an example of what such a reason *might* be.

Critical responses to the argument from evil—at least responses by philosophers—usually take just this form. A philosopher who responds to the argument from evil typically does so by telling a story, a story in which God allows evil to exist. This story will, of course, represent God as having reasons for allowing the existence of evil, reasons that, if the rest of the story were true, would be good ones. Such a story philosophers call a *defense*. If I offer a story about God and evil as a defense, I hope for the following reaction from my audience: "Given that God exists, the rest of the story might well be true. I can't see any reason to rule it out." The reason I hope for this reaction should be clear. If the story I have told is true, then the argument from evil (any version of the argument from evil) has a false premise. More precisely: given that the argument from evil is logically valid (that is, given that the conclusion of the argument follows logically from its premises), at least one of the premises of the argument has to be false if my story, my "defense", is true. If, therefore, my audience reacts to my story about God and evil as I hope they will, they will immediately draw the conclusion I want them to draw: that, for all they know, at least one of the premises of the argument from evil is false.[7]

Some people, if they are familiar with the usual conduct of debates about the argument from evil may be puzzled by my bringing the notion "a very real possibility" into my fictional debate at this early point. It has become something of a custom for critics of the argument from evil first to discuss the so-called logical problem of evil, the problem of finding a defense that satisfies no stronger condition than this, that it be free from internal logical contradiction; when the critics have dealt with this problem to their own satisfaction, as they always do, they go on to discuss the so-called evidential (or probabilistic) problem of evil, the problem of finding a defense that (among certain other desirable features) represents, in my phrase, a real possibility. If defense counsels followed a parallel strategy in courts of law, they would first try to prove that their clients' innocence was logically consistent with the evidence by telling stories (by presenting "alternative theories of the crime") involving things like twins separated at birth, operatic coincidences, and mental telepathy; only after they had shown by this method that their clients' innocence was logically consistent with the evidence, would they go on to try to raise *real* doubts in the minds of jurors about the guilt of their clients.

As I said in the first lecture, I find this division of the problem artificial and unhelpful—although I think it is easy to see why it arose. It arose because the earliest attempts to use the argument from evil to prove the non-existence of God—I mean the earliest attempts by analytical philosophers—were attempts to prove that the statement 'God and evil both exist' was logically self-contradictory. And various philosophers, most notably Nelson Pike and Alvin Plantinga, attempted to show that these supposed proofs of logical self-contradiction were far from convincing.[8] The debate evolved fairly quickly out of this early, "logical" stage into a discussion of a much more interesting question: whether the statement 'God and evil both exist' could be shown to be *probably false* or *unreasonable to believe*. Discussions of the problem of evil even today tend to recapitulate this episode in the evolution of the discussion of the argument from evil.

Since I find the distinction artificial and unhelpful, I am, of course, not going to allow it to dictate the form that my discussion of the argument from evil will take. I am, as it were, jumping right into the evidential problem (so-called; I won't use the term) without any consideration of the logical problem. Or none as such, none under the *rubric* "the logical problem of evil". Those who know the history of the discussions of the argument from evil in the Fifties and Sixties of the last century will see that many of the points I make, or have my creatures Atheist and Theist make, were first made in discussions of the logical problem.

All right. Theist's response will take the form of an attempt to present one or more defenses, and his hope will be that the response of the audience of agnostics to this defense, or these defenses, will be, "Given that God exists, the rest of the story might well be true. I can't see any reason to rule it out." What form could a plausible defense (a defense having a real chance of eliciting this reaction from an audience of neutral agnostics following an ideal debate) take?

One point is clear: A defense cannot simply take the form of a story about how God brings some great good out of the evils of the world, a good that outweighs those evils. At the very least, a defense will have to include the proposition that God was *unable* to bring about the greater good without allowing the evils we observe (or some other evils as bad or worse). And to find a story that can plausibly be said to have this feature is no trivial undertaking. The reason for this lies in God's omnipotence. A human being can often be excused for allowing, or even causing, a certain evil if that evil was a necessary means, or an unavoidable consequence thereof, to some good that outweighed it—or if it was a necessary means to the prevention of some greater evil. The eighteenth-century surgeon who operated without anesthetic caused unimaginable pain to his patients, but we do not condemn him because (at least if he knew what he was about) the pain was an unavoidable consequence of the means necessary to a good that outweighed it—saving the patient's life, for example. But we should not excuse a present-day surgeon who had anesthetics available and who nevertheless operated without using them—not even if his operation saved the patient's life and thus resulted in a good that outweighed the horrible pain the patient suffered.

A great many of the theodicies or defenses that one sees are insufficiently sensitive to this point. Many undergraduates at the University of Notre Dame, for example, seem inclined to say something like the following: if there were no evil, no one would appreciate—perhaps no one would even be aware of—the goodness of the things that *are* good. You know the idea: you never really appreciate health till you've been ill, you never really understand how great and beautiful a thing friendship is till you've known adversity and known what it is to have friends who stick by you through thick and thin—and so on. Now the obvious criticism of this defense is so *immediately* obvious that it tends to mask the point that led me to raise it. The immediately obvious criticism is that this defense may be capable of accounting for a certain amount of, for example, physical pain, but it certainly doesn't account for the degree and the duration of the pain that many people are subject to—and it doesn't account for the fact that many of the people who experience horrible physical pain do not seem to be granted any subsequent goods to appreciate. If, for example, the final six months of the life of a man dying of cancer are one continuous chapter of excruciating pain, the "appreciation" defense (so to call it) can hardly be said to provide a plausible account of why God would allow someone's life to end this way. (Admittedly, this is not a conclusive point: the Notre Dame undergraduate will probably add to his or her defense at this point the thesis that the sufferer better appreciates the goods of Heaven because of his earthly sufferings.) But I have brought up the "appreciation" defense—which otherwise would not be worth spending any time on—to make a different point. It is not at all evident that an omnipotent creator would need to allow people really to experience *any* pain or grief or sorrow or adversity or illness to enable them to appreciate the good things in life. An omnipotent being would certainly be able to provide the knowledge of evil that human beings in fact acquire by bitter experience of real events in some other way. An omnipotent being could, for example, so arrange matters that at a certain point in each person's life—for a few years during his adolescence, say—that person have very vivid and absolutely convincing *nightmares* in which he is a prisoner in a concentration camp or dies of some horrible disease or watches his loved ones being raped and murdered by soldiers bent on ethnic cleansing. Whether such dreams would be "worth it", I don't know. That is, I don't know whether people in a world in which nothing bad ever happened in reality would be better off for having such nightmares—whether the nightmares would lead to an appreciation of the good things in their lives that outweighed the intrinsic unpleasantness of having them. But it seems clear that a world in which horrible things occurred *only* in nightmares would be better than a world in which the same horrible things occurred in reality, and that a morally perfect being would, all other things being equal, prefer a world in which horrible things were confined to dreams to a world in which they existed in reality. The general point this example is intended to illustrate is simply that the resources of an omnipotent being are unlimited—or are limited only by what is intrinsically possible—and that a defense must take account of these unlimited resources.

There seems to me to be only one defense that has any hope of succeeding, and that is the so-called free-will defense.[9] In saying this, I place myself in a long tradition that goes back at least to St Augustine, although I do not propose, like many in that tradition, to offer a theodicy. I do not claim to know that free will plays any central part in God's reasons for allowing the existence of evil. I employ the free-will defense as just precisely a defense, a story that includes both God and evil and, given that there is a God, is true for all anyone knows. If I have anything to add to what others in this tradition have said, it derives from the fact (I firmly believe it to be a fact) that today we understand free will better than philosophers and theologians have in the past. Those of you who know my work on free will may be puzzled by this last statement, for I have always insisted (though not always as explicitly and vehemently as I have in recent years) that free will is a mystery, something we don't understand at all. Am I not, therefore, saying that we now understand something we don't understand at all better than philosophers used to understand it? And is it not a form of obscurantism to argue for the conclusion that the argument from evil, which is a very straightforward argument indeed, is a failure by telling a story that essentially involves a mystery?

These are good questions, but I am confident I have good answers to them. Here is what I mean by saying that free will is a mystery: Anyone who has thought carefully about the problem of free will and who has come to a conclusion about free will that is detailed and systematic enough to be called a theory of free will must accept *some* proposition that seems self-evidently false. To choose what theory of free will to accept is to choose *which* seemingly self-evidently false proposition one accepts. And this choice cannot be evaded by accepting some deflationary or "commonsense" or naturalistic theory of free will. To do that is simply to choose a theory of free will, and, if I am right, it is therefore to choose to accept some proposition that seems self-evidently false. Well, this is a controversial thesis; that is, it is controversial whether free will is in this sense a mystery. And, fortunately, my use of the free-will defense in these lectures will not depend on it. I mention it only to absolve myself of the charge of contradiction, for I believe that it is consistent to say that free will is a mystery in this sense and that philosophers today understand free will better than philosophers of the past have understood it. I claim to have a better philosophical understanding of free will than, for example, Augustine and Aquinas. By this I mean that, although I find free will an impenetrable mystery, I have at my disposal a better family of ideas, a set of unambiguous, sharply defined, and more useful technical terms relating to the problem of free will than Augustine and Aquinas had. And I know of all manner of arguments pertaining to free will that were unknown (or only vaguely, gropingly formulated) before the 1960s.

As to the charge of obscurantism—well, free will is a real thing. (If anyone denies that free will exists, *that* is a theory about free will, or an important part of one, and it commits its adherents to the seemingly self-evidently false proposition that free will does not exist.) I will, of course, include in my version of the free-will defense (that is, in the version of the free-will defense that I put into the mouth of Theist), some statements that imply the existence of free will. In my view, however, none of these statements are ones that are *known* to be false or probably false or unreasonable to believe. Remember that the free-will defense is a defense, not a theodicy, and that the person who offers a defense is not obliged to include in it only statements that are known to be true. I shall, for example, suppose that free will is incompatible with determinism, but that is not a thesis that is known to be false. There are philosophical arguments that can be brought against "incompatibilism" of course, but that fact is nicely accommodated by my methodology, by my placing Theist's use of the free-will defense in the context of a debate: Atheist is perfectly free to bring these arguments to the attention of the agnostics.

Let us now return to that debate. I am going to imagine Theist putting forward a very simple form of the free-will defense; I will go on to ask what Atheist might say in response:

God made the world and it was very good. An indispensable part of the goodness he chose was the existence of rational beings: self-aware beings capable of abstract thought and love and having the power of free choice between contemplated alternative courses of action. This last feature of rational beings, free choice or free will, is a good. But even an omnipotent being is unable to control the exercise of the power of free choice, for a choice that was controlled would *ipso facto* not be free. In other words, if I have a free choice between x and y, even God cannot ensure that I choose x. To ask God to give me a free choice between x and y and to see to it that I choose x instead of y is to ask God to bring about the intrinsically impossible; it is like asking him to create a round square, a material body that has no shape, or an invisible object that casts a shadow. Having this power of free choice, some or all human beings misused it and produced a certain amount of evil. But free will is a sufficiently great good that its existence outweighs the evils that have resulted and will result from its abuse; and God foresaw this.

We should note that the free-will defense depends on the Thomist, as opposed to the Cartesian, conception of omnipotence, for, according to Descartes, an omnipotent being *can* bring about the intrinsically impossible. But that is no real objection to Theist's defense. In adopting the Thomist conception of omnipotence, Theist actually makes things harder for himself—for on the Cartesian conception of omnipotence, it is absurdly easy to reply to the argument from evil in any of its forms. (Absurdly easy, *I* would say, because the Cartesian conception of omnipotence is absurd.) The Cartesian need only say that there is no evil. And, in saying this, he need not be in agreement with Leibniz and Pope, who refuse to say that there *is* evil. He can say that there is evil—and also that there isn't. After all, if God *can* bring it about that evil both exists and does not exist, who's to say that he hasn't? (Well, *Descartes* says that God in fact hasn't brought about the truth of any self-contradictory statements, but that thesis is not inherent in his theory of omnipotence.) "But a morally perfect God, even if he could bring about the truth of contradictions, wouldn't bring it about that there both is and isn't evil; he'd do something even better: he'd bring it about that there isn't evil, and *not* bring it about that there is; he'd bring it about that there isn't any evil, full stop." I agree, replies the Cartesian theodicist, but that doesn't count against my argument, for he has done just that. "But that contradicts what you just said. You said that God has brought it about that there both is and isn't evil, and then you said that he brought it about that there isn't any evil, full stop." "Yes," the Cartesian theodicist replies, "that's a contradiction all right. But there's nothing wrong with asserting a contradiction if it's true, and that one is, for God has brought about its truth. He's omnipotent, you know." And there is no reply to the Cartesian theodicist; a *reply* is a species of rational discourse, and anyone who, like the Cartesian theodicist, affirms the truth of contradictions, has the resources to make rational discourse about the argument from evil (or any other topic) impossible.[10] Let us leave him to his own devices and presuppose the Thomist account of omnipotence, which at least makes rational discourse about what an omnipotent being can do possible. Theist's presentation of the free-will defense immediately suggests several objections. Here are two that would immediately occur to most people:

How could anyone possibly believe that the evils of this world are outweighed by the good inherent in our having free will? Perhaps free will is a good and would outweigh, in Theist's words "a certain amount of evil", but it seems impossible to believe that it can outweigh the amount of physical suffering (to say nothing of other sorts of evil) that actually exists.

Not all evils are the result of human free will. Consider, for example, the Lisbon earthquake or the almost inconceivable misery and loss of life produced by the Asian tsunami of December 2004. Such events are not the result of any act of human will, free or unfree.

In my view, the simple form of the free-will defense I have put into Theist's mouth is unable to deal with either of these objections. The simple form of the free-will defense can deal with at best the existence of *some* evil—as opposed to the vast amount of evil we actually observe—and the evil with which it can deal is only the evil that is caused by the acts of human beings. I believe, however, that more sophisticated forms of the free-will defense do have interesting things to say about the vast amount of evil in the world and about those evils that are not caused by human beings. Before I discuss these "more sophisticated" forms of the free-will defense, however, I want to examine some objections that have been raised against the free-will defense that are so fundamental that, if valid, they would refute any elaboration of the defense, however sophisticated. These objections have to do with the nature of free will. I am not going to inject them into my dialogue between Atheist and Theist, for the simple reason that—in my view, anyway—they have not got very much force, and I do not want it to be accused of fictional character assassination; my Atheist has more interesting arguments at her disposal. Nevertheless, I am going to discuss these arguments. One of them I will discuss because it played an important part in early debates about the argument from evil. (From my parochial point of view, the "early" debates about the argument from evil took place in the Fifties and Sixties.) I will discuss the others because, although they cannot be said to have played an important part in the debate, they have some currency. Since, like the first, they involve philosophical problems about free will, it will be convenient to discuss them in connection with the first.

I will begin the next lecture with a discussion of these three arguments: the argument that, since free will is compatible with determinism, an omnipotent and omniscient being could indeed determine the free choices of its creatures; the argument that, although free will and determinism are incompatible, God is able to ensure that human beings freely choose one course of action over another *without* determining their actions (owing to his having what is called "middle knowledge"); and the argument that since God's omniscience is incompatible with free will, the free-will defense is logically self-contradictory.

Lecture 5

The Global Argument Continued

I said that I would begin this lecture with a discussion of some problems involving free will. The first of the three problems I shall consider arises from the contention that free will is compatible with strict causal determinism: that is, with the thesis that the past and the laws of nature together determine a unique future. Many philosophers—Hobbes, Hume, and Mill are the most illustrious representatives of their school—have held that free will and determinism are perfectly compatible: that there could be a world in which at every moment the past determined a unique future and whose inhabitants were nonetheless free beings.[1] Now if this school of philosophers is right, the free-will defense fails, for if free will and determinism are compatible, then an omnipotent being *can*, contrary to a central thesis of the free-will defense, create a person who has a free choice between *x* and *y* *and* ensure that that person choose *x* rather than *y*. Those philosophers who accept the compatibility of free will and determinism defend their thesis as follows: being free is being free to do what one wants to do. Prisoners in a jail, for example, are unfree because they want to leave and can't. The man who desperately wants to stop smoking but can't is unfree for the same reason—even though no barrier as literal as the bars of a cell stands between him and a life without nicotine. The very words 'free will' testify to the rightness of this analysis, for one's will is simply what one wants, and a free will is just exactly an unimpeded will. Given this account of free will, a Creator who wants to give me a free choice between *x* and *y* has only to arrange the components of my body and my environment in such a way that the following two 'if' statements are both true: *if* I were to want *x*, I'd be able to achieve that desire, and *if* I were to want *y*, I'd be able to achieve *that* desire. And a Creator who wants to ensure that I choose *x*, rather than *y*, has only to implant in me a fairly robust desire for *x* and see to it that I have no desire at all for *y*. And these two things are obviously compatible. Suppose, for example, that there was a Creator who had put a woman in a garden and had commanded her not to eat of the fruit of a certain tree. Could he so arrange matters that she have a free choice between eating of the fruit of that tree and not eating of it—and also *ensure* that she not eat of it? Certainly. To provide her with a free choice between the two alternatives, he need only see to it that two things are true: first, that if she wanted to eat of the fruit of that tree, no barrier (such as an unclimbable fence or paralysis of the limbs) would stand in the way of her acting on that desire, and, secondly, that if she wanted *not* to eat of the fruit, nothing would force her to act contrary to *that* desire. And to ensure that she not eat of the fruit, he need only see to it that not eating of the fruit be what she desires. This latter end could be achieved in a variety of ways; the simplest, I suppose, would be to tell her not to eat of it after having built into her psychological makeup a very strong desire to do whatever he tells her to and a horror of disobedience—a horror like that experienced by the acrophobe who is forced to approach the edge of a cliff. An omnipotent and omniscient being could therefore bring it about that every creature with free will always freely did what was right; there would then be no creaturely abuse of free will, and evil could not, therefore, have entered the world through the creaturely abuse of free will. And that is what a morally perfect being would, of necessity, do—at least assuming that free will is a good that a morally perfect Creator would have wanted to include in his creation. The so-called free-will defense is thus not a defense at all, for it is an impossible story.

Here, then, is an argument for the conclusion that the story called the free-will defense essentially incorporates a false proposition. But how plausible is the account of free will on which the argument rests? Not very, I think. It certainly yields some odd conclusions. Consider the lower social orders in *Brave New World*, the "deltas" and "epsilons". These unfortunate people have their deepest desires chosen for them by others—by the "alphas" who make up the highest social stratum. What the deltas and epsilons primarily desire is to do what the alphas (and the beta and gamma overseers who are appointed to supervise their labors) tell them. This is their primary desire because it is imposed on them by pre-natal and post-natal conditioning. (If Huxley were writing today, he would no doubt add genetic engineering to the alphas' list of resources for determining the desires of their willing slaves.) It would be hard to think of beings who better fitted the description 'lacks free will' than the deltas and epsilons of *Brave New World*. And yet, if the compatibilist account of free will is right, the deltas and epsilons not only have free will, but are much freer than you and I. Each of them is at every moment doing exactly what he wants, and, therefore, according to the compatibilist account of free will, each of them enjoys a life of perfect freedom. What each of them wants, of course, is to do as he is told to do by those appointed over him, but the account of free will we are examining says nothing about the *content* of a free agent's desires: it requires only that there be no barrier to the agent's acting on them. The deltas and epsilons are not very intelligent, and are therefore incapable of philosophizing about their condition, but the alphas' techniques could as easily be applied to highly intelligent people. It is interesting to ask what conclusions such people would arrive at if they reflected on their condition. If you said to one of these willing but highly intelligent slaves, "Don't you realize that you obey your masters only because your desire to obey them was implanted in you by pre-natal conditioning and genetic engineering?", he would, I expect, reply by saying something like this: "Yes, and a good thing, too, because, you see, they had the foresight to implant in me a desire that my desires be so formed. I'm really very fortunate: I'm not only doing exactly what I want, but I want to want what I want, and I want what I want to be caused by pre-natal conditioning and genetic engineering." Again, such a being can hardly be said to have free will. I have no theory of what free will is—lots of philosophers do; unfortunately, all their theories labor under the disadvantage of being wrong—but I can see that this isn't a case of it. Therefore the argument we are considering, the argument for the conclusion that an omnipotent being could determine the free choices of its creatures, rests on a false theory of free will.

Now *my* argument, my argument for the falsity of the compatibilist theory of free will is, of course, a philosophical argument and is therefore, by my own testimony, inconclusive. But let us remember the dialectical situation in which my inconclusive argument occurs. You will remember that at the end of the previous lecture I declined, out of courtesy to my fictional creation Atheist, to represent her as replying to Theist's presentation of the free-will defense by employing any of the three arguments about free will that we are now considering. But let's suppose that Atheist has a rather dim sister—Village Atheist, I'll call her—and let's suppose for a moment that Village Atheist and Theist are engaged in debate, and that Village Atheist is dim enough to employ the compatibilist response to the free-will defense, and that Theist replies to the compatibilist response more or less as I have. Let us pay attention to where we are in the debate when this much has happened; that is, let us remember who is trying to prove what and to whom and in what dialectical circumstances. Village Atheist has opened the discussion by trying to convince the agnostics of the truth of atheism; to this end, she employs the global argument from evil. Theist responds by producing the free-will defense and contends that this defense shows that evil does not prove the non-existence of God. Village Atheist's rejoinder is that the story called the free-will defense can be shown to be impossible by reflection on the nature of free will. Theist replies that Village Atheist has got the nature of free will wrong, and he offers a philosophical argument for this conclusion, an argument that, like all philosophical arguments falls short of being a proof, but nevertheless seems fairly plausible. If this is the end of the exchange, it seems that Theist has got the better of Village Atheist. When we think about it, we see that, for all Village Atheist has said, the story called the free-will defense *may well* be a true story—at least given that there is a God. One cannot show that a story involving creatures with free will is impossible by pointing out that the story would be impossible if a certain theory about free will were true. To show that, one would also have to show that the theory of free will that one has put forward was true. To show that the story was *probably* impossible, one would have to show that the theory of free will that one has put forward was *probably* true. And neither Village Atheist nor anyone else has shown that the theory of free will to which her argument appeals, the compatibilist or "no barriers" theory, is true or probably true; for the objections to the "no barriers" theory of free will that I have set out show that this theory faces very serious objections indeed, objections to which no one has ever adequately replied. It is Village Atheist, remember, and not Theist, who is trying to prove something. She is trying to prove something to the audience of agnostics: namely, that they should stop suspending judgment about whether there is a God and instead believe that there is no God. Theist offers the free-will defense only to frustrate her attempt to prove this conclusion to the agnostics. If Village Atheist's reply to the free-will defense is to succeed, she must convince the agnostics that compatibilism is the *correct* theory of free will, or is at least probably correct; Theist need only elicit this response from the agnostics: "For all we know, compatibilism is *not* the correct theory of free will." And he has certainly made a sufficiently strong case against the "no barriers" theory of free will for this to be the reasonable response.

I will now pass on to the other two arguments for the conclusion that any form of the free-will defense must fail that I promised to talk about. Both these arguments turn on old philosophical disputes about

God and free will. The first rests on a philosophical theory that, unlike compatibilism, has been very popular among theists. This is the theory that there are "true counterfactuals of creaturely freedom"—and in fact so many of them that an omniscient being would know what a creature with free will *would freely do* in any circumstance.[2] That there are true counterfactuals of creaturely freedom—for example, 'If there had been a peal of thunder at the moment Eve was trying to decide whether to eat the apple, she would freely have decided not to eat it'—has been accepted by a wide range of theists, among them most (if not all) Dominicans and Thomists, the sixteenth-century Spanish Jesuits, and Alvin Plantinga.[3] An atheist might try to make use of the thesis that such propositions exist to refute the free-will defense, to exhibit it as an impossible story. The argument would be a generalization of this example: Suppose the conditional proposition I just now used as an example—'If there had been a peal of thunder at the moment Eve was trying to decide whether to eat the apple, she would freely have decided not to eat it'—is true. Then God could have brought it about that Eve *freely* decided not to eat the apple. Being omniscient, he would have known that the conditional was true; all he would then have had to do to bring it about that she freely decided not to eat the apple would have been to cause its antecedent to be true—that is, to produce a peal of thunder at the crucial moment. By adopting as a general strategy the technique illustrated in this example, he could bring it about that *every* creature with free will always freely did what was right; there would then be no creaturely abuse of free will, and evil could not, therefore, have entered the world through the creaturely abuse of free will. And that is what a morally perfect being would, of necessity, do—at least assuming that free will is a good that a morally perfect Creator would have wanted to include in his creation. The so-called free-will defense is thus not a defense at all, for it is an impossible story.

Plantinga has an enormously elaborate response to this argument, a response that depends on a Molinist, rather than a Thomist, view of the relation between God's power and the true counterfactuals of creaturely freedom.[4] (Thomists have generally held that each counterfactual of creaturely freedom had the truth-value it did because God *decreed* that it should have that truth-value; Luis de Molina and his followers held that, as a matter of contingent fact, certain members of the set of counterfactuals of freedom were true and the others false, and that God was just *stuck* with a certain distribution of truth-values over the members of this set, the distribution that *happened* to obtain, by chance and independently of his will. As for the Thomist view, I do not see any way for theists to respond to the argument we are considering if it is supposed that God has decided the truth-value of every counterfactual of freedom.) To make a very long story very short, Plantinga suggests that, for all we know, for all anyone can say, it may be that the distribution of truth-values on the set of counterfactuals of creaturely freedom that God is stuck with is, from his, God's, point of view, a particularly unfortunate one: the true counterfactuals of creaturely freedom happen to be ones with antecedents and consequents such that no matter which of their antecedents God caused to be true, there would be some evil-producing free actions on the part of some creatures—provided only that God created any free beings at all. For my part, I would simply deny the common premise of the Thomists and Molinists; I would deny, that is, that there are *any* true counterfactuals of creaturely freedom. The thesis that no counterfactuals of creaturely freedom are true has been defended by several philosophers, among them Robert Adams, William Hasker, and myself.[5] I will say no more about the subject here—largely because I find the idea of there being true counterfactuals of creaturely freedom just enormously implausible. I will leave further exploration of the problems related to them to philosophers who take their possibility seriously (and there are very able ones—Plantinga and Flint, for example). The argument we are considering can be met by separation of cases: either there are true counterfactuals of creaturely freedom or there are not. If there are not, the argument has a false premise; in the other case, since "Plantinga's hypothesis" is true for all anyone knows, if the set of true counterfactuals of creaturely freedom is non-empty—if there are *some* true counterfactuals of creaturely freedom—it does not follow that this set has the *right* members for God to be able to create a world containing free creatures who never cause any bad things.

Now for the third of the three arguments against the free-will defense that I have promised to discuss. (Doubly promised, in this case, for in the second lecture I briefly mentioned the philosophical problem on which this argument is based and said I would discuss it in connection with the free-will defense.) The free-will defense, of course, entails that at least some human beings have free will. But the existence of a being who knows the future is incompatible with free will, and an omniscient being knows the future, and omniscience belongs to the concept of God. Hence, the so called free-will defense is not a possible story, and hence is not a defense at all. Most theists, I think, would reply to this argument by trying to show that divine omniscience and human free will are compatible, for that is what most theists believe. But I find the arguments—which I will not discuss—for the incompatibility of omniscience and freedom, if not indisputably correct, at least pretty convincing. I will, rather, respond to the argument by engaging in some permissible tinkering with the concept of omniscience. At any rate, I believe it to be permissible. (You will recall that I discussed the question of what constitutes permissible tinkering with the list of divine attributes in the second lecture.)

In what follows, I am going to suppose that God is everlasting but temporal, not outside time. I make this assumption for two reasons. First, I do not really know how to write coherently and in detail about a non-temporal being's knowledge of what is to us the future. Secondly, it would seem that the problem of God's knowledge of what is to us the future is particularly acute if this knowledge is *fore*knowledge, if what is from our point of view the future is the future from God's point of view as well.[6]

In the second lecture, I considered two definitions of omniscience. Let us look at the problem from the perspective provided by the second definition: An omniscient being is a being who, for every proposition believes either that proposition or its denial, and whose beliefs cannot (this is the 'cannot' of metaphysical impossibility) be mistaken. Now consider these two propositions:

X will freely do A at the future moment *t*.

Y, a being whose beliefs cannot be mistaken, believes now that X will do A at *t*.

These two propositions are consistent with each other or they are not. If they are consistent, there is no problem of omniscience and freedom. Suppose they are inconsistent. Then it is impossible for a being whose beliefs cannot be mistaken now to believe that someone will at some future moment freely perform some particular action. Hence, if free will exists, it is impossible for any being to be omniscient. (More exactly: no being is omniscient in any possible world in which there are free agents.[7]) Now this conclusion would seem, at least to the uninitiated, to tell against not only the possibility of omniscience (given free will), but the possibility of omnipotence as well. For if the two propositions are incompatible, then it is intrinsically or metaphysically impossible for a being whose beliefs cannot be mistaken now to *find out* what the future free acts of any agent will be. But this argument is invalid on both the Cartesian and the Thomist conceptions of omnipotence. A being that is omnipotent in the Cartesian sense is able to do intrinsically impossible things; a being that is omnipotent in the Thomist sense is, as it were, excused from the requirement that it be able to do things that are intrinsically impossible. This suggests a solution to the problem of free will and divine foreknowledge: why should we not qualify the "standard" definition of omniscience in a way similar to that in which St Thomas, if you will forgive the prolepsis, qualified the Cartesian definition of omnipotence?[8] Why not say that even an omniscient being is unable to know certain things—those such that its knowing them would be an intrinsically impossible state of affairs. Or we might say this: an omnipotent being is also omniscient if it knows everything it is able to know. Or if, as I prefer, we frame our definition of omniscience in terms of belief and the impossibility of mistake: an omnipotent being is also omniscient if it is impossible for its beliefs to be mistaken *and* it has beliefs on every matter on which it is able to have beliefs. (The way that had to be worded is rather complicated; perhaps an example will make its point clearer. Suppose that today I made a free choice between lying and telling the truth, and that I told the truth. Suppose that this proposition is logically inconsistent with the proposition that yesterday a being whose beliefs cannot be mistaken believed that today I should tell the truth. Then any being whose beliefs cannot be mistaken must yesterday *not* have believed that today I should tell the truth; and, of course, it can't be the case that yesterday it believed that today I should lie. That is, such a being must yesterday have had *no* beliefs about what I should do freely today. And if that being was also omnipotent, it was unable, despite its omnipotence, then to have or then to acquire beliefs about what I should freely do today. To ask it to have or to acquire any belief about my future free actions would be to ask it to bring about a metaphysically impossible state of affairs.)

This qualification of the "standard" definition of omniscience is in the spirit of what I contended in the second lecture were permissible revisions of the properties in our list of divine attributes—or of our accounts of them. If we say, first, that the omnipotent God is omniscient in this sense: he knows everything that, in his omnipotence, he is able to know, and, secondly, that he does not know what the future free acts of any agent will be, we do not, for the reasons I have just given, contradict ourselves. I propose then that we revise our earlier definition in just this way. If it is possible, metaphysically or intrinsically possible, for God, to know the truth-value of every proposition, the two definitions will coincide. If it is not, God will be omniscient (given the Thomist account of omnipotence) by the weaker definition, and not omniscient by the stronger. But even in the latter case, he will possess knowledge in the highest degree that is metaphysically possible, and will therefore not be debarred from the office "greatest possible being".

I must admit that this solution to the problem of free will and divine foreknowledge raises a further problem for theists: Are not most theists committed (for example, in virtue of the stories told about God's actions in the Bible) to the proposition that God at least sometimes foreknows the free actions of creatures? This is a very important question. In my view, the answer is No, at least as regards the Bible.[9] But a discussion of this important question is not possible within the scope of these lectures.

I conclude that neither an appeal to the supposed compatibility of free will and determinism, nor an appeal to the supposed existence of true counterfactuals of creaturely freedom, nor an appeal to the supposed incompatibility of free will and divine foreknowledge can undermine the free-will defense.

Let us return to Atheist, who, as I said, has better arguments than these at her disposal. What shall she say in response to the free-will defense? Her most promising course of action, I think, is to concede a certain limited power to the free-will defense and go on to argue that this power is *essentially* limited. Her best course is to admit that the free-will defense shows that there might, for all anyone can say, be a certain amount of evil, a certain amount of pain and suffering, in a world created by an all-powerful and morally perfect being, and to conduct her argument in terms of the amounts and the kinds of evil that we actually observe. Her best course is to argue for the conclusion that neither the simple version of the free-will defense that I have had Theist present nor any elaboration of it can constitute a plausible account of the evil, the bad things, that actually exist. In the previous lecture I mentioned two facts about the evils we actually observe that, I said, would probably occur to anyone who heard Theist's preliminary statement of the free-will defense: that the amount of suffering (and other evils) is enormous, and that some evils are not caused by human beings and cannot therefore be ascribed to the abuse of free will by creatures. If they would occur to anyone, they would occur to Atheist. Let us imagine that she takes them up in the following speech to the audience of agnostics:

I will concede that the free-will defense shows that the mere existence of *some evil or other* cannot be used to prove that there is no God. If we lived in a world in which everyone, or most people, suffered in certain relatively minor ways, and if each instance of suffering could be traced to the wrong or foolish acts of human beings, you would be making a good point when you tell these estimable agnostics that, for all they know, these wrong or foolish acts are free acts, that even an omnipotent being is unable to determine the outcome of a free choice, and that the existence of free choice is a good thing, sufficiently good to outweigh the bad consequences of its occasional abuse. But the evils of the world as it is are not at all like that. First, the sheer *amount* of evil in the world is overwhelming. The existence of free will may be worth some evil, but it certainly isn't worth the amount we actually observe. Secondly, there are lots of evils that aren't productions of the human will, be it free or unfree. Earthquakes and tornados and genetic defects and . . . well, one hardly knows where to stop. The free-will defense, therefore, is quite unable to deal either with the amount of evil that actually exists or with one of the kinds of evil that actually exists: evil that is not a consequence of human acts.

How is Theist to reply to this argument? I am going to put a very long speech into his mouth:

The free-will defense, in the simple form in which I first stated it suggests—though it does not entail—that God created human beings with free will, and then just left them to their own devices. It suggests that the evils of the world are the more or less unrelated consequences of countless millions of largely unrelated abuses of free will by human beings. Let me now propose a sort of plot to be added to the bare and abstract free-will defense that I stated above. Consider the story of creation and rebellion and expulsion from paradise that is told in the first three chapters of Genesis. Could this story be true—I mean literally true, true in every detail? Well, no. It contradicts what science has discovered about human evolution and the history of the physical universe. And that is hardly surprising, for it long antedates these discoveries. The story is a reworking—with much original material—by Hebrew authors (or, as *my* author, Mr van Inwagen, believes, *a* Hebrew author) of elements found in many ancient Middle Eastern mythologies. Like the *Aeneid*, it is a literary refashioning of materials drawn from myth and legend, and it retains a strong flavor of myth. It is possible, nevertheless, that the first three chapters of Genesis are a mythico-literary representation of actual events of human pre-history. The following story is consistent with what we know of human pre-history. Our current knowledge of human evolution, in fact, presents us with no particular reason to believe that this story is false:

> For millions of years, perhaps for thousands of millions of years, God guided the course of evolution so as eventually to produce certain very clever primates, the immediate predecessors of *Homo sapiens*. At some time in the last few hundred thousand years, the whole population of our pre-human ancestors formed a small breeding community—a few thousand or a few hundred or even a few score. That is to say, there was a time when every ancestor of modern human beings who was then alive was a member of this tiny, geographically tightly knit group of primates. In the fullness of time, God took the members of this breeding group and miraculously raised them to rationality. That is, he gave them the gifts of language, abstract thought, and disinterested love—and, of course, the gift of free will. Perhaps we cannot understand *all* his reasons for giving human beings free will, but here is one very important one we *can* understand: He gave them the gift of free will because free will is necessary for love. Love, and not only erotic love, implies free will.[10] The essential connection between love and free will is beautifully illustrated in Ruth's declaration to her mother-in-law Naomi:

> And Ruth said, Intreat me not to leave thee, or to return from following after thee: for whither thou goest, I will go; and where thou lodgest, I will lodge: thy people shall be my people, and thy God my God: Where thou diest, will I die, and there will I be buried: the LORD do so to me, and more also, if ought but death part thee and me. (Ruth 1: 16–17)

It is also illustrated by the vow that *my* creator, Mr van Inwagen, made when he was married:

> I, Peter, take thee, Elisabeth, to my wedded wife, to have and to hold from this day forward, for better for worse, for richer for poorer, in sickness and in health, to love and to cherish, till death us do part, according to God's holy ordinance; and thereto I plight thee my troth.

God not only raised these primates to rationality—not only made of them what we call human beings—but also took them into a kind of mystical union with himself, the sort of union that Christians hope for in Heaven and call the Beatific Vision. Being in union with God, these new human beings, these primates who had become human beings at a certain point in their lives, lived together in the harmony of perfect love and also possessed what theologians used to call preternatural powers—something like what people who believe in them today call "paranormal abilities". Because they lived in the harmony of perfect love, none of them did any harm to the others. Because of their preternatural powers, they were able somehow to protect themselves from wild beasts (which they were able to tame with a look), from disease (which they were able to cure with a touch), and from random, destructive natural events (like earthquakes), which they knew about in advance and were able to escape.[11] There was thus no evil in their world. And it was God's intention that they should never become decrepit with age or die, as their primate forebears had. But, somehow, in some way that must be mysterious to us, they were not content with this paradisal state. They abused the gift of free will and separated themselves from their union with God.

The result was horrific: not only did they no longer enjoy the Beatific Vision, but they now faced destruction by the random forces of nature, and were subject to old age and natural death. Nevertheless, they were too proud to end their rebellion. As the generations passed, they drifted further and further from God—into the worship of false gods (a worship that sometimes involved human sacrifice), inter-tribal warfare (complete with the gleeful torture of prisoners of war), private murder, slavery, and rape. On one level, they realized, or some of them realized, that something was horribly wrong, but they were unable to do anything about it. After they had separated themselves from God, they were, as an engineer might say, "not operating under design conditions". A certain frame of mind had become dominant among them, a frame of mind latent in the genes they had inherited from a million or more generations of ancestors. I mean the frame of mind that places one's own desires and perceived welfare above everything else, and which accords to the welfare of one's immediate relatives a subordinate privileged status, and assigns no status at all to the welfare of anyone else. And this frame of mind was now married to rationality, to the power of abstract thought; the progeny of this marriage were continuing resentment against those whose actions interfere with the fulfillment of one's desires, hatreds cherished in the heart, and the desire for revenge. The inherited genes that produced these baleful effects had been harmless as long as human beings had still had constantly before their minds a representation of perfect love in the Beatific Vision. In the state of separation from God, and conjoined with rationality, they formed the genetic substrate of what is called original or birth sin: an inborn tendency to do evil against which all human efforts are vain. We, or most of us, have some sort of perception of the distinction between good and evil, but, however we struggle, in the end we give in and do evil. In all cultures there are moral codes (more similar than some would have us believe), and the members of every tribe and nation stand condemned not only by alien moral codes but by their own. The only human beings who consistently do right in their own eyes, whose consciences are always clear, are those who, like the Nazis, have given themselves over entirely to evil, those who say, in some twisted and self-deceptive way, what Milton has his Satan say explicitly and clearly: "Evil, be thou my Good."

When human beings had become like this, God looked out over a ruined world. ("And God saw that the wickedness of man was great in the earth, and that every imagination of the thoughts of his heart was only evil continually" (Gen. 6.5).) It would have been just of him to leave human beings in the ruin they had made of themselves and their world. But God is more than a God of justice. He is, indeed, more than a God of mercy—a God who was merely merciful might simply have brought the story of humanity to an end at that point, like a man who shoots a horse with a broken leg. But God is more than a God of mercy: he is a God of love. He therefore neither left our species to its own devices nor mercifully destroyed it. Rather, he set in motion a rescue operation. He put into operation a plan designed to restore separated humanity to union with himself. This defense will not specify the nature of this plan of atonement. The three Abrahamic religions, Judaism, Christianity, and Islam, tell three different stories about the nature of this plan, and I do not propose to favor one of them over another in telling a story that, after all, I do not maintain is true. This much must be said, however: the plan has the following feature, and any plan with the object of restoring separated humanity to union with God would have to have this feature: its object is to bring it about that human beings once more love God. And, since love essentially involves free will, love is not something that can be imposed from the outside, by an act of sheer power. Human beings must choose freely to be reunited with God and to love him, and this is something they are unable to do by their own efforts. They must therefore cooperate with God. As is the case with many rescue operations, the rescuer and those whom he is rescuing must cooperate. For human beings to cooperate with God in this rescue operation, they must know that they need to be rescued. They must know what it means to be separated from him. And what it means to be separated from God is to live in a world of horrors. If God simply "canceled" all the horrors of this world by an endless series of miracles, he would thereby frustrate his own plan of reconciliation. If he did that, we should be content with our lot and should see no reason to cooperate with him.

Here is an analogy. Suppose Dorothy suffers from angina, and that what she needs to do is to stop smoking and lose weight. Suppose her doctor knows of a drug that will stop the pain but will do nothing to cure the condition. Should the doctor prescribe the drug for her, in the full knowledge that if the pain is alleviated, there is no chance that she will stop smoking and lose weight? Well, perhaps the answer is Yes—if that's what Dorothy insists on. The doctor is Dorothy's fellow adult and fellow citizen, after all. Perhaps it would be insufferably paternalistic to refuse to alleviate Dorothy's pain in order to provide her with a motivation to do what is to her own advantage. If one were of an especially libertarian cast of mind, one might even say that someone who did that was "playing God". It is far from clear, however, whether there is anything wrong with God's behaving as if he were God. It is at least very plausible to suppose that it is morally permissible for God to allow human beings to suffer if the inevitable result of suppressing the suffering would be to deprive them of a very great good, one that far outweighs the suffering. But God does shield us from *much* evil, from a great proportion of the sufferings that would be a natural consequence of our rebellion. If he did not, all human history would be at least this bad: every human society would be on the moral level of Nazi Germany. (I say *at least this bad* because I don't really know how bad human beings can get. The Third Reich is my model for the moral nadir, but, for all I know, this model is naively optimistic. Perhaps there are levels of moral horror that surpass even that of the Nazis. One lesson of Hitler's Germany is that our great-grandparents did not know how bad it was possible for human beings to be; for all we know, *our* great-grandchildren will say that *we* didn't know how bad it was possible for human beings to be.) But, however much evil God shields us from, he must leave in place a vast amount of evil if he is not to deceive us about what separation from him means. The amount he has left us with is so vast and so horrible that we cannot really comprehend it, especially if we are middle-class Europeans or Americans. Nevertheless, it could have been much worse. The inhabitants of a world in which human beings had separated themselves from God and he had then simply left them to their own devices would regard their world as a comparative paradise. All this evil, however, will come to an end. At some point, for all eternity, there will be no more unmerited suffering: this present darkness, "the age of evil", will eventually be remembered as a brief flicker at the beginning of human history. Every evil done by the wicked to the innocent will have been avenged, and every tear will have been wiped away. If there is still suffering, it will be merited: the suffering of those who refuse to cooperate with God's great rescue operation and are allowed by him to exist forever in a state of elected ruin—those who, in a word, are in Hell.

One aspect of this story needs to be brought out more clearly than I have. (Indeed, I have done no more than hint at this aspect of the story. These were the hints: the phrases "random, destructive natural events" and "the random forces of nature".) If the story is true, much of the evil in the world is due to chance. (And this statement applies to the evils caused by human beings as well as to those caused by "the random, destructive forces of nature". It could well happen that a woman was raped and murdered only because she yielded to a sudden impulse to pull over to the side of the road and consult a map. There may be, quite literally, no more to say than that in response to the question, "Why *her*?")

According to the story I have told, there is generally no explanation of why *this* evil happened to *that* person. What there is, is an explanation of why evils happen to people without any reason. If a much-loved child dies of leukemia, there may well be no explanation of why that happened—although there is an explanation of why events of that *sort* happen. And the explanation is: that is part of what being separated from God means; it means being the playthings of chance. It means living in a world in which innocent children die horribly, and it means something worse than that: it means living in a world in which innocent children die horribly *for no reason at all*. It means living in a world in which the wicked, through sheer luck, often prosper. Anyone who does not want to live in such a world, a world in which we are the playthings of chance, had better accept God's offer of a way out of that world.[12]

Here ends the very long story I—it is still Theist who is speaking—said was consistent with what we know of human prehistory. I will call this story the *expanded* free-will defense. I mean it to include the "simple" free-will defense as a part. Thus, it is a feature of the expanded free-will defense that even an omnipotent being, having raised our remote ancestors to rationality and having given them the gift of free will, which included a free choice between remaining united with him in bonds of love and turning away from him to follow the devices and desires of their own hearts, was not able to *ensure* that they have done the former—although we may be sure that he did everything omnipotence could do to raise the probability of their doing so. But the omniscient God knew that, however much evil might result from the elected separation from himself, and consequent self-ruin, of his creatures—if it should occur—the gift of free will would be, so to speak, worth it. For the existence of an eternity of love depends on this gift, and that eternity outweighs the horrors of the very long but, in the most literal sense, temporary period of divine–human estrangement. And he has done what he can to keep the horrors of estrangement to a minimum—if there is a minimum. [Here is a brief parenthesis *in propria persona*: in the next lecture I shall defend the thesis that there is no minimum amount of suffering consequent on our separation from our Creator that is consistent with his plan of Atonement. This point will in fact turn out to be extremely important in connection with local arguments from evil.] At any rate, he has made them vastly less horrible than they might have been.

The expanded free-will defense includes evils in the amounts and of the kinds that we find in the actual world, including what is sometimes called natural evil, such as the suffering caused by the Lisbon earthquake. (Natural evil, according to the expanded free-will defense, is a special case of evil that is caused by the abuse of free will; the fact that human beings are subject to destruction by earthquakes is a consequence of an aboriginal abuse of free will.) I contend that the expanded free-will defense is a possible story (internally consistent, at least as far as we can see). I contend that, given that the central character of the story, God, exists, the rest of the story might well be true. I contend that, in the present state of human knowledge, we could have no reason for thinking that the story was false unless we had some reason—a reason other than the existence of evil—for thinking that there was no God.

I concede that the expanded free-will defense does not help us with cases like "Rowe's fawn"—cases of suffering that occurred before there were human beings or which are in some other way causally unconnected with human choice. Those I will consider presently. [I'm not going to allow Theist to keep this promise. I'll discuss "pre-lapsarian horrors" in the seventh lecture, but I'll lay out the arguments on both sides of the case myself, without feigning that these arguments are presented in the context of an ideal debate.] But it is unwise to try to do everything at once. I should like to turn the floor back to Atheist and ask her whether my story doesn't have the features I claim for it.

Here ends Theist's long speech. Theist has told a story, a story he calls "the expanded free-will defense". The purpose of the story is to raise doubts in the minds of the agnostics about one of the premises of the argument from evil: namely, the conditional premise, 'If there were a God, we should not find vast amounts of horrendous evil in the world'. Theist hopes that the agnostics will say something like the following when they have heard the expanded free-will defense: "If there is a God, the rest of that story might well be true. But then there is no reason to accept Atheist's conditional premise. It may be true, but it also may well not be true." And if Theist's hope is fulfilled, if that is how the agnostics do react to his story, then, by my definition of 'failure', the global argument from evil is a failure.

I believe that that is indeed how the agnostics would react.

No doubt you have questions about the story. You may, for example, want to ask whether an audience of neutral agnostics *would* react to the story by saying, "If there is a God, the rest of that story might well be true". Perhaps you think not. Perhaps you think it's a bizarre story. Perhaps you think that the agnostics ought to react to it as any jury composed of normal, reasonable people would have reacted if Clarence Darrow had tried to raise doubts in their minds about whether Leopold and Loeb had murdered Bobby Franks by telling a story that turned on the murder's having been committed not by his clients but by their evil twins, clones created by the super-science of malevolent extra-terrestrial beings. We should expect a normal, reasonable jury member to react to such a story by saying something like, "Darrow wants me to believe that if his clients are innocent, the rest of that story he has told us might well be true, too. Well, I don't think that. I think that even if those two young men are somehow innocent of the murder they're accused of, the rest of the story is certainly false." I have to say that I don't think that *our* rational jurors, the members of the audience of agnostics, would have the corresponding reaction to the expanded free-will defense. The jurors in the criminal case know enough about how things stand in the world to know that the "evil twins" story is certainly false ("certainly" in the sense that the probability of its truth is so close to zero that the possibility that it is true—it is, strictly speaking, a *possible* story—should be ignored by anyone engaged in practical deliberation) even if the accused are innocent. But would it be rational for the agnostics to say that the creation-fall-and-atonement story is certainly false even if there is a God? You, perhaps, think that the story is certainly false—so vastly improbable that the possibility of its truth must be ignored in serious intellectual inquiry. But then (perhaps) you think that the existence of God is vastly improbable. Suppose, however, you were suddenly converted to theism, to the belief that there was a being who, among his other features, was omnipotent and morally perfect. Do you think that you would *still* say that the creation-fall-and-atonement story was vastly improbable? If you think that, I have to disagree with you. That's not what you would say. I don't mean that, having been converted to theism, you would accept the story, or think it more probable than not. I do mean that you would say that it was the sort of story that *could* be true, that it represented a real possibility, that it was true for all you knew.

Here is another question you might want to ask: whether I *believe* the story I have put into Theist's mouth. Well, I believe parts of it, and I don't disbelieve any of it. (Even the part I believe does not, for the most part, belong to my faith; it merely comprises some of my religious opinions. They are on a par with my belief that Anglican orders are valid.) I am not at all sure about "preternatural powers", for example, or about the proposition that God shields us from much evil, and that the world would be far worse if he did not. But what *I* believe and don't believe is not really much to the point. The story I have told is, I remind you, only supposed to be a defense. Theist does not put forward the expanded free-will defense as a theodicy, as a statement of the real truth of the matter concerning the co-presence of God and evil in the world. Nor would I, if I told it. Theist contends only, I contend only, that the story is—given that God exists—true for all anyone knows. And I certainly don't see any reason to reject any of it. In particular, I see no reason to reject the thesis that a small population of our ancestors were miraculously raised to rationality on, say, June 13th, 190,027 BC—or on some such particular date. It is not a discovery of evolutionary biology that there are no miraculous events in our evolutionary history. It *could* not be, any more than it could be a discovery of meteorology that the weather at

Dunkirk during those fateful days in 1940 was not due to a specific and local divine action. Anyone who believes either that the coming-to-be of human rationality or the weather at Dunkirk had purely natural causes must believe this on philosophical, not scientific, grounds. In fact, the case for this is rather stronger in the matter of the genesis of rationality, for we know a lot about how the weather works, and we know that the rain clouds at Dunkirk are the sort of thing that could have had purely natural causes. We most assuredly do not know that rationality could have arisen through natural causes—or, at any rate, we do not know this unless we somehow know that *everything* in fact *has* purely natural causes. This is because everyone who believes that human rationality could have arisen from purely natural causes believes this solely on the basis of the following argument: Everything has purely natural causes; human beings are rational; hence, the rationality of human beings could have arisen from purely natural causes because it did so arise in fact.

It could, I concede, be a discovery of evolutionary biology that the genesis of rationality was not a sudden, local event, and such a discovery would imply the falsity of the expanded free-will defense. But no such discovery has been made. If someone, for some reason, put forward the theory that extraterrestrial beings once visited the earth, and by some prodigy of genetic engineering, raised some population of our primate ancestors to rationality in a single generation—something like this happened in the movie *2001: A Space Odyssey*—this theory could not be refuted by any facts known to physical anthropology.

I am not going to have Atheist raise any scientific objections to this story; I could have done that, of course. If I had, I should have had Theist reply to them by saying what I have just said. And I don't see that an audience of really impartial agnostics would find any purely scientific barriers to agreeing that, for all they knew, given that there was a God, the rest of the story might be true. I want to reserve Atheist for the office of raising philosophical rather than scientific objections to the expanded free-will defense. (In the seventh lecture, the lecture devoted to the suffering of animals, I will say more about the question whether the expanded free-will defense faces scientific difficulties, and I will discuss some philosophical questions that are closely related to this question. These philosophical questions are ramifications of this question: Why does the expanded free-will defense represent the genesis of rationality as a sudden, miraculous event? My discussion of these questions will arise naturally from certain considerations concerning the suffering of animals.)

The most important philosophical question that can be asked about the story is this: Suppose, for the sake of argument, that the expanded free-will defense is a true story. Does it justify the evils of the world? Or put the question this way: Suppose there were an omnipotent and omniscient being and that this being acted just as God has acted in the expanded free will defense. Could any moral case be made against the actions of this being? Is there any barrier to saying that this being is not only omnipotent and omniscient but morally perfect as well?

In the next lecture, I will look at an argument that Atheist might offer for the conclusion that a morally perfect being would not do what the expanded free-will defense says that God has done.

Lecture 6

The Local Argument from Evil

At the conclusion of the previous lecture, I said that in today's lecture, I would see what sort of argument Atheist might offer for the conclusion that a morally perfect being would not do what the expanded free-will defense says God has done. Her best response to the expanded free-will defense, I think, would along these lines:

You, Theist, may have told a story that accounts for the enormous amount of evil in the world, and for the fact that much evil is not caused by human beings. But there is a challenge to theism that is based on the evils we find in the world, and not simply on what might be called the general fact of evil. There is an argument that is based on the obvious gratuitousness of many particular evils. I will present such an argument, and I will try to convince these estimable agnostics that even if you have effectively answered what our creator, Mr van Inwagen, has called the global argument from evil, your response to this argument does not touch what he has called local arguments from evil.

Let us consider certain particular very bad events—"horrors" I will call them. Here are some examples of what I call horrors: a school bus full of children is crushed by a landslide; a good woman's life is gradually destroyed by the progress of Huntington's Chorea; a baby is born without limbs. Some horrors are consequences of human choices, and some are not. But whether a particular horror is connected with human choices or not, it is evident, at least in many cases, that God could have prevented the horror without sacrificing any great good or allowing some even greater horror. (If you tell me that among the children in the school bus there might have been a child who would have been the twenty-first-century counterpart of Hitler, and that enormous amounts of evil were therefore prevented by the crushing of the school bus, I reply that that case is exactly like the case of the surgeon who saves a patient's life by amputating a limb but perversely refuses to use an anaesthetic; the same good result could have been achieved in a way that involved much less suffering, and an omniscient God would have known that and acted accordingly.)

Now a moment ago, I mentioned the enormous amount of evil in the world, and it is certainly true that there is an enormous amount of evil in the world. The phrase "the amount of evil" suggests—perhaps it even implies—that evil is quantifiable, like distance or weight. That may be false or unintelligible, but if it is true, even in a rough-and-ready sort of way, it shows that horrors raise a problem for the theist that is distinct from the problem raised by the enormous amount of evil. If evil can be, even roughly, quantified, as talk about amounts seems to imply, it might be that there was *more* evil in a world in which there were thousands of millions of relatively minor episodes of suffering (broken ribs, for example) than in a world in which there were a few horrors. But an omnipotent and omniscient creator could be called to moral account for creating a world in which there was even *one* horror. And the reason is obvious: that horror could have been "left out" of creation without the sacrifice of any great good or the permitting of some even greater horror. And leaving it out is just what a morally perfect being would do; such good things as might depend causally on the horror could—given the being's omnipotence and omniscience—be secured by (if the word is not morally offensive in this context) more "economical" means. Thus, the sheer amount of evil (which might be distributed in a fairly uniform way) is not the only fact about evil that Theist needs to take into account. He must also take into account what we might call (again with some risk of using morally offensive language) *high local concentrations* of evil—that is, horrors. And it is hard to see how the free-will defense, however elaborated, could provide any resources for dealing with horrors.

Rowe's well-known example of a horror, the fawn that died an agonizing death in a forest fire that was not caused, in any way, however remote, by human beings—and whose death leaves no trace that could ever be discovered by human beings—is a particularly difficult case for Theist. (If the episode left no trace, how do we know it occurred? Well, we're not really talking about a particular event, but about a *type* of event. Our knowledge of nature and our acceptance of the principle of the uniformity of nature make it impossible for us to believe that no events of this type have ever occurred.) True, however sentimental we may be about animals, this is not much of a horror compared with, say, Auschwitz. The *degree* of horror involved in the event is not what creates the special difficulty for theists in this case, but rather its complete causal isolation from the existence and activities of human beings. No appeal to considerations in any way involving human free will or future benefits to human beings can possibly be relevant to the problem with which this case confronts Theist, the difficulty of explaining why an omnipotent and morally perfect being would allow such a thing to happen.

There are many horrors, vastly many, from which no discernible good results—and certainly no good, discernible or not, that an omnipotent being couldn't have achieved without the horror; in fact, without any suffering at all. Here is a true story. A man came upon a young woman in an isolated place. He overpowered her, chopped off her arms at the elbows with an axe, raped her, and left her to die. Somehow she managed to drag herself on the stumps of her arms to the side of a road, where she was discovered. She lived, but she experienced indescribable suffering, and although she is alive, she must live the rest of her life without arms and with the memory of what she had been forced to endure.[1] No discernible good came of this, and it is wholly unreasonable to believe that any good could have come of it that an omnipotent being couldn't have achieved without employing the raped and mutilated woman's horrible suffering as a means to it. And even if this is wrong, and some good came into being with which the woman's suffering was so intimately connected that even an omnipotent being couldn't have obtained the good without the suffering, it wouldn't follow that that good outweighed the suffering. (It would certainly have to be a very great good for it to do that.) I will now draw on these reflections to construct a version of the argument from evil, a version that, unlike the version I presented earlier, refers not to all the evils of the world, but just to this one event. (The argument is modeled on the central argument of William Rowe's classic essay, "The Problem of Evil and Some Varieties of Atheism".) I will refer to the events in the story I have told collectively as 'the Mutilation'. I argue:

> (1) If the Mutilation had not occurred, if it had been, so to speak, simply *left out* of the world, the world would be no worse than it is. (It would seem, in fact, that the world would be significantly *better* if the Mutilation had been left out of it, but my argument doesn't require that premise.)

> (2) The Mutilation in fact occurred (and was a horror).

(3) If a morally perfect creator could have left a certain horror out of the world he created, and if the world he created would have been no worse if that horror had been left out of it than it would have been if it had included that horror, then the morally perfect creator would have left the horror out of the world he created—or at any rate he would have left it out if he had been able to.

(4) If an omnipotent being created the world, he was able to leave the Mutilation out of the world (and was able to do so in a way that would have left the world otherwise much as it is).

There is, therefore, no omnipotent and morally perfect creator.

I do not claim that this argument—one of the many "local arguments from evil"—is formally valid, but obviously it could easily be made formally valid by the addition of suitably chosen additional premises. Since it is obvious that all the additional premises that would be needed to make the argument formally valid would be indisputably true, it would be pedantic actually to search them out. You, Theist, must deny at least one of the four premises I have explicitly stated; or at any rate you must show that serious doubts can be raised about at least one of them. But which?

So speaks Atheist. How might Theist reply? Atheist has said that her argument is modeled on an argument of William Rowe's. If Theist models his reply on the replies made by most of the theists who have written on Rowe's argument, he will attack the first premise. He will try to show that, for all anyone knows, the world (considered under the aspect of eternity) is a better place for containing the Mutilation. He will defend the thesis that, for all anyone knows, God has brought, or will at some future time bring, some great good out of the Mutilation, a good that outweighs it, or else has employed the Mutilation as a means to the prevention of some even greater evil; and he will contend that, for all anyone knows, the great good achieved or the great evil prevented could not have been, respectively, achieved or prevented, even by an omnipotent being, in any other way than by some means that involved the Mutilation or some other horror at least as bad as the Mutilation.

I am not going to have Theist reply to Atheist's argument in this way. I find (1) fairly plausible, even if I am not as sure as Atheist is (or as sure as most atheists who have discussed the issue seem to be) that (1) is true. And I find it even more plausible, very plausible indeed, to suppose that the following existential generalization of (1) is true:

There has been, in the history of the world, at least one horror such that, if it had not existed, if it had been, so to speak, simply *left out* of the world, the world would be no worse than it is.

If this generalization is true, then, even if (1) is false, there has been at least one horror in the history of the world that Atheist could use to show that the world was not created by an omnipotent and morally perfect being—given, of course, that the other three premises of her argument, suitably adjusted, are true.

I am going to represent Theist as employing another line of attack on Atheist's response to his expanded free-will defense. I am going to represent him as denying premise (3) or, more precisely, as trying to show that the expanded free-will defense casts considerable doubt on premise (3). In order to enable you the better to follow what Theist says, I will attempt to fix the essential content of premise (3) in your minds by restating it in terms of a rather fanciful metaphor. Consider a morally perfect creator who is taking a final look at the four-dimensional blueprint of the world he is about to create. His eye falls on a patch in the blueprint that represents a horror. He reflects a moment and sees that if he simply erases that patch, replaces it with something innocuous, and does a little smoothing around the spatiotemporal edges to render the lines of causation in the revised blueprint continuous (or nearly so), a world made according to the revised blueprint will contain at least as favorable a balance of good and evil as a world made according to the unrevised blueprint. He therefore perceives a moral obligation to revise the blueprint in the way he has thought of and to incorporate the revision into his creation, and, being morally perfect, necessarily revises and creates accordingly. (Or, to be pedantic, he necessarily so revises and so creates if he is able so to revise and so to create.) Premise (3) simply says that this is what *must* happen when a morally perfect creator perceives in his plan for the world a horror that can be "edited out" without significantly altering the balance of good and evil represented in that plan.

Now that we have, I hope, got the content of premise (3) into our minds in an intuitive and memorable form, we are ready to hear Theist's reply to Atheist's rejoinder to the expanded free-will defense:

Why should we accept this premise? I have had a look at Rowe's defense of the corresponding premise of his argument, the entirety of which I will quote:

[This premise] seems to express a belief that accords with our basic moral principles, principles shared both by theists and non-theists.[2] This is not what anyone would call an extended piece of close reasoning. Still, let us consider it. We must ask, what are these "basic moral principles... shared both by theists and non-theists"? Rowe does not say; but I believe there is really just one moral principle that it would be plausible to appeal to in defense of premise (3). It might be stated like this:

> If one is in a position to prevent some evil, one should not allow that evil to occur—not unless allowing it to occur would result in some good that would outweigh it or preventing it would result in some other evil at least as bad.

(It should be noted that this principle does *not* say that if allowing the evil to occur would result in some good that would outweigh the evil or preventing it would result in some other evil at least as bad, then one *should* allow the evil to occur—or even that it's morally permissible to allow the evil to occur.)

A word about the phrase 'in a position to'. I mean it to imply both "is able to" and "is morally permitted to". As to the latter implication, perhaps—no matter what the utilitarians may say—it is sometimes simply *not one's place* to prevent certain evils. Some threatened evils may be such that to prevent them would constitute officious meddling in the lives of one's fellow citizens, a disregard of everyone's right to go to hell in his or her own custom-made hand-basket. (Remember the case of Dorothy and her doctor, which figured in the previous lecture.) Or to prevent certain evils might be to presume a legal or moral authority one does not have (consider the case of a police officer who secretly murders a serial killer whom the law cannot touch). Insisting on the moral component of 'in a position to' is probably necessary to make the principle that (I suggest) Rowe is appealing to plausible. But having said this, I can proceed to ignore it, since, it would seem, it is never morally impermissible for *God* to prevent an evil; not at any rate on the ground that to do so would be to interfere in a matter that is really none of his business or on the ground that it falls outside the scope of his moral authority. God is not our fellow citizen but our Maker, and all moral authority is his.

Now: Is the moral principle correct? I think not. Consider this case. Suppose you are an official who has the power to release anyone from prison at any time. Blodgett has been sentenced to ten years in prison for felonious assault. His sentence is nearing its end, and he petitions you to release him from prison a day early. Should you? Well, the principle says so. A day spent in prison is an evil—if you don't think so, I invite you to spend a day in prison. (Or consider the probable reaction of a prisoner who is, by bureaucratic foot-dragging, kept in prison one day longer than the term of his sentence.) Let's suppose that the only good that results from someone's being in prison is the deterrence of crime. (This assumption is made to simplify the argument I am going to present. That it is false introduces no real defect into the argument.) Obviously, 9 years and 364 days spent in prison is not going to have a significantly different power to deter felonious assault from 10 years spent in prison. So: no good will be secured by visiting on Blodgett that last day in prison, and that last day spent in prison is an evil. The principle tells you, the official, to let him out a day early. This much, I think, is enough to show that the principle is wrong, for you have no such obligation. But the principle is in more trouble than this simple criticism suggests.

It would seem that if a threatened punishment of n days in prison has a certain power to deter felonious assault, $n - 1$ days spent in prison will have a power to deter felonious assault that is not significantly less. Consider the power to deter felonious assault that belongs to a threatened punishment of 1,023 days in prison. Consider the power to deter felonious assault that belongs to a threatened punishment of 1,022 days in prison. There is, surely, no significant difference? Consider the power to deter felonious assault that belongs to a threatened punishment of 98 days in prison. Consider the power to deter felonious assault that belongs to a threatened punishment of 97 days in prison. There is, surely, no significant difference? Consider the power to deter felonious assault that belongs to a threatened punishment of one day in prison. Consider the power to deter felonious assault that belongs to a threatened punishment of no time in prison at all. There is, surely, no significant difference? (In this last case, of course, this is because the threat of one day in prison would have *no* power to deter felonious assault.)

A moment's reflection shows that if this is true, as it seems to be, then the moral principle entails that Blodgett ought to spend no time in prison at all. For suppose that Blodgett had lodged his appeal to have his sentence reduced by a day not shortly before he was to be released but before he had entered prison at all. He lodges this appeal with you, the official who accepts the moral principle. For the reason I have set out, you must grant his appeal. Now suppose that when it has been granted, clever Blodgett lodges a second appeal: that his sentence be reduced to 10 years less *two* days. This second appeal you will also be obliged to grant, for there is no difference between 10 years less a day and 10 years less two days as regards the power to deter felonious assault. I am sure you can see where this is going. Provided only that Blodgett has the time and the energy to lodge 3,648 successive appeals for a one-day reduction of his sentence, he will escape prison altogether.

This result is, I take it, a *reductio ad absurdum* of the moral principle. As the practical wisdom has it (but this is no compromise between practical considerations and strict morality; this *is* strict morality), "You have to draw a line somewhere". And this means an *arbitrary* line. The principle fails precisely *because* it forbids the drawing of morally arbitrary lines. There is nothing wrong, or nothing that can be determined a priori to be wrong, with a legislature's setting 10 years in prison as the minimum punishment for felonious assault—and this despite the fact that 10 years in prison, considered as a *precise span of days*, is an arbitrary punishment. If the terrestrial day were about 25 seconds shorter, the law would no doubt be stated in the same words, and it would be neither more nor less effective than it in fact is; the interval of time denoted by the phrase '10 years' would, however, be about one day shorter than the interval of time actually denoted by that phrase. It is obvious, when you think about it, that the lengths of the prison sentences written into our laws depend on accidents of astronomy, the (to some degree) accidental fact that we use a decimal rather than a binary or duodecimal system of numerical representation, and many other arbitrary factors—such as our preference for numbers that can be specified concisely. And there is nothing wrong with this. Since, however we "draw the line", its exact position will be an arbitrary matter, we might as well let its exact placement depend partly on the set of (morally speaking) arbitrary preferences that nature has dropped into our collective lap.

So: the moral principle is false—or possesses whatever defect is the analogue in the realm of moral principles of falsity in the realm of factual statements. What are the consequences of its falsity, of its failure to be an acceptable moral principle, for the local argument from evil? Let us return to the expanded free-will defense. This story accounts for the existence of horrors—that is, that there are horrors is a part of the story. The story explains why there are such things as horrors, although it says nothing about any particular horror. (It in fact implies that many individual horrors have no explanation whatever.) And to explain why there are horrors is not to meet the local argument from evil. I will consider this point in a moment, but first I will qualify my statement that the expanded free-will defense accounts for the existence of horrors. What is strictly correct is that the story accounts for the existence of what we might call "post-lapsarian" horrors—horrors that are consequences of humanity's separation from God. It cannot account for "pre-lapsarian" horrors (such as a "Rowe's fawn" case if the fawn's horrible death is imagined to have occurred before there were human beings). I shall first discuss post-lapsarian horrors (like the Mutilation); only when this discussion is complete shall I turn to the difficult topic of pre-lapsarian horrors. [As I said in the previous lecture, I'm not going to allow Theist to keep this promise. I'll discuss pre-lapsarian horrors in the next lecture, but in my own person.]

A general account of the existence of horrors does not constitute a reply to the argument from horrors, because it does not tell us which premise of the argument to deny. Let us examine this point in detail. According to the expanded free-will defense, the answer to the question, "Why are there horrors in a world created by an all-powerful and morally perfect God?" is this:

When human beings misused their free will and separated themselves from God, the existence of horrors was one of the natural and inevitable consequences of this separation. Each individual horror, however, may well have been due to chance. Let us, in fact, say that all horrors are individually due to chance. (Remember, the expanded free-will defense is a defense, not a theodicy. If a theist believes that some horrors are brought about by God, in each case to achieve some specific end—and both the Hebrew Bible and the New Testament imply this[3]—that is no reason for that theist to object to a philosopher's employing as a *defense* a story according to which every individual horror is due to chance.) As regards physical suffering and untimely death, rebelling against God is like disregarding a clearly worded notice, climbing a fence, and wandering about in a mine field. If someone does that, it's very close to a dead certainty that sooner or later something very bad will happen to him. But whether it's sooner or later, when and where it happens, may well be a matter of chance. In separating ourselves from God, we have become, as I said, the playthings of chance. Even those horrors most closely connected with human planning and deliberation are due to chance. Winifrid may have carefully planned her husband's murder for months, but it was by chance they met on that bus 28 years before. Now why doesn't God miraculously prevent each horror? Why didn't he see to it that the man responsible for the Mutilation broke his ankle earlier in the day that would have been the day of his encounter with his victim—or something of that sort? And why hasn't he done the same *mutatis mutandis* with respect to every horror? According to the expanded free-will defense, he has not done this because to have done it would have frustrated his plan for restoring human beings to their original union with him by removing an essential motive for cooperating with him—namely, the realization that there is something horribly wrong with the world they live in. The best that could come of a miraculous prevention of each of the horrors that resulted from our separation from God would be a state of perfect natural happiness—like the state of the souls of infants who die unbaptized, according to traditional Roman Catholic theology. But allowing horrors to occur opens the possibility of a supernatural good for humanity that is infinitely better than perfect natural happiness. God's strategy, so to call it, is like the strategy contemplated by Dorothy's doctor: to refuse to give Dorothy a drug that would stop the pains in her chest because doing so would frustrate the doctor's project of getting her to stop smoking and lose weight. (And such a strategy is morally permissible for God, whether or not it is for a human physician.) Now God perhaps does act to prevent any number of horrors. For all we know, he reduces the number of horrors in our world to some very small fraction of what it would have been if not for his specific and local miraculous action. Still, he has to leave the unredeemed world a horrible place or his plan for the redemption of humanity will fail.

This is what the expanded free-will defense says. This much we have already said. And this much, we have said, is not a reply to the argument from horrors, because it does not—by itself—seem to entail the falsity of any of the premises Atheist set out. But we are now in a position to imagine how one might reply to her invitation to Theist to say which of the premises of the argument to ask the agnostics to declare "not proven".

God, then, removes many horrors from the world—that is, in many cases, he sees that if he interacts with the world simply by sustaining the existence and normal causal propensities of its inhabitants, a horror will occur, and he does more than this; he makes specific local changes in the world in such a way that what would have happened doesn't, and the threatened horror is prevented. But he cannot remove *all* the horrors from the world, for that would frustrate his plan for reuniting human beings with himself. And if he prevents only some horrors, how shall he decide which ones to prevent? Where shall he draw the line?—the line between threatened horrors that are prevented and threatened horrors that are allowed to occur? I suggest that wherever he draws the line, it will be an arbitrary line. That this must be so is easily seen by thinking about the Mutilation. If God had added that particular horror to his list of horrors to be prevented, and that one alone, the world, considered as a whole, would not have been a significantly less horrible place, and the general realization of human beings that they live in a world of horrors would not have been significantly different from what it is. The existence of that general realization is just that factor in his plan for humanity that (according to the expanded free-will defense) provides his general reason for allowing horrors to occur. Therefore, preventing the Mutilation would in no way have interfered with his plan for the restoration of our species' original perfection. If the expanded free-will defense is a true story, God has made a choice about where to draw the line, the line between the actual horrors of history, the horrors that are *real*, and the horrors that are mere averted possibilities, might-have-beens. And the Mutilation falls on the "actual horrors of history" side of the line. And this fact shows that the line is an arbitrary one; for if he had drawn it so as to exclude the Mutilation from reality (and had excluded no other horror from reality), he would have lost no good thereby and he would have allowed no greater evil. He had no reason for drawing the line where he did. And what justifies him in doing this? What justifies him in allowing the Mutilation to occur in reality when he could have excluded from reality it without losing any good thereby? Has the victim of the Mutilation not got a moral case against him? He could have saved her, and he did not; and he does not even *claim* to have achieved some good by not saving her. It would seem that God is, in C. S. Lewis's words, in the dock; if he is, then I, Theist, am playing the part of his barrister, and you, the agnostics, are the jury. I offer the following obvious defense. There was no non-arbitrary line to be drawn. Wherever he drew the line, there would have been countless horrors left in the world—his plan requires the actual existence of countless horrors—and the victim or victims of any of those horrors could bring the same charge against him that we have imagined the victim of the Mutilation bringing against him.

But I see Atheist stirring in protest; she is planning to tell you that, given the terms of the expanded free-will defense, God should have allowed the *minimum* number of horrors consistent with his project of reconciliation, and that it is obvious he has not done this. She is going to tell you that there *is* a non-arbitrary line for God to draw, and that it is the line that has the minimum number of horrors on the "actuality" side. But there is no such line to be drawn. There is no minimum number of horrors consistent with God's plan of reconciliation, for the prevention of any one particular horror could not possibly have any effect on God's plan. For any *n*, if the existence of at most *n* horrors is consistent with God's plan, the existence of at most *n* − 1 horrors will be equally consistent with God's plan.[4] To ask what the minimum number of horrors consistent with God's plan is, is like asking, What is the minimum number of raindrops that could have fallen on France in the twentieth century that is consistent with France's having been a fertile country in the twentieth century? France *was* a fertile country in the twentieth century, and if God had prevented any one of the raindrops that fell on France in the twentieth century from reaching the earth, France would still have been a fertile country. And the same, of course, goes for any two raindrops, or any thousand raindrops, or any million raindrops. But, of course, if God had allowed *none* of the raindrops that in fact fell from the clouds over France in the twentieth century to reach the earth, France would have been a desert. And France would have been a desert if he had allowed only one, or only a thousand, or only a million, of those raindrops to reach the earth. And no one, I expect, thinks that there is some number *n* such that (1) if God had prevented *n* or fewer of the raindrops that fell on France in the twentieth century from reaching the earth, France would have been fertile, and (2) if God had prevented *n* + 1 or more of those raindrops from reaching the earth, France would not have been fertile.

I *expect* no one thinks this. But the operative concept in this case is vagueness—the vagueness of fertility—and vagueness is *such* a puzzling topic that philosophers who have banged their heads against it for extended periods have said some very startling things. *Very* able philosophers, for example, have been heard to say that there is a perfectly sharp cutoff point between "being tall" and "not being tall", a height such that someone of that height is tall and someone one millimeter shorter is not tall, even though no one knows, and no one can find out, precisely where that cutoff point lies. So perhaps there *is* someone, Timothy Williamson, perhaps, who would say that there is and *has to be* a smallest number of raindrops that could have fallen on France during the twentieth century consistently with France's having been a fertile country during that century. Well, if there is such a person, that person is wrong.

I want to point out, however, that any theist who accepts this thesis has, from his own point of view, a very simple way to answer the local argument from evil: "There *is* a smallest number of horrors such that the real existence of horrors in that number is consistent with the openness of human beings to the idea that human life is horrible and that no human efforts will ever alter this fact. And, since God is good, the horrors that actually exist—past, present, and future—are of just that number. If, therefore, the Mutilation had not happened, and if all else had been much the same, human beings wouldn't have been open to the idea that human life is horrible and that no human efforts would ever alter this fact. The first premise of the local argument is therefore false. You may find this counterfactual hard to believe, but I don't. After all, I believe that there is a smallest number of raindrops such that raindrops in that number falling on France in the twentieth century is consistent with the twentieth-century fertility of France, and I therefore believe that it is possible (although immensely improbable: it is immensely improbable that the number of raindrops that fell on France in the twentieth century is 'right at the cutoff point') that every twentieth-century French raindrop is such that, if it hadn't fallen on France in the twentieth century, France would not have been a fertile country in the twentieth century. If I can believe *that*, I can easily enough believe that if the Mutilation hadn't occurred, human beings wouldn't have been open to the idea that human life is horrible and that no human efforts would ever alter this fact. Here is a simple analogy of proportion: a given horror is to the openness of human beings to the idea that human life is horrible and that no human efforts will ever alter this fact as a given raindrop is to the fertility of France." Here ends the promised simple reply to the local argument from evil. Having presented this reply, let us leave to their own devices those philosophers who say that the boundaries which natural language draws are always sharp, that vagueness does not exist, that apparent cases of vagueness are in reality cases in which one is ignorant of where some of the sharp boundaries that one's language has drawn lie. Let us leave them and return to the bright world of good sense.

In the bright world of good sense, *this* is why God did not prevent the Mutilation—insofar as there is a "why". He had to draw an arbitrary line, and he drew it. And that's all there is to be said. This, of course, is cold comfort to the victim. Or, since we are merely telling a story, it would be better to say: if this story were true, and known to be true, knowing its truth would be cold comfort to the victim. But the purpose of the story is not to comfort anyone. It is not to give an example of a possible story that would comfort anyone if it were true and that person knew it to be true. If a child dies on the operating table in what was supposed to be a routine operation and a board of medical inquiry finds that the death was due to some factor that the surgeon could not have anticipated and that the surgeon was not at fault, that finding will be of no comfort to the child's parents. But it is not the purpose of a board of medical inquiry to comfort anyone; the purpose of a board of medical inquiry is, by examining the facts of the matter, to determine whether anyone was at fault. And it is not my purpose in offering a defense to provide even hypothetical comfort to anyone. It is to determine whether the existence of horrors entails that God is at fault—or, rather, since by definition God is never at fault, to determine whether an omnipotent and omniscient creator of a world that contained horrors would necessarily be at fault.

It is perhaps important to point out that we might easily find ourselves in a moral situation like God's moral situation according to the expanded free-will defense, a situation in which we must draw an arbitrary line and allow some bad thing to happen when we could have prevented it, and in which, moreover, no good whatever comes of our allowing it to happen. In fact, we do find ourselves in this situation. In a welfare state, for example, we use taxation to divert money from its primary economic role in order to spend it to prevent or alleviate various social evils. And how much money, what proportion of the gross national product, shall we—that is, the state—divert for this purpose? Well, not none of it and not all of it (enforcing a tax rate of 100 percent on all earned income and all profits would be the same as not having a money economy at all). And where we draw the line is an arbitrary matter. However much we spend on social services, we shall always be able to find some person or family who would be saved from misery if the state spent (in the right way) a mere £1,000 more than it in fact plans to spend. And the state can *always* find another £1,000, and can find it without damaging the economy or doing any other sort of harm. But this example takes us

into the troublesome real world—troublesome because the real world is
a world of all but infinite complexity, and if we talk of the real world,
we shall never come to the end of the conversation, for there will always
be more to say. I offer in place of this real example an artificially simple
philosopher's example. If this example does not correspond very closely
to anything in the real world, it can at any rate be discussed within the
restricted scope of a lecture like this one:

> One thousand children have a disease that is fatal if untreated. We
> have a certain amount of a medicine that is effective against the
> disease. Effective, that is, if the dose is large enough. If we distribute
> it evenly, if we give one one-thousandth of the medicine we have on
> hand to each of the children, all one thousand of them will certainly
> die, for one one-thousandth of the medicine is definitely too little
> to do anyone any good. We decide to divide the medicine into N
> equal parts (N being some number less than one thousand) and
> divide it among N of the children. (The N children will be chosen
> by lot, or by some other "fair" means.) Call each of these N equal
> parts a "unit". And where do we get the number N? Well, we get
> it somewhere—perhaps it is the result of some sort of optimality
> calculation; perhaps no optimality calculation is a practical possibility,
> and some expert on the disease has made an educated guess, and N
> is that guess. But we have *somehow* to come up with a number, for,
> of logical necessity, once we have decided to distribute the medicine
> in equal doses, a certain number of children are going to get doses in
> that amount. Now, since N is less than one thousand, less than the
> number of children who have the disease, *whatever* we do *must* have
> the following consequence: at most 999 of the children will live; at
> least one of them will die.

Now consider any one of the children who die if this plan is carried
out (the lots have been drawn but the medicine has not yet been
distributed); suppose the child's name is Charlie. Our plan, as I said,
is this: to give each of N children one unit of medicine. But suppose
now that Charlie's mother proposes an alternative plan. She points to
the N units of medicine laid out in N little bottles on the table, waiting
to be distributed, and says: Take $1/N + 1$ units from each bottle
and give $N/N + 1$ units to my Charlie. Then each of the N children
who would have received one unit will instead receive $1 - (1/N + 1)$
units—which is $(N + 1/N + 1) - (1/N + 1)$, which is $N/N + 1$.

If this redistribution is carried out, each of the N children *and* Charlie will receive N/N + 1 units. Now, thus algebraically represented, her plan is rather too abstract to be easily grasped. Let us look at a particular number. Suppose N is 100. Then here is what will happen if the "original" plan of distribution is carried out: each of 100 children will get 1 unit of medicine and live (at least if 100 was a small enough number); 900 children will die. And here is what will happen if Charlie's mother's plan is carried out: Charlie and each of 100 other children get 100/101 units of medicine—about 99 percent of a unit—and live; 899 children will die. Or, if you like, we can't say that this is what would have happened; we can't assert this counterfactual without qualification. (For that matter, we weren't able to predict with certainty that all 100 children would live in the actual case.) But we can say this: this is almost certainly what would have happened. "So," Charlie's mother argues, "you see that you can avert the certain death of a child at very small risk to the others; perhaps no risk at all, for your guess that N should be set at 100 was just that, a guess. One hundred and one would have been an equally good guess." We can make her argument watertight if we assume that for any determination of what number to set N equal to, that number plus 1 would have been an equally reasonable determination. That seems plausible enough to me; if you don't find it plausible, we can always make it plausible by making the number of children larger: suppose there were not 1,000 children but 1,000 million, and that everyone's best guess at N is somewhere around 100 million. You will not, I think, find it easy to deny the following conditional: if a certain amount of some medicine or drug has a certain effect on someone, then that amount minus one part in 100 million would not have a significantly different effect.

"Well," someone may say, "Charlie's mother has a good point. But the fact that she has a good point just shows that the authorities haven't picked the optimum value for N. N should have been some larger number." But I had my fictional authorities choose the number 100 only for the sake of having a concrete number with which to illustrate Charlie's mother's argument. She could have presented essentially the same argument no matter what number the authorities chose, and they had to choose *some* number. And what shall the authorities say to Charlie's mother? They must either accept her proposal or reject it. If (on the one hand) they accept it, they will have to deal with Alice's father, who will say, "You have 101 bottles of medicine on the table, each of which contains the same amount of medicine. Call that amount a 'dose'. I want you to take 1/102nd of a dose from each bottle and give what you collect by this method to Alice." If (on the other hand) they reject Charlie's mother's proposal, they will have to condemn Charlie to death without achieving any good thereby. We cannot evade this conclusion: No matter what the authorities do, they will have to permit the death of a child they could have saved, or almost certainly could have saved, without achieving any good by permitting that child's death.

It seems clear, therefore, that there can be cases in which it is morally permissible for an agent to permit an evil that agent could have prevented, despite the fact that no good is achieved by doing so. But then, it would seem, if the expanded free-will defense is a true story, this is exactly the moral structure of the situation in which God finds himself when he contemplates the world of horrors that is the consequence of humanity's separation from him. The local argument from evil, the argument from horrors, therefore, fails.

Here ends Theist's speech in reply to Atheist's presentation of the local argument from evil—or, more exactly, to her presentation of any local argument that appeals to a post-lapsarian horror (such as the Mutilation). It seems to me that if the audience of agnostics has been convinced by Theist's response to the global argument (a big 'if', you may want to say), they will be convinced by his reply to the local argument.

But Atheist has at least one arrow left in her quiver, the arrow I just mentioned. If the local argument has failed, it is the local argument with the restriction under which we have been considering it: that it be based on a *post-lapsarian* horror. There is still to be considered the matter of pre-lapsarian horrors, horrors such as a fawn who dies horribly in a forest fire long before there are human beings. There were certainly sentient animals long before there were sapient animals, and the paleontological record shows that, and a priori considerations having to do with the uniformity of nature strongly suggest that, for much of the long pre-human past, sentient creatures died agonizing deaths in natural disasters (not to mention agonizing deaths due to predation, parasitism, and disease). Obviously the free-will defense cannot be expanded in such a way as to account for these agonizing deaths, for only sapient creatures have free will, and these deaths cannot therefore have resulted from the abuse of free will.[5] It would seem that any approach to the problem of animal suffering must take account of the fact that there were sentient animals long before there were rational animals. (I believe that science has made only two contributions to the data of natural theology. The discovery of this fact is one of them; the other is the discovery that the physical world does not have an infinite past.) In the next lecture, we shall take up the problem of the sufferings of sentient but non-rational animals.

Lecture 7

The Sufferings of Beasts

In this lecture, I will present a defense that accounts for the sufferings of non-human terrestrial animals—"beasts"—or, more exactly, for the sufferings of beasts that cannot be ascribed to the actions of human beings. Since non-human animals presumably do not have free will, and since some (most, in fact) of the sufferings of non-human animals occurred before there were human beings, no extension or elaboration of the free-will defense can account for all animal suffering. (Or not unless it attributed the suffering of beasts to the free actions of angels or non-human rational animals. At the end of this lecture, I will briefly consider a version of the free-will defense that has this feature.)

I maintain that the defense I shall present, when it is conjoined with the free-will defense, will constitute a composite defense that accounts for the sufferings of both human beings and beasts, both rational or sapient animals and merely sentient animals.

In this lecture, I will abandon explicit reference to Atheist, Theist, and their debate before the audience of agnostics. I will present the second half of my composite defense in my own narrative voice. But I remind you that the ideal debate I have imagined remains my standard for evaluating a defense. In my view, the question we should attend to is not what I think of a defense or what you think of it, not what religious believers or committed atheists think of it, but what genuinely neutral agnostics think of it (or what they would think of it if there were any of them). My role in relation to a defense is to present it in as strong a form as possible; the role of atheists is to see to it that those who evaluate it are made aware of all its weak points; it is agnostics, neutral agnostics, who should be assigned the role of evaluating it.

I will now tell a story, a story that, I maintain, is true for all anyone knows, a story according to which God allows beasts to suffer (and in which the extent of their suffering and the ways in which they suffer are the actual extent and the actual ways). The story comprises the following four propositions:

(1) Every world God could have made that contains higher-level sentient creatures either contains patterns of suffering morally equivalent to those of the actual world, or else is massively irregular.[1]

(2) Some important intrinsic or extrinsic good depends on the existence of higher-level sentient creatures; this good is of sufficient magnitude that it outweighs the patterns of suffering found in the actual world.

(3) Being massively irregular is a defect in a world, a defect at least as great as the defect of containing patterns of suffering morally equivalent to those found in the actual world.

(4) The world—the cosmos, the physical universe—has been created by God.

The four key terms contained in this story may be explained as follows.

Higher-level sentient creatures are animals that are *conscious* in the way in which (*pace* Descartes) the higher non-human mammals are conscious.

Two patterns of suffering are *morally equivalent* if there are no morally decisive reasons for preferring one to the other: if there are no morally decisive reasons for creating a world that embodies one pattern rather than the other. To say that A and B are in this sense morally equivalent is not to say that they are in any interesting sense comparable. Suppose, for example, that the Benthamite dream of a universal hedonic calculus is an illusion, and that there is no answer to the question whether the suffering caused by war is equal to, the same as, or greater than the suffering caused by cancer. It does not follow that these two patterns of suffering are not morally equivalent. On the contrary: unless there is some "non-hedonic" morally relevant distinction to be made between a world that contains war and no cancer and a world that contains cancer and no war (i.e. a distinction that does not depend on comparing the amounts of suffering caused by war and cancer), it follows that the suffering caused by war and the suffering caused by cancer *are*, in the present technical sense, morally equivalent.

A *massively irregular world* is a world in which the laws of nature fail in some massive way.[2] A world, a physical universe, containing all the miracles recorded in the Old and New Testaments would not, on that account, be massively irregular, for those miracles were too small (if size is measured in terms of the amounts of matter directly affected) and too few and far between. But a world would be massively irregular if it contained the following state of affairs:

God, by means of an ages-long series of ubiquitous miracles, causes a planet inhabited by the same animal life as the actual earth to be a hedonic utopia. On this planet, fawns are (like Shadrach, Meshach, and Abednego) saved by angels when they are in danger of being burnt alive. Harmful parasites and micro-organisms suffer immediate supernatural dissolution if they enter a higher animal's body. Lambs are miraculously hidden from lions, and the lions are compensated for the resulting restriction on their diets by physically impossible falls of high-protein manna. On this planet, either God created every species by a separate miracle, or else, although all living things evolved from a common ancestor, a hedonic utopia has existed at every stage of the evolutionary process. (The latter alternative implies that God has, by means of a vast and intricately coordinated sequence of supernatural adjustments to the machinery of nature, guided the evolutionary process in such a way as to compensate for the fact that a hedonic utopia exerts no selection pressure.[3])

It would also be possible for a world to be massively irregular in a more systematic, or "wholesale", way. A world that came into existence five minutes ago, complete with memories of an unreal past, would be on that account alone massively irregular—if indeed such a world was metaphysically possible. A world in which beasts (beasts having the physical structures of and exhibiting the pain-behavior of actual beasts) felt no pain would be on that account alone massively irregular—if indeed such a world was metaphysically possible.

Finally, a *defect in a world* is a feature of a world that (whatever its extrinsic value might be in various worlds) a world is intrinsically better for not having. Our four technical terms have now been defined.

Our story, our defense, comprises propositions (1), (2), (3), and (4).[4] I believe that we have no reason to assign any probability or range of probabilities to this story. (With the following qualification: if we have a reason to regard the existence of God as improbable—a reason other than the sufferings of beasts—then we shall have a reason to regard the story as improbable.) That is to say, I regard this case as like the following case. I have drawn one of the numbers from 0 to 100 in a fair drawing from a hat, but I am not going to tell you what it is. I have put that many black balls into an empty urn and have then added 100-minus-that-many white balls. Now: What proportion of the balls in the urn are black? You have no way of answering this question: no answer you could give is epistemically defensible: "35 percent" is no better than "6 percent"; "about half" is no better than "about a quarter"; "a large proportion" is no better than "a small proportion", and so on. (More exactly, no answer is better than any *equally specific* competing answer. Of course there are answers like "between 1 percent and 90 percent" that have a pretty good crack at being right. But this answer is no better than "between 7 percent and 96 percent" or "either between 4 percent and 6 percent, or else between 10 percent and 97 percent".) And, because you have no way of answering the question, What proportion of the balls in the urn are black, you have no way of assigning a probability to the hypothesis that the first ball drawn from the urn will be black.[5]

Here is a case that is less artificial. Ask me what proportion of the galaxies other than our own contain intelligent life, and I'll have to say that I don't know;[6] no answer I could give is epistemically defensible for me. The answer could be "all" or "none" or "all but a few" or "about half". I see no reason to prefer any possible answer to this question to any of its equally specific competitors. (Or such is my judgment, a judgment based on what I think I know. I could be wrong about the implications of what I think I know, but then I could be wrong about almost anything.) And if I am right to think that I cannot say what proportion of the galaxies contain intelligent life, I have no way to assign a probability to the hypothesis that a given galaxy, one chosen at random, contains intelligent life.

In my view, our epistemic relation to the defense I have presented is like the epistemic relations illustrated by my examples.[7] It is like your epistemic relation to the hypothesis that the first ball drawn will be black or my relation to the hypothesis that Galaxy X, which was chosen at random, contains intelligent life.[8] That is to say, we have no way to answer the following question: Given that God exists, how likely is it that the other components of the defense are true? We should have reason to reject the defense if we had reason to believe that an omnipotent being could create a world—a world that was not massively irregular—in which higher-level sentient creatures inhabited a hedonic utopia. Is there any reason to think that an omnipotent being could create such a world? I suppose that the only kind of reasons one could have for believing that it was possible for an omnipotent being to create a world having a certain feature would be the reasons one acquired in the course of a serious attempt to "design" a world having that feature. Let us consider doing that. How should one go about designing a world?

One should start by describing in some detail the laws of nature that govern that world—and one should not neglect to include in one's description of the laws the values of the numerical parameters that occur in them, parameters like the fine-structure constant and the universal constant of gravitation. (Physicists' actual formulations of quantum field theories and the general theory of relativity provide the standard of required "detail".) One should then go on to describe the boundary conditions under which those laws operate: the topology of the world's spacetime, its average density as a function of time, its initial entropy, the number of particle families to be found in it, and so on. Then one should tell in convincing detail the story of cosmic evolution in that world: the story of the development of large objects like galaxies and stars and of small objects like carbon atoms. Finally, one should tell the story of the evolution of life. These stories, of course, must be coherent, given one's specification of laws and boundary conditions. Unless one proceeds in this manner, one's statements about what is intrinsically or metaphysically possible—and thus one's statements about an omnipotent being's "options" in creating a world—will be entirely subjective, and therefore without value.[9]

Our own universe provides the only model we have for the formidable task of designing a world.[10] (For all we know, in every possible world that exhibits any degree of complexity, the laws of nature are the actual laws, or at least have the same structure as the actual laws. There are, in fact, philosophically minded physicists who believe that there is only one possible set of laws of nature, and it is epistemically possible that they are right.) Our universe has—apparently—evolved out of an initial singularity in accordance with certain laws of nature. Might these laws be deterministic? And if they are, might it not have been possible for an omnipotent and omniscient being to have carefully selected the initial state of a universe like ours so as to render an eventual universal hedonic utopia causally inevitable? Well, there is this point: if a world evolves out of a singularity, it *has* no initial state. To create a world that has an initial state and, like ours, *appears* to have evolved out of a singularity, an omnipotent creator would have to create that world *ex nihilo* at some moment "complete with memories of an unreal past" (if only a very brief one). And, as I have said, that would be a case of massive irregularity. But let us set this point aside and assume that, if the laws of nature are deterministic, an omnipotent being could have "fine-tuned" the initial state of the universe so as to produce, in the fullness of time, a hedonic utopia. Could the omnipotent being have also done this if the laws were *indeterministic?* There is certainly no guarantee of this. If the laws of nature are indeterministic, then, for all we know, any initial state of the world that permitted the eventual existence of complex animals, however carefully selected that state was, *might* (if the world were left to its own devices once it had been created) eventually be succeeded by states that involved vast amounts of suffering. A deterministic creation would therefore seem to be the only option for a creator who wishes to make a world that contains complex animals that never suffer: even if only a minuscule proportion of the possible initial states of the world would yield the desired outcome, if even one did, he could choose to create a world with that initial state. But is a deterministic world (a deterministic world containing complex organisms like those of the actual world) possible? Have we any reason to think that a deterministic world is possible? These questions raise many further questions, questions that mostly cannot be answered. Nevertheless, the following facts would seem to be relevant to any attempt to answer them, and they suggest that there is at least good reason to think that a deterministic world that contains complex life—or any life at all—may not be possible. Life depends on chemistry, and chemistry depends on atoms, and atoms depend on quantum mechanics (classically speaking, an atom cannot exist: the electrons of a "classical" atom would spiral inward, shedding their potential energy in the form of electromagnetic radiation, till they collided with the nucleus), and, according to the "Copenhagen interpretation", which is the interpretation of quantum mechanics favored by most working physicists, quantum mechanics is essentially indeterministic. If the laws of nature are quantum-mechanical, it is unlikely that an omnipotent being could have "fine-tuned" the initial state of a universe like ours so as to render an eventual universal hedonic utopia causally inevitable. It would seem to be almost certain that, owing to quantum-mechanical indeterminacy, a universe that was a duplicate of ours when ours was, say, 10^{-45} seconds old could have evolved into a *very* different universe from our present universe.

Our universe is, as I said, our only model of how a universe might be designed. And that universe is not without its mysteries. The very early stages of the unfolding of the cosmos (the incredibly brief instant during which the laws of nature operated under conditions of perfect symmetry), the formation of the galaxies, and the origin of life on the Earth are, in the present state of natural knowledge, deep mysteries.

Nevertheless, it seems reasonable to assume that all these processes involved only the operation of the laws of nature.[11] One important thing that is known about the evolution of the universe into its present state is that it has been a very tightly structured process. A large number of physical parameters have apparently arbitrary values such that if those values had been only slightly different (very, *very* slightly different) the universe would contain no life, and *a fortiori* no intelligent life. A similar point applies to some of the boundary conditions on which these laws operate: the entropy of the early universe, for example. It may or may not be the "purpose" of the cosmos to constitute an arena in which the evolution of intelligent life takes place, but it is certainly true that this evolution did take place, and that if the universe had been different by an all but unimaginably minute degree, it wouldn't have. My purpose in citing this fact—it is reasonable to believe that it is a fact—is not to produce an up-to-date version of the Design Argument. It is, rather, to suggest that (at least, for all we know) only in a universe very much like ours could intelligent life, or indeed life of any sort, develop by the operation of the laws of nature, unsupplemented by miracles. And the natural evolution of higher sentient life in a universe like ours essentially involves suffering, or there is every reason to believe it does. The mechanisms underlying biological evolution may be just what most biologists seem to suppose—the production of new genes by random mutation and the culling of gene pools by environmental selection pressure—or they may be more subtle. But no one, I believe, would take seriously the idea that the highest subhuman animals, the immediate evolutionary precursors of human beings, could have evolved naturally without hundreds of millions of years of ancestral suffering. (If I am wrong and there are those who would take this idea seriously, even these people must admit that it is *true for all we know* that pain is an essential component of the evolution of higher-level sentient organisms. And this concession will be sufficient for our argument.) Pain would seem to be an indispensable component of the evolutionary process after organisms have reached a certain stage of complexity.[12] And, for all we know, the amount of pain that organisms have experienced in the actual world, or some amount morally equivalent to that amount, is necessary for the natural evolution of conscious animals. I conclude that the first part of our defense is true for all we know: Every world God could have made that contains higher-level sentient creatures either contains patterns of suffering morally equivalent to those of the actual world, or else is massively irregular.[13]

Let us now consider the second component of our defense: Some important intrinsic or extrinsic good depends on the existence of higher-level sentient creatures; this good is of sufficient magnitude that it outweighs the patterns of suffering contained in the actual world. It is not very hard to believe (is it?) that a world that was as the Earth was just before the appearance of human beings would contain a much larger amount of intrinsic good, and would, in fact, contain a better balance of good over evil, than a world in which there were no organisms higher than worms. (Which is not to say that there could not be worlds lacking intelligent life that contained a still better balance of good over evil—say, worlds containing the same organisms, but significantly less suffering.) And then there is the question of extrinsic value. One consideration immediately suggests itself: intelligent life—creatures made in the image and likeness of God—could not evolve directly from worms or oysters; the immediate evolutionary precursors of intelligent animals must possess higher-level sentience.

We now turn to the third component of our defense: Being massively irregular is a defect in a world, a defect at least as great as the defect of containing patterns of suffering morally equivalent to those contained in the actual world. We should recall that a defense is not a theodicy, and that I am not required to show that it is *plausible to suppose* that massive irregularity is a defect in a world, a defect so grave that creating a world containing animal suffering morally equivalent to the animal suffering of the actual world is a reasonable price to pay to avoid it. I am required to show only that *for all anyone knows* this judgment is correct.

The third component of our defense is objectionable only if we have some prima facie reason for believing that the actual sufferings of beasts are a graver defect in a world than massive irregularity would be. Have we any such reason? It seems to me that we do not. To begin with, it does seem that massive irregularity is a defect in a world. One minor point in favor of this thesis is the witness of deists and other thinkers who have deprecated the miraculous on the ground that *any* degree of irregularity in a world is a defect, a sort of unlovely jury-rigging of things that is altogether unworthy of the power and wisdom of God. Presumably such thinkers would regard *massive* irregularity as a very grave defect indeed. And perhaps there is something to this reaction. It does seem that there is something right about the idea that God would include no more irregularity than was necessary in his creation. A second point is that many, if not all, massively irregular worlds are not only massively irregular but massively *deceptive*. This is obviously true of a world that now looks like the actual world but which began five minutes ago, or a world that looks like the actual world but in which beasts feel no pain. (And it is not surprising that massively irregular worlds should be massively deceptive, for our beliefs about the world depend in large measure on our habit of drawing conclusions that are based on the assumption that the world is regular.) But it is plausible to suppose that deception, and, *a fortiori*, massive deception, is inconsistent with the nature of a perfect being. These points, however, are no more than suggestive, and, even if they amounted to proof, they would prove only that massive irregularity was a defect; they would not prove that it was a defect comparable to the actual suffering of beasts. In any case, proof is not the present question: the question is whether there is a prima facie case for the thesis that the actual sufferings of beasts constitute a graver defect in a world than does massive irregularity.

Let us imagine a philosopher, Frank, who proposes to set out a prima facie case for this thesis. What considerations might he appeal to? I would suppose that he would have to rely on his moral intuitions, or, more generally, on his intuitions of value. He would have to regard himself as in a position to say, "I have held the two states of affairs—the actual sufferings of beasts and massive irregularity—before my mind and carefully compared them. My considered judgment is that the former is worse than the latter." This judgment presupposes that these two states of affairs are, in the sense that was explained above, comparable: one of them is worse than the other, or else they are of the same value (or "disvalue"). It is not clear to me that there is any reason to suppose that this is so. If it is *not* so, then, as we have seen, it can plausibly be maintained that the two states of affairs are morally equivalent, and a creator could not be faulted on moral grounds for choosing either over the other. But let us suppose that the two states of affairs are comparable. In that case, if Frank's value-judgment is to be trusted, he possesses (and, presumably, most other people do as well) a faculty that enables him correctly to judge the relative values of states of affairs of literally cosmic magnitude, states of affairs, moreover, that are in no way (as some states of affairs of cosmic magnitude may be) connected with the practical concerns of human beings. But why should Frank suppose that his inclinations—why should anyone suppose that anyone's inclinations—to make judgments about the relative value of various states of affairs are reliable guides to the true relative values of states of affairs of cosmic magnitude that have no connection with the business of human life? One's intuitions about value are either a gift from God or a product of evolution or socially inculcated or stem from some combination of these sources. Why should we suppose that any of these sources would provide us with the means to make correct value-judgments concerning matters that have nothing to do with the practical concerns of everyday life? (As I said in Lecture 4, I think we must be able to speak of *correct* value-judgments if the argument from evil is to be at all plausible. An eminent philosopher of biology has said in one place that God, if he existed, would be indescribably wicked for having created a world like this one, and, in another place, that morality is an illusion, an illusion that we are subject to because of the evolutionary advantage that being subject to it confers. These two theses do not seem to me to add up to a coherent position.[14]) When I addressed the question, How does one go about designing a world?, I (in effect) advocated a form of modal skepticism: our modal intuitions, while they are no doubt to be trusted when they tell us that the table could have been placed on the other side of the room, are not to be trusted on such matters as whether there could be a "regular" universe in which there were higher sentient creatures that did not suffer.[15] And if this is true, it is not surprising. Assuming that there are "modal facts of the matter", why should we assume that God or evolution or social training has given us access to modal facts knowledge of which is of no interest to anyone but the metaphysician? God or evolution has provided us with a capacity for making judgments about size and distance by eye that is very useful in hunting mammoths and driving cars, but which is of no use at all in astronomy. It seems that an analogous restriction applies to our capacity for making modal judgments. How can we be sure that an analogous restriction does not also apply to our capacity for making *value*-judgments? My position is that we cannot be sure, and that, for all we know, the value-judgments that people are inclined to make about cosmic matters unrelated to the concerns of everyday life are untrustworthy. (Not that our inclinations in this area are at all uniform. I myself experience no inclination to come down on one side or the other of the question of whether massive irregularity or vast amounts of animal suffering is the graver defect in a world. I suspect that others do experience such inclinations. If they don't, of course, then I'm preaching to the converted.) But then there is no prima facie case for the thesis that the actual sufferings of beasts constitute a graver defect in a world than does massive irregularity. Or, at least, there is no case that is grounded in our intuitions about value. And in what else could such a case be grounded?

These considerations have to do with intrinsic disutility, with the comparison of the intrinsic disutility of states of affairs. There is also the matter of extrinsic disutility. Who can say what the effects of creating a massively irregular world might be? Who can say what things of intrinsic value might be impossible in a massively irregular world? *We* cannot say. Here is one example of a consideration that may, for all I know, be relevant to this question. Christians have generally held that at a certain point God plans to hand over the government of the world to humanity. Would a massively irregular world be the sort of world that could be "handed over"? Perhaps a massively irregular world would immediately dissolve into chaos if an infinite being were not constantly making adjustments to it. Again, we cannot say. If anyone maintains that he has good reason to believe that nothing of any great value depends on the world's being regular, we must ask him why he thinks he is in a position to know things of that sort. We might remind him of the counsel of epistemic humility that was spoken to Job out of the whirlwind:

Gird up now thy loins like a man; for I will demand of thee, and answer thou me.

Where wast thou when I laid the foundations of the earth? declare, if thou hast understanding.

Knowest thou it, because thou wast then born? or because the number of thy days is great?

Canst thou bind the sweet influences of Pleiades, or loose the bands of Orion?

Knowest thou the ordinances of heaven? canst thou set the dominion thereof in the earth?[16]

I have urged extreme modal and moral skepticism (or, one might say, humility) in matters unrelated to the concerns of everyday life. If such skepticism is accepted, then we have no reason to accept the proposition that an omniscient and omnipotent being will be able so to arrange matters that the world contains sentient beings and does not contain patterns of suffering morally equivalent to those of the actual world. More precisely, we have no reason to suppose that an omniscient and omnipotent being could do this without creating a massively irregular world; and, for all we know, either the disutility, intrinsic or extrinsic, of massive irregularity in a world is greater than the intrinsic disutility that is a consequence of containing vast amounts of animal suffering, or else the disutility of massive irregularity and the disutility of containing vast amounts of animal suffering are incomparable.

What I have said so far is, or purports to be, a defense, a response to the global argument from animal suffering, to the argument whose premise is the fact that animal suffering exists. Let us now turn to the local argument, to the argument (to any argument) whose premise is the existence of some particular episode in which a beast suffers. Let us begin by noting that two patterns of suffering may be morally equivalent even if they are comparable and one of them involves *less* suffering than the other. That this is so can be shown by reflection on some considerations having to do with vagueness, reflections similar to our reflections on vagueness in the previous lecture. As I pointed out in that lecture, there is no morally decisive reason to prefer a prison term of 10 years less a day as a penalty for armed assault to a term of 10 years, despite the indubitable facts that these two penalties would have the same deterrent effect and that the former is a lighter penalty than the latter. And it may well be that for any amount of suffering that somehow serves God's purposes, some smaller amount of suffering would have served them just as well. It may be, therefore, that God has had to choose *some* amount of suffering as the amount contained in the actual world, and could, consistently with his purposes, have chosen any of a vast array of smaller or greater amounts, and that all the members of this vast array of alternative amounts of suffering are morally equivalent. (Similarly, a legislature has to choose *some* penalty as the minimum penalty for armed assault, and—think of penalties as prison terms measured in minutes—must choose among the members of a vast array of morally equivalent penalties.) Or it may be that God has decreed, with respect to this vast array of alternative, morally equivalent amounts of suffering, that *some* member of this array shall be the actual amount of suffering, but has left it to chance which member of this array is the amount of suffering that actually exists.[17]

In the previous lecture, we saw that it may be morally necessary for God to draw a morally arbitrary line through the set of threatened or possible or potential evils, a line that divides those evils that are actually to occur from those that will be averted. And we saw that if this is so, it opens the way to a reply to the local argument from evil to anyone who has a satisfactory reply to the global argument from evil. The logic of the case is the same whether our subject is the sufferings of human beings or the sufferings of beasts. If theists know of a story that explains why, in general, God allows beasts to suffer (I have offered such a story), they may reply to any local argument from evil that is based on a particular case of suffering in the subhuman world in the following way: Even if no good came of the instance of suffering cited in the argument, the occurrence of that event does not tell against the existence of an omnipotent, morally perfect being; for it may be that the omnipotent, morally perfect Creator of the world was morally required to draw a morally arbitrary line through the set of threatened evils, and that the instance of suffering that the argument cites fell on the "actuality" side of the particular line he chose.

But this is rather abstract. Let us consider a concrete case that illustrates these abstract points. Let us consider a famous case we have mentioned or alluded to a number of times, the case of "Rowe's fawn". (We will imagine—Rowe doesn't say this—that the fawn's horrible death took place long before there were human beings.) Rowe contends, first, that an omnipotent and omniscient being could have prevented the fawn's suffering without thereby losing some greater good or permitting some evil as bad or worse, and, secondly, that an omniscient, omnipotent wholly good being *would* have prevented the fawn's suffering—unless it could not have done so without losing some greater good or permitting some evil as bad as or worse than the fawn's suffering. Whatever might be said about the first of Rowe's two premises, it should be clear that if God has some good reason for allowing the world to contain the sufferings of beasts, and if there are alternative, morally equivalent amounts of (intense) suffering that would serve God's purposes equally well, then the second premise may well be false. God, everyone will agree, could have miraculously prevented the fire, or miraculously saved the fawn, or miraculously caused its agony to be cut short by death. And—I will concede this for the sake of argument[18]—if he had done so, this would have thwarted no significant good and permitted no significant evil. But what of the hundreds of millions (at least) of similar incidents that have, no doubt, occurred during the long history of life? Well, I concede, he could have prevented any one of them, or any two of them, or any three of them ... without thwarting any significant good or permitting any significant evil. But could he have prevented them all? No, or not necessarily. For if God has some good reason for allowing beasts to suffer, this good reason would not be served if he prevented all cases of such suffering. There may well be no *minimum* number of cases of intense suffering that God could allow without forfeiting whatever good depends on the suffering of beasts—just as there is no shortest sentence that a legislature can establish as the penalty for armed assault without forfeiting the good of effective deterrence. It may well be, therefore, that the fawn suffered simply because its sufferings fell on the "actuality" side of the particular line through the set of possible instances of suffering that God chose. If, therefore, theists can tell a story according to which God has a good reason for permitting the sufferings of beasts, if theists have a defense that can be used successfully to counter the global argument from animal suffering, they need not be embarrassed by the fact that they are unable to see what outweighing good might depend on some particular instance of animal suffering. It might be that they cannot see what good might have this feature for the simple reason that no possible good has this feature; but, as we have seen, a morally perfect God might have allowed this instance of suffering even though no good at all came of it.[19]

I will now consider some questions raised by, and possible objections to, the defense I have used to counter the global argument from animal suffering.

I will begin by remarking that I make no apology for the fact that my "total" defense, the composite defense, comprises two quite different parts. If there is a God who permits the sufferings of both beasts and human beings, it seems to me to be not at all implausible to suppose that he has one reason for permitting the sufferings of beasts and another, entirely different, reason for permitting the sufferings of human beings. This seems to me to be plausible because human beings are radically different from all other terrestrial animals, even the most intelligent primates. We may share 98 percent of our DNA (or whatever the latest figure is) with chimpanzees, but that other 2 percent is the genetic substrate of a great gulf. It may be surprising that we are so different from chimpanzees if our DNA is (as I am told) more similar to theirs than the DNA of grizzly bears is to the DNA of Kodiak bears; but there it is. The world is full of surprises. It is, after all, we human beings, or some of us, who are surprised by this fact. The chimps—perhaps you will have noticed this—aren't in a position to be surprised by the fact that surprises us.

Although it is not strictly to our purpose, I will point out that a "two-part" defense, a defense that treats the sufferings of beasts and the sufferings of human beings differently, is consonant with the most usual Christian view of suffering. On the one hand, Christians have typically held that human suffering is not a part of God's plan for the world, but exists only because that plan has gone awry. On the other:

Thou makest darkness, that it may be night; wherein all the beasts of the forest do move.

The lions, roaring after their prey, do seek their meat from God. The sun ariseth, and they get them away together, and lay them down in their dens. (Ps. 104: 20–2)

This and many other biblical texts seem to imply that the whole subrational natural world proceeds according to God's plan (except insofar as we human beings have corrupted nature). And this, as the Psalmist tells us in his great hymn of praise to the order that God has established in nature, includes the phenomenon of predation.[20]

However this may be, the composite defense I have offered raises—by the very fact that I have offered it—an obvious question. Why need my defense be a composite defense? Why did I bother with the lengthy and elaborate expanded free-will defense when I had the anti-irregularity defense (so to call it) at my disposal? After all, human beings are sentient animals. If the anti-irregularity defense satisfactorily explains the sufferings of sub-rational sentient animals, why does it not satisfactorily explain the sufferings of rational sentient animals, of human beings?

I have two things to say in reply to this question. First, or so it seems to me, the sufferings of human beings are a much worse evil than the sufferings of beasts. And it is not only I to whom things seem this way. Almost all human beings agree that, although it is a bad thing for animals to suffer, the sufferings of human beings are to be prevented, if there is no other way to do it, at the cost of animal suffering—even quite large amounts of animal suffering. Not everyone agrees, of course—not Peter Singer, for example. Still, this judgment of mine is not an idiosyncratic one. It seems to me, in fact, that the suffering of human beings, the actual total suffering of human beings, is so much worse a thing than the suffering of beasts, the actual total suffering of beasts, that, although I am confident that I do not know whether a pattern of suffering like the actual suffering of beasts constitutes a graver moral defect in a world than massive irregularity, I am not willing to say that I have no idea whether the pattern of suffering actually exhibited by human beings constitutes a graver moral defect in a world than massive irregularity. In fact, I am inclined to deny this thesis; I am inclined to say that the mere avoidance of massive irregularity cannot be a sufficient justification for the actual sufferings of human beings. (And there is this point to be made: there have been so few human beings, compared with the number of sentient living things that there have been, that it is not evident that a world in which all human suffering was miraculously prevented *would* be a massively irregular world.)

Secondly, suppose that, contrary to what I am inclined to think, the anti-irregularity defense *does* provide good reason to think that no moral case could successfully be made against an omnipotent creator of a world containing human suffering in the amount and of the kinds found in the actual world. It never hurts to have more than one defense. The counsel for the defense who has a plausible story that explains away the prosecuting attorney's apparently damning evidence does well. But the defense counsel who has *two* such plausible stories—*different* stories, stories that are not trivial variations on a single theme—does better. (This sort of case, by the way, shows that a defense need not be *probable* on the existence of God and evil and what is known to the audience of agnostics. If Theist had *ten* defenses, defenses that were logically inconsistent with one another, the average probability of these defenses on any proposition could not be greater than 10 percent. But it would be a good thing, from Theist's point of view, to have ten independent defenses, despite the fact that this would necessitate a low average probability for the individual defenses.)

It might also be argued that there was a certain tension between the anti-irregularity defense and the expanded free-will defense, since the anti-irregularity defense implies that there is at least a prima facie case against God's employing a miracle on any given occasion, and the expanded free-will defense entails that the raising of our immediate non-human ancestors to human or rational status was a miraculous event. This argument has little force, however, for the raising of our primate ancestors to rationality could have taken place in a world that contained very little in the way of miraculous irregularity. It would, in fact, require nothing more than a genotypic and phenotypic transformation of a few score or a few hundred, or, at most, a few thousand organisms. It might be asked why the expanded free-will defense need postulate that the genesis of human rationality requires divine intervention at all. There are two reasons. First, human beings and beasts are, as I have noted, radically different. Between us and the highest primates there is a vast gulf. I have a hard time believing that this gulf was bridged by the ordinary mechanisms of evolution in the actual time in which it was bridged. Whenever the first rational primates existed, it is clear that our ancestors of one million years ago were mere animals, no more rational than present-day chimpanzees or gorillas, and a million years is not much time for the evolutionary development of radical novelty.

In a similar way, I'd have a hard time believing a paleontologist who told me that at some point in the history of life there was an organism with eyes comparable to those of present-day birds and mammals, and that, a mere million years earlier, the ancestors of that organism had no visual apparatus at all, not even photosensitive spots. If I may judge by some unguarded remarks I've heard, I think that some adherents of philosophical naturalism are a bit uneasy about the time span in which the gulf between non-rationality and rationality was bridged—but, unlike us theists, they have no alternative to supposing that the gulf was bridged by purely natural mechanisms within this time span, and, in one way or another, they have made their peace with it.

This, however, is not my primary reason for ascribing a miraculous origin to human rationality in the expanded free-will defense. (For one thing, although it seems to me very hard to see how human rationality could have had a purely natural origin, I cannot say that it is *evident* that it did not. The world, and particularly the biological world, is a thing of enormous complexity, and it is very dangerous to reach conclusions about it on the basis of a priori argument. When I think about it, I have to say that *for all I know* rationality had a purely natural origin. And I think I could expect—I think Theist could expect—that an audience of neutral agnostics would agree with me on this point. If, therefore, there were something to be gained by including in the expanded free-will defense the proposition that rationality had a natural origin, there would be no barrier to doing so.) My primary reason is that the plausibility of the story would be greatly reduced if it did not represent the genesis of rationality as a sudden, sharp event. If the story represented the genesis of rationality as a long, vague event, an event comprising thousands of generations, this would open the way for Atheist to raise all sorts of awkward questions about the plausibility of the story. Here was my description of the miraculous raising of humanity to rationality:

... there was a time when every ancestor of modern human beings who was then alive was a member of [a] tiny, geographically tightly knit group of primates. ... God took the members of this breeding group and miraculously raised them to rationality. That is, he gave them the gifts of language, abstract thought, and disinterested love—and, of course, the gift of free will.

The story goes on to tell how these newly human primates abused the gift of free will and, as it were, laid violent hands on the Creation and attempted to turn it to their own purposes. But suppose I, or Theist, had told the story this way: there was no first generation of human beings; the genesis of human rationality was a gradual event covering hundreds of thousands of years; but our ancestors were definitely rational by 190,000 BC; on February 26, 187,282 BC; they rebelled against God—and, from this point, the rest of our story is the same. If I were Atheist, and if I heard this version of the story told to the agnostics, I should have all sorts of pointed questions to ask. For example: "At the time of the Edenic rebellion, there had been rational human beings for many thousands of years. What happened to all those rational beings? Where did they go? They can't have *died*, for according to your story, human death is a consequence of the rebellion." Well, Theist might respond that, after a certain period of life in Paradise, during which they married and raised families, Edenic human beings were taken up into some other mode of existence; in Tolkien's words, "removed for ever from the circles of the world". This reply might save the coherence of the story, but it does not remove the miraculous element from it, for the passage from paradisal to transcendent existence would be a miraculous event. And the miraculous element in the story was supposed to be the problem. Or Theist might say that the earlier human beings didn't go anywhere. They never died, and the human population gradually increased from a few hundred to several million (at the time of the rebellion). Now this might raise empirical difficulties. (Would a vast deposit of more or less simultaneous skeletal remains not mark the deaths of those who participated in the rebellion and their immediate descendants?) And any proposed revision of the expanded free-will defense that, like the two we have considered, represents the genesis of rationality as a vague, smudgy event will raise a problem more fundamental than those I have mentioned. If the genesis of rationality was a vague event, there would have to have been a long, a very long, period during which our ancestors were neither fully rational nor simply beasts. Atheist will certainly ask what part these "intermediate" creatures played in God's plan for humanity. And she will ask Theist to tell his audience at what point they became immorbid—at what point they stopped dying after the fashion of their purely animal ancestors. Must the genesis of immorbidity, if not the genesis of rationality, have been a sudden, sharp event? After all, an organism either ages and dies, or it doesn't.

All in all, the story seems to raise the fewest problems in the form in which I had Theist tell it in the fifth lecture. That is to say, it raises the fewest problems if it represents the genesis of human rationality as taking place in a single generation. And it is hard to see how, if this happened, it could have been anything other than a miracle. (Anyone who *does* think that a "sudden" genesis of rationality could have happened in the natural course of evolution can, if he likes, introduce a disjunction into the story: at a certain point in time, a population of our ancestors suddenly became rational beings, either miraculously *or* as the result of the workings of purely natural causes. I don't think that this disjunction does much for the plausibility of the story, but some may.) It is necessary to point out, too, that even if a sharp genesis of rationality need not involve a miracle, the taking of our first human ancestors into union with God must certainly have been miraculous. That miracle might bother some people less than a miraculous genetic and physiological transformation of the human organism, but this, I think, is an unphilosophical reaction. The taking of an individual, call him Adam, into union with God must involve some sort of rearrangement of the matter of which Adam is composed. If Adam is, in his own nature, in a suitable state for union with God, after all, so will a perfect physical duplicate of Adam be in that state. And a miraculous rearrangement of matter is a miraculous rearrangement of matter, whether it effects rationality or the capability of entering into union with God.

This, then, is why the story I have had Theist tell contains a miracle—or two miracles (or two miracles times n, where n is the number of human beings who were raised first to rationality and then to the Beatific Vision). These miracles are in the story because (in my judgment) the story would be less plausible without them. But, as I have contended, even the totality of these miracles is not comparable to the huge set of miracles that (according to the anti-irregularity defense) would be needed to maintain a hedonic utopia for hundreds of millions of years.

Having answered these objections to the anti-irregularity defense, I will now raise the question of what alternatives there might be to it. If we leave aside a thesis endorsed by various Eastern religions and by Absolute Idealists, that the world of space and time and individual objects and causal relations is an illusion (and that the suffering of beasts is therefore an illusion, as indeed are the beasts themselves), and if we leave aside the absurd Cartesian idea that non-human animals do not feel pain, I know of two.

First, there is C. S. Lewis's suggestion that there may have been pain in the pre-human natural world only because fallen angels had corrupted nature.[21] (On this suggestion, the free-will defense can account for the sufferings of beasts, for the suggestion is, of course, that angelic free will is a great good, and that an omnipotent being is no more able to ensure the outcome of a free angelic choice than the outcome of a free human choice.) I do not take Lewis's suggestion seriously enough to be able to make a reliable guess about how plausible it would seem to an audience of neutral agnostics. I must concede, however, that my reaction to this suggestion is at least in part a product of theological convictions that the audience of agnostics will not share. I am convinced that the teaching of the Bible is that the natural world is and always has been, apart from the effects that fallen human beings have had on it, just as God made it. (See, for example, Psalm 104, quoted earlier in this lecture, and the remarks that follow the quotation.) And I don't see how to apply anything like the expanded free-will defense to the case of angels in a way that is consistent with the rather standard Christian theology that I accept; for, according to this theology, fallen angels are forever fallen, and God has no plan of atonement for them. Perhaps my dislike of the "angelic corruption of nature" defense is rooted in a moral tendency analogous to that of the defense attorney who is reluctant to explain away the prosecution's evidence by telling a story (not as the truth, but as representing a real possibility) he himself regards as certainly false. There is, however, one point that might be made against the angelic corruption defense that does not rest on theology. The anti-irregularity defense included this proposition: The immediate evolutionary precursors of human beings could not have evolved naturally without many millions of years of ancestral suffering. And this proposition, I contended, is true for all anyone knows. I in fact think that it is more than true for all anyone knows: I think that it is extremely plausible. I therefore find it correspondingly implausible to suppose that the sufferings of pre-human animals are due to the actions of malevolent angels (even supposing—as I do—that such beings exist). I am inclined to think that an audience of neutral agnostics would share this reaction.

Secondly, there is an argument due to Professor Geach, who finds the problem of the suffering of beasts to be no problem at all. We human beings must be concerned with the sufferings of beasts (in a narrowly circumscribed set of cases: we have no obligation to dedicate our lives to saving rabbits from foxes or to end our "genocidal war with the rat"), Geach says, because we and they share the same animal nature, and we can thus feel sympathy toward them and therefore have (certain very limited) moral obligations to them. God, however, is not an animal and cannot feel pain, and can therefore feel no sympathy with suffering animals; he is, therefore, under no moral obligation to eliminate or ameliorate their sufferings.[22]

This argument seems to me to have two defects.

First, it proves too much: if it shows that God is under no obligation to eliminate or minimize the physical sufferings of beasts, an exactly parallel argument shows that he is under no obligation to eliminate or minimize the physical sufferings of human beings. Geach writes:

God is not an animal as men are, and if he does not change his designs to avoid pain and suffering to animals he is not violating any natural sympathies as Dr Moreau did. Only anthropomorphic imagination allows us to accuse God of cruelty in this regard. (p. 80)

But why would someone who accepted this argument not also accept the following argument:

God is not an animal as men are, and if he does not change his designs to avoid pain and suffering to human beings he is not violating any natural sympathies as Hitler did. Only anthropomorphic imagination allows us to accuse God of cruelty in this regard.[23]

Secondly, the argument assumes that if God is under any moral obligation to remove or lessen the sufferings of beasts, this obligation must be grounded in sympathy. But why should this be so? The suffering of a higher animal is an intrinsically bad thing, and the incompatibility of physical suffering with the divine nature is no barrier to God's knowing this to be true. This, surely, is enough to place him under a moral obligation to eliminate or ameliorate the sufferings of higher animals (a prima facie obligation, to be sure, an obligation that may well be overridden by some other consideration). Or, if this is not evident, owing perhaps to considerations pertaining to the differences between God and creatures, it is at any rate evident that the fact that a certain being cannot feel sympathy with physical suffering does not show that that being is not under a prima facie obligation to eliminate or ameliorate physical suffering. If even *that* much is not evident to you, I invite you to consider the following analogy. In the distant future, human beings visit a planet orbiting the star Epsilon Eridani, and discover that it is inhabited by a species of rational beings. We establish communication with the Eridanans, but only with great difficulty, and with much uncertainty about *what* is being communicated because they're very, well, alien. But we're clear on one thing, at least: that they have urgently warned us not to release any significant quantities of the inert gas argon into their atmosphere. If we do, they tell us, something very bad will happen to them. We try to learn the nature of this bad thing, but the statements about it that we can understand are mostly negative: it will not involve physical suffering or illness or famine or a diminution of their population or diminished mental capacities—indeed, for every bad thing we can think of, we learn that it isn't *that* thing or in any way like it (apart from its badness). The Eridanans insist, however, that it is a bad thing whose badness is as *objective* as the badness of widespread physical suffering. (It's not, they assure us, that their religions teach that argon is an "unclean gas" or anything else that is "subjective" or dependent on some cultural contingency.) Suppose we believe them. Should we not then regard ourselves as being under a moral obligation (prima facie, at least) not to release argon into their atmosphere? And is it not clear that this moral obligation would not rest on sympathy? (If we did release the argon, and if the Eridanans then said, "Well, you did it, and the very bad thing we warned you of has now happened to us," we could feel no sympathy with them.) Is it not clear that the obligation arises simply from the fact that we believe that the release of argon would cause something very bad to happen to the Eridanans?

Neither of these two alternatives to the anti-irregularity defense, therefore—neither the angelic-corruption-of-nature defense nor the no-divine-sympathy-with-beasts defense, is satisfactory. It is my conviction that the most promising defense as regards the sufferings of beasts is the anti-irregularity defense. How plausible an audience of neutral agnostics would find this defense is a question I will leave to you to answer.

Lecture 8

The Hiddenness of God

I will begin by laying out an argument for your consideration:

If God existed, that would be a very important thing for us human beings to know. God, being omniscient would know that this would be an important thing for us to know, and, being morally perfect, he would act on this knowledge. He would act on it by providing us with indisputable evidence of his existence. St Paul recognized this when he in effect said (Rom. 2: 18–23) that the blasphemies of the pagans were without excuse because God *had* provided humanity with indisputable evidence of his existence—simply by placing humanity in a world in which, to quote a text we can be sure Paul approved of, the heavens declare the glory of God and the firmament showeth his handiwork. But Paul was wrong to think we had such evidence. It's quite obvious that we don't have it and never have had it, for the unprejudiced know that the heavens are quite silent about the glory of God and that the firmament displays nothing of his handiwork. And, therefore, the absence of evidence for the existence of God should lead us to become atheists, and not merely agnostics.

This argument is in some ways very similar to the global argument from evil.[1] It contends that if there were a God, the world would, owing to his moral perfection, his knowledge, and his power, have certain observable features; it contends, moreover, that the world can be seen not to have these features; it concludes that God does not exist. In a way, it *is* an argument from evil, for, if God *does* exist, then a rational creature's being ignorant of his existence is an evil. It might also be said that this argument stands to a famous theological problem called "the problem of the hiddenness of God" or "the problem of divine hiddenness" as the argument from evil stands to the problem of evil. But if the problem of the hiddenness of God is indeed a famous theological problem, it is not so famous a theological problem as the problem of evil, and perhaps not everyone will be familiar with the problem of the hiddenness of God, or will even have heard of it.[2] I will, therefore, take some time to lay out this problem. As is the case with the problem of evil, the problem of the hiddenness of God is more often referred to than precisely stated. Theologians often refer to this problem as if it were perfectly clear what it was, but their writings on the subject do not always make it wholly clear what the problem is. In some writers, it is hard to distinguish the problem of the hiddenness of God from the problem of evil. The writers I am thinking of introduce the problem of the hiddenness of God with reflections along the following lines. The world is full of terrible things, and we observe no response from God when these terrible things happen: the heavens do not rain fire on the Nazis, the raging flood does not turn aside just before it sweeps away the peaceful village, the paralyzed child remains paralyzed.

Nevertheless, I think it is possible to make an intuitive distinction between what is naturally suggested by the words "the problem of divine hiddenness" and what is naturally suggested by the words "the problem of evil". I think I can imagine worlds in which it would not be right or natural by anyone's lights to say that God was "hidden" but in which evil was as much a problem for theists as it is in the actual world.

Imagine, for example, that to every Jew who was to perish in the Holocaust there had come, a few weeks before his or her death, a vision of a seraph, a being of unutterable splendor, who recited Psalm 91 in Hebrew—and then vanished. The doomed recipients of these visions, comparing notes, found that the visions were remarkably consistent. Learned Jews understood the seraph's words perfectly. Less learned Jews recognized the psalm and understood bits and pieces of it, just as they would have if they had heard it recited in a synagogue. Others, less learned still, recognized the language as biblical Hebrew, and said things like, "It sounded like poetry—maybe a psalm". A few wholly secularized Jews did not even recognize the language, but gave an account of the visual aspect of the apparition consistent with everyone else's, and said that the apparition spoke to them in a language they did not understand. (But those victims of the Holocaust who were not Jews according to the Law but were Jews according to the Nazi Race Laws did not experience the vision at all; some of them, however, experienced other visions, of a kind I will describe in a moment.) There were, then, these visions, but that was all. Nothing else happened: not a single life was saved, not a single brutal incident was in any way mitigated. With the exception of the visions, the Holocaust proceeded exactly as it did in the actual world. And let us further imagine that many other victims of horrendous evil in our imaginary world, victims of horrendous evils throughout all its recorded history, have received, shortly before their final suffering and death, analogous or comparable "signs" in the form of visions incorporating religious imagery—every victim, in fact, who belonged to any cultural tradition that provided religious images he could recognize and interpret. It would seem that in this imaginary world, the problem of evil is no less pressing than it is in ours, but "the problem of the hiddenness of God" does not arise. Or at least we can say this: if the existence of the visions is generally known among the inhabitants of the imaginary world, writers of the sort who in our world speak of "the hiddenness of God" will not use that phrase (they will perhaps speak instead of the "passivity of God").

The problem of evil and the problem of the hiddenness of God are, therefore, not identical. But is the latter essentially connected with suffering and other forms of evil? Would, or could, this problem exist in a world without suffering? I think that trying to answer this question will help us understand what the problem is. Let us imagine a world without suffering—not a world in which everyone enjoys the Beatific Vision, but a world that is as much like our world (as it is at present) as the absence of suffering permits. I will call such a world a "secular utopia", because my model for this world is just that future of alabaster cities undimmed by human tears that secularists yearn for.

In the world I imagine, human beings are benevolent, and nature is kind. There is no physical pain, or very little of it (just enough to remind people to take care not to damage their extremities). There is no premature death, whether by violence, accident, or disease. There are, in fact, no such things as violence and disease, and accidents are never very serious. (The inhabitants of this world all enjoy a vigorous old age and die peacefully in their sleep when they are well over 100 years old—and the fear of death is unknown.) No one is a cripple or mentally retarded or mentally unbalanced or even mildly neurotic. There is no racial prejudice or prejudice of any sort. No one is ugly or deformed. Everyone is provided with all the physical necessities and comforts of life—but great wealth and luxury are as unknown as poverty. Consumer goods are produced in a way that does no violence to nature: the human and non-human inhabitants of the world live in perfect harmony.[3] Everyone has interesting and rewarding work to do, and this work is appropriately rewarded with respect and, if appropriate, admiration. No one covets anyone else's possessions. There is no lying or promise breaking or cheating or corruption—there is in fact nothing for anyone to be corrupt *about*, for there are no laws and no money, and there is essentially no government. If there is any unhappiness in this world, it arises only in cases like these: Alfred has fallen in love with Beatrice, but Beatrice is in love with Charles; Delia has devoted her life to proving Goldbach's Conjecture, and Edward has published a proof of it when Delia had a proof almost within her grasp. And even in such cases, everyone involved behaves with perfect rationality and complete maturity, thereby keeping the resulting unhappiness to an irreducible (and usually transient) minimum.

Now let us suppose that in this world, as in ours, some people believe in God—in a necessarily existent, omniscient, omnipotent, omnipresent creator and sustainer of the world. (The inhabitants of our invented world would have trouble grasping the concept "moral perfection"—but, if you could get them to understand it, the theists among them wouldn't hesitate to ascribe moral perfection to God.) And, as in our world, some people believe that there is no such being. Could someone in this world, perhaps one of its atheists, raise the problem of divine hiddenness? I think so. I think we can imagine a dialogue in which the problem is raised, a dialogue "purer" than any that could be imagined to take place in our world, purer because neither of the participants has ever known or heard of any horrendous evil.

Atheist. This God of yours—why does he hide himself? Why doesn't he come out in the open where we can see him?

Theist. Your question doesn't make any sense. God is omnipresent. That is, he is totally present everywhere and locally present nowhere. A thing is locally present in a place (that is, a region of space) if it occupies or takes up or fills that place. And God occupies neither any particular place (as does a cat or a mountain) nor all places (as the luminiferous aether would, if it existed). He is totally present everywhere in that the totality of his being is reflected in the sustaining power that keeps every spatial thing everywhere in the physical universe in existence from moment to moment. Similarly, we might say that Rembrandt is locally present nowhere in "Aristotle Contemplating a Bust of Homer" and totally present everywhere in this painting. (But the analogy is imperfect, since the three-dimensional objects and spatial relations "in" the painting are fictional, illusory, or imaginary, whereas the ones in the physical universe are—of course—real.)

Only a locally present thing can reflect light, and thus only a locally present thing can be visible. Only a locally present thing can exclude other things from the space it occupies, and thus only a locally present thing can be tangible. And only a visible or tangible thing can "show itself". Someone who wants God to "show himself" just doesn't understand the concept of God. Asking for that is like demanding that Rembrandt "show himself" in a painting. The complaint "I can't find God anywhere in the world" is as misplaced as the complaint "I can't find Rembrandt anywhere in 'Aristotle Contemplating a Bust of Homer' ".[4]

Atheist. Well, if he can't show himself by being present in the world, why can't he show himself by his effects on some of the things that *are* present in the world?

Theist. You haven't been listening. Everything in the world is his "effect". He "shows himself by his effects" in the world just as Rembrandt "shows himself by his effects" in his paintings.

Atheist. That sounds good, but I wonder if it's anything more than words. What I want is not "general effects" but, if I may coin a phrase, "special effects". Given your picture of God's relation to the world, everything will look just the same whether there is a God or not—wait, stop, don't tell me that that's like saying that one of Rembrandt's paintings will look the same whether there is a Rembrandt or not! I couldn't bear it. Let me put the problem this way. I have bought one of the modal telescopes invented by the great metaphysician Saul Kripke, and I have looked into other possible worlds. In one of them I caught a glimpse of the following argument, in a book by a man named Thomas Aquinas (evidently a sound atheist like myself):

Objection 2. It is, moreover, superfluous to suppose that what can be accounted for by a few principles has been produced by many. But it seems that everything we see in the world can be accounted for by other principles, without supposing God to exist. For all natural things can be accounted for by one principle, which is nature; and all voluntary things can be accounted for by one principle, which is human reason or will. Hence, there is no need to suppose that a God exists. [*ST* I, q. 2, art. 3]

Surely this argument is unanswerable? Surely one should not believe in the existence of an unobservable entity unless its existence is needed to explain some observed phenomenon?

Theist. So what you are looking for is a particular event, an event that is not caused by any human action, whose occurrence resists any natural or scientific explanation, and which is evidently the work of someone trying to send human beings a message or signal whose content is that there is such a being as God. How about the stars in the sky rearranging themselves to spell out 'I am who am'? [Exod. 3: 14] Would that be satisfactory?

Atheist. It would.

Theist. You don't want much, do you? But it happens I can supply something of the sort you want. My own religion is called Julianism, after its founder, Julia, the great prophetess and author of *The Book of Julia* and the forty volumes of sermons we call *The Words of Julia*. Julia's message was so important that God granted her three times a natural span of life, as a sign of his special favor and to ensure that her teachings would have a chance to put down deep roots. Julia lived 326 years. And every physiologist agrees that it is physiologically impossible for a human being to live 326 years. Therefore, Julia's preternaturally long life must have been a sign from God.

Atheist. Well, that would be pretty impressive if it actually happened. But when did Julia live, and how do you Julianists know that she really did live that long?

Theist. Julia lived about 2,000 years ago. We know of her long life and lots of other things about her because the facts of her biography are carefully set out in the Holy Records of the Julian Church, which originally derive from the testimony of eyewitnesses.

Atheist. Forgive me if I'm skeptical. Even if we discount the possibility of some mixture of fraud and simple factual error on the part of your "eyewitnesses", we must concede that stories can become distorted as they pass from mouth to mouth. As stories are passed from one teller to another, people unconsciously fill in or change minor details in the story. These minor distortions can accumulate, and, given long enough, the accumulation of minor distortions can change a story till it's no longer really the same story. We know that this happens. Just last month, there was a rumor in Neapolis of a terrible tragedy somewhere in Asia—a woman had actually lost a *finger* in an industrial accident! The whole town was in an uproar. But when the dust settled, it turned out that what had really happened was that the

Asian woman had got her finger badly mauled in a piece of machinery while she was daydreaming. The finger, of course, healed perfectly within a week. Now since we know from experience that stories can become distorted in this fantastic way—the very idea of someone's losing a finger!—and since we know from experience that no one in our modern record-keeping era has lived even 150 years, the most reasonable thing to suppose is that, although Julia may indeed have lived to be remarkably old, she certainly did not live to be 326; the reasonable thing to suppose is that what experience tells us often happens happened this time (that is, the story grew in the telling; it certainly had plenty of time to grow), and that what experience tells us never happens did not happen.[5]

Theist. What you are saying seems to come down to this. You contend that if God is to make his existence credible to human beings, he must cause some particular, unmistakable sign to occur somewhere in the world of space and time. But when you hear a story of some event that would have been such a sign if it had actually occurred, you refuse, on general epistemological grounds, to believe the story.

Atheist. My position is not so extreme as that, or so unreasonable as you make it sound. Take your first, hypothetical example. If the stars in the sky were suddenly rearranged so as to spell out 'I am who am', I'd believe in the existence of God then, all right.[6] That would be a good, clear case of what I'd call "God's coming out of hiding". In such a case, God would be making it evident to human beings that Reality contained another intelligence than human intelligence—and not just any non-human intelligence, but an intelligence grand enough to be a plausible candidate for the office "God". And, obviously, this—or something along the same lines—is what such a grand intelligence would do if it wanted us to believe in it. If, *per impossibile*, the figures in a Rembrandt painting were conscious beings and aware of (and only of) the objects in their little two-dimensional world, what reason could they have for believing in Rembrandt but something he put specially into the painting that was not a part of the natural order of things in the painting (his signature, perhaps). If he didn't do that, how could he blame the denizens of the painting for not believing in him?

Theist. Let me make two points. First, these signs you want God to place in the world would have to recur periodically, or, after a few generations had passed, people like you would say that the stories about the signs had grown in the telling—perhaps from the seed of an astronomical prodigy that, remarkable as it was, had some purely natural explanation. Secondly, even the 'I am who am' story wouldn't make the existence of *God* evident to a sufficiently determined skeptic—for even the (apparent) rearrangement of the stars could be the work of a lesser being than God. We can imagine no sign that would *have* to be the work of a necessary, omnipresent, omnipotent being. Any sign one might imagine could be ascribed to a contingent, locally present being whose powers, though vastly greater than ours, were finite. I should expect that someone like you would say that if two hypotheses explain the data equally well, and if they are alike but for the fact that one of them postulates an unobservable *infinite* being and the other an unobservable *finite* being, one should always prefer the latter hypothesis, since it does the same explanatory work as the former, but is, literally, infinitely weaker.

Atheist. Well, perhaps you're right when you say that to be convincing the signs would have to recur periodically. I don't see why I shouldn't ask for that, and I don't see that it will weaken my argument if I do. And the more I think about it, the more inclined I am to accept your second point as well. Your argument has convinced me of something you didn't foresee: that you theists have invented a being whose existence no one could possibly rationally believe in, since the hypothesis that he exists is necessarily infinitely stronger than other hypotheses that would explain any possible observations equally well. And if you haven't invented him, if he really does exist, even *he* couldn't provide us—or any other finite beings he might create—with evidence that would render belief in him rational. If he exists, he should approve of me for not believing in him, and disapprove of you for believing in him.

Let us at this point leave our dialogue and the secular utopia in which it was imagined to occur, and return to the real world. The lesson of the dialogue is that in a world that lacks any real suffering, the problem of the hiddenness of God is a purely epistemological problem, or a cluster of epistemological problems: can one rationally believe in God in a world devoid of signs and wonders?[7] Under what conditions would it be rational to believe a story that reports signs and wonders? Could any possible sign or wonder or series of signs and wonders make it reasonable to believe in a necessarily existent, omnipresent, omnipotent Creator and Sustainer of the world of locally present things?

These epistemological questions obviously have the same force in the real world as in our secular utopia. The most pointed of them, the one I wish to discuss, is this: Why does God not show us that he exists by providing us with signs and wonders? Anyone who thinks that this question has no answer can present an argument for the non-existence of God whose premise is the absence of signs and wonders. We have seen a simple version of this argument. Here is a more careful version of the argument—a version that turns on one component of knowledge, belief, rather than knowledge itself:

(1) If God exists, he wants all finite rational beings to believe in his existence.

(2) If every finite rational being observed signs and wonders of the right sort, every finite rational being would believe in God.

(3) There is, therefore, something that God could do to ensure that every finite rational being believed in his existence.

(4) If God wants all finite rational beings to believe in his existence and there is something he can do to bring this about, he will do something to bring it about.

(5) But not all finite rational beings believe in God.

Hence,

(6) God does not exist.

I will make two observations about this argument, which I will call the doxastic argument. First, it is not formally valid, but it could easily be made so, and it hardly seems plausible to suppose that any of the premises that would have to be added to make the argument formally valid would be false. If there is any defect in this argument, it must be that one or more of the premises of the argument as I have stated it are false. And these premises seem to be, to say the least, plausible. It is certainly true that not all people believe in God. Although no one is likely to dispute this premise, I want to make it clear that widespread unbelief is almost certainly not a recent thing, even in officially Christian cultures. Here are some remarkable words, written by one Peter of Cornwall, Prior of Holy Trinity, Aldgate, around the year 1200:

There are many people who do not believe that God exists, nor do they think that a human soul lives on after the death of the body. They consider that the universe has always been as it is now and is ruled by chance rather than by Providence.[8]

If this was the best God could do in twelfth-century England, it would seem that he just wasn't trying! (And, obviously, he hasn't done any better since.)

My second observation is that some might find this argument more persuasive if 'rational belief' were substituted for 'belief' in it. If this substitution is made, the first two premises of the argument read:

If God exists, he wants all finite rational beings to believe rationally in his existence.

If every finite rational being observed signs and wonders of the right sort, every finite rational being would believe in God rationally.

I am not sure which version of the argument is the more persuasive, but I mean my remarks to apply equally to either.

Now how should the theist respond to this argument? I propose that the theist's response be strictly parallel to Theist's response to the global argument from evil. That is, that the theist should attempt to tell a story that has the following logical consequences:

The world was created and is sustained by a necessary, omnipresent, omniscient, omnipotent, morally perfect being—that is, by God. There are rational beings in this world, and God wants these beings, or some of them at some times, to believe in his existence. The world is devoid of signs and wonders—of "special effects". Or if the world contains any such events, they are so rare that very few people have actually observed one or even encountered anyone who claims to have observed one. (In the latter case, among those people whom God wants to believe in his existence are many of the people who are distant in space and time from any of the very rare signs and wonders.)

And I propose that the doxastic argument should be judged a failure just in the case that the theist is able to tell a story with these consequences such that an audience of ideal agnostics (who have been presented with the doxastic argument and have been trying to decide whether it is convincing) will respond to it by saying, "Given that God exists, the rest of that story may well be true. I don't see any reason to rule it out." And, of course, we require that this reaction be achieved in the presence of an ideal atheist who does everything possible to block this reaction, everything possible to defend the truth of the premises of the argument against the doubts raised by the theist's story. We may as well call such a story what we called stories that played an analogous role in relation to the argument from evil: we may as well call it a defense. The term is appropriate enough because God is, once more, in the dock—the charge being that he has not presented us with indisputable evidence in the form of signs and wonders in the important matter of his existence—and the theist is the counsel for the defense. We may remember at this point the famous story of Lord Russell's reply to a woman at a London dinner party (or an American undergraduate—the story comes in various versions) who had asked him what he would say to God on the Day of Judgment (if, contrary to his expectations, there should be such a day): "Lord, you gave me insufficient evidence."[9] Russell's indignant post-mortem protest is one formulation of the accusation that the God in the dock faces. How should counsel for the defense reply?

In discussions of the global argument from evil, the kernel of every defense is a *reason* (or a set of reasons), God's reason or reasons for permitting the existence of evil. So it should be with discussions of the doxastic argument: the kernel of every defense should be a reason or reasons, God's reason or reasons for not providing the human species with ubiquitous signs and wonders, despite the fact that he thinks it very important that they believe in his existence.

I will try to present such a defense. This defense will build upon the expanded free-will defense that I had Theist present in our discussion of the argument from evil. The essential idea of that defense was that the elimination of all evil from the world by an enormous congeries of local miracles would frustrate God's plan of atonement, his plan for reuniting separated humanity with himself. The essential idea of the defense I shall present in response to the doxastic argument is that ubiquitous signs and wonders would also frustrate God's plan of atonement.

I begin with an observation. Note that the proposition

God wants people to believe in his existence

does not entail the proposition

God wants people to believe in his existence—*and* he does not care why anyone who believes in him has this belief.

The former proposition, in fact, is consistent with the proposition that God would regard the following list as presenting three states of affairs in order of decreasing value:

(1) Patricia believes, for reason A, that God exists.

(2) Patricia believes that God does not exist.

(3) Patricia believes, for reason B, that God exists.

It is, for example, consistent with God's wanting Patricia to believe in him that he regard (1) as a good state of affairs, (2) as a bad state of affairs, and (3) as a bad state of affairs that is *much* worse than (2). (And this would be consistent with reason B's being an epistemically unobjectionable reason for belief in God: reason B might be, from the point of view of someone interested only in justification or warrant, a perfectly good reason for believing in the existence of God.) And this is no idle speculation about a logical possibility. Most theists hold that God expects a good deal more from us than mere belief in his existence. As James says in his epistle, "You believe in the one God—that is creditable enough, but the demons have the same belief, and they tremble with fear" (2: 19).[10] God expects a complex of things, of which belief in his existence is a small (although essential) part. It is certainly conceivable that someone's believing in him for a certain reason (because, say, that person has witnessed signs and wonders) might make it difficult or even impossible for that person to acquire other features God wanted him or her to have.

Can we make this seem plausible? Let us wander a bit, and look at some examples and analogies. Let us consider a second New Testament text. Remember the story of the rich man in Hell in chapter 16 of Luke's Gospel. The rich man, who had in life treated the poor with contemptuous neglect, is in Hell (for that very reason), and petitions Abraham (who is somehow able to converse with him across a "great gulf") that a messenger should be sent to his still living brothers, who also have starving beggars at their sumptuous gates, to warn them to mend their ways before it is too late. Abraham replies, "If they do not hear Moses and the Prophets, neither will they be persuaded though one rose from the dead." A very striking parable, but can its message really be true? That is, can it be true that witnessing a miracle, even a very personal and pointed miracle, would have no effect on the character of values of someone who witnessed it, no effect on the type of person he or she is? In order that our imaginations may not be distracted by the quaint literary devices of an old book, let us imagine a parable for our own time. This parable has two central characters. The first is the Russian strategist whose contribution to his country's cause in Afghanistan was the clever idea of placing powerful bombs disguised as bright shiny toys in the vicinity of unreliable villages. This man dies (in bed, of course) and receives an appropriate reward in the afterlife. He begs Abraham to be allowed, after the fashion of Marley's ghost,[11] to be allowed to appear to his living brother (who is, let us say, the general whose forces carried out the distribution of the "toys" in the Afghan countryside) and warn him of what awaits him. In this case the petition is granted. He appears to his brother and says to him, "Listen, brother, we were wrong. There is a God and there is a judgment. I am in Hell because of the terrible things I did. Repent and change your life and avoid my unhappy fate." What would the result be?

I would suppose that the best result one could hope for would be this—and remember, we're talking about someone who distributed anti-personnel bombs disguised as toys. This is a man who, in the words of the Wisdom of Solomon, had made a covenant with death: that is, who had, in his own mind, traded eternal extinction after death for the privilege of behaving any way he liked, with impunity, during life.[12] Such a man could only regard what his brother told him as bad news—as a bad child who was told that Santa Claus would bring him no toys if he behaved according to his normal inclinations would regard this information as bad news. The general's reaction would, or so it seems to me, be articulable along these lines: "All right, it seems I was badly out in my calculations. The nature of the universe is entirely different from what I thought it was. It has a personal creator, a being of such great power that it is hopeless to oppose his will. This being has some rules, and the penalty for disobeying them is terrible, and it seems that these rules are, are to put it mildly, inconsistent with the kind of life I want to live. It seems that if I kill and maim Afghan children and their families in order to curry favor with my political bosses, I'll be subjected to eternal torment. This is the worst news of my life; all my plans have to be rethought. Well, I'd better get on with it. What I have to do is to figure out how to obey these damned rules in a way that will require a minimum modification of my goals in life." (Or, at least, that's one way the general might react. Another possibility would be simple rebellion. The infernal debate in Pandaemonium in Book II of *Paradise Lost*, which is a debate about the best way to conduct a rebellion against an authority whose power is immeasurably greater than one's own, lays out various possibilities that the general might want to consider.) If the general resolves to modify his behavior and his goals in response to be the bad news he has received from his dead brother, it is far from clear that even this resolution could be expected to last very long. The effect of hell-fire sermons—on those who are affected by them at all—is in general a repentance and an attempt at amendment of life that are transitory indeed. I shouldn't be surprised if our general would, before too long, find some way to convince himself that his vision of his brother was some sort of illusion, perhaps a transient psychotic episode, and to push it out of his mind altogether. But whether he does or doesn't continue to believe that the miracle he witnessed was real, it's not going to produce any change in his behavior that God would be interested in. It's not going to cause him to realize that the world is a horrible place and to seek a way out of this horrible world. It's not going to make of him a man who believes that the world is a horrible place *because* human beings are separated from God, and that the world can be healed only if humanity is reunited with God. It's not going to convince him that *he* is a moral horror, and that his only hope of being anything else is to be united with God in bonds of love. No, he likes things just the way they are—or just the way they seemed to be before the visitation. He doesn't think the world is a horrible place, although he no doubt realizes that it's a horrible place for many *other* people. But other people are of interest to him only as instruments. His only objection to the world as he perceived it before the visitation was that he didn't enjoy enough power in it, a deficiency he was devoting every minute of his waking life to correcting.

I would generalize this contention. If God were to convince us of his existence by ubiquitous miracles, this would contribute nothing to his plan of atonement. And it seems to me likely that it would interfere with it. If I were an atheist or agnostic who witnessed such things as the following:

The stars in the skies spell out 'I am who am';

A voice heard in the thunder tells us that there is a God and that we had better mend our ways;

Microscopic examination of grains of sand reveals that each of them carries the inscription "Made by God" (this amusing example is due to John Leslie);

I suppose I should conclude that God existed—or at least that some being I should probably refer to as 'God' existed. (It isn't clear that I'd conclude that a being who was God, properly speaking, existed; for, as I had my characters in the story of the secular utopia point out, any series of miraculous events can always be explained by postulating a finite being of great power and knowledge.) But I should also probably infer that this being's main project for me was this: he wanted me to believe in his existence, and, no doubt, to behave in some way that would be a natural consequence of this new piece of knowledge. And this isn't really what God wants at all. From the point of view of theism, or at least from the point of view of the theistic religions—Judaism, Christianity, and Islam—it is indeed *true* that God wants us human beings to believe in his existence,[13] but, like many truths, this truth can be very misleading if it is asserted out of context. I want my wife to believe in my existence; if I say this, I say something true; but it's not a thing I would ever say outside a philosophical example. What I want is for my wife and me to stand in a certain complex set of relations that, as a matter of fact, have her believing in my existence as an essential component or logical consequence. If my marriage were destroyed, if this complex set of relations ceased to obtain, she would no doubt still believe in my existence, but that, by itself, would be of no value to me. And God does not place any particular value on anyone's believing in *his* existence, not *simpliciter*, not by itself. What he values is, as I noted earlier, a complex of which belief in his existence is a logical consequence, a complex some of whose features I had Theist spell out in Lecture 5 in his description of God's plan for the reconciliation of humanity with himself. Is it not possible, does it not seem plausible, that if God were to present the world with a vast array of miracles attesting to the existence of a personal power beyond nature, this action would convey to us the message that what he desired of us was simply that we should believe in his existence?—and nothing more?—or nothing more than believing in his existence and taking account of it as one important feature of reality, a feature that has to be factored into all our practical reasoning? If that is so, then the vast array of miracles would not only be useless from God's point of view, but positively harmful, a barrier to putting his plan of reconciliation into effect.

If it is hard to see what I am getting at here, perhaps a sort of analogy will help. There are *many* propositions God wants everyone to accept that people don't generally accept, or haven't generally accepted in the course of human history. One of them would be "Women are not intellectually, emotionally, or spiritually inferior to men." But if God wants everyone to accept this proposition, everyone at all times and in all places, why has he not (as Russell might have asked) provided us with *more evidence* for it? Why doesn't a voice from a whirlwind or a burning bush inform everyone of its truth on their eighteenth birthday? Why isn't every woman born with a tastefully small but clearly legible birthmark that says (perhaps in the native language of her parents) "*Not* intellectually, emotionally, or spiritually inferior to men"? If God had done any of these things, he'd have vastly changed the course of human history. There would have been no sexism, no male domination, no clitoral circumcision, no prostitution, no sexual slavery, no foot-binding or purdah or suttee. So why hasn't God "provided us with more evidence"? Part of the answer, I think, is that he has already given us all the evidence we need or should ever have needed to be convinced—to *know*—that women are not the intellectual, emotional, or spiritual inferiors of men. And this is, simply, the evidence that is provided by normal human social interaction. Another part of the answer is that it would be useless for him to do this if his purpose were a real transformation of the attitude of fallen male humanity toward women. The best that such "external" evidence could produce would be a sort of sullen compliance with someone else's opinion—even if that "someone else" were God. (If you doubt this, consider how a present-day radical feminist would be likely to respond if it suddenly came to pass that male babies began to be born with scientifically inexplicable birthmarks that spelled out "The superior sex" and female babies began to be born with scientifically inexplicable birthmarks that spelled out "The inferior sex".) What is really needed to eliminate sexism is not sullen compliance forced on one by evidence that has no natural connection with life in the human social world. What is needed is natural conviction that proceeds from our normal cognitive apparatus operating on the normal data of the senses. Sexism will be really eliminated (as opposed to repressed) only when everyone, using his normal cognitive capacities, applying them to the data of everyday social interaction, believes in the intellectual, emotional, and spiritual equality of the sexes in the same way in which everyone now believes in the equality of the auditory and visual capacities of the sexes. And might it not be that miraculous evidence for the equality of the sexes would actually interfere with our capacity to come to a belief in the equality of the sexes in the right way? If most men at most times (and perhaps most women, too) have believed that men were superior to women—and they have—they have managed to do this in a world in which they were positively swimming in evidence to the contrary. Something, therefore, must have been wrong with their ability to process the data of everyday experience. They must have been epistemically defective (and not innocently so like the natural philosophers who believed that heavy bodies fell faster than light ones,[14] but culpably epistemically defective, like Holocaust deniers). Might it not be that external, miraculous evidence for the equality of the sexes would simply raise such emotional barriers, such waves of sullen resentment among the self-deceived, that there would be no hope of their gradually coming to listen to what their senses were saying to them in the course of ordinary human social interaction? If there is, as St Paul has said, a natural tendency in us to see the existence and power and deity of the maker of the world in the things around us (Rom. 2: 20), and if many people do not see this because they do not want to see it, is it not possible that grains of sand bearing the legend "Made by God" (or articulate thunder or a rearrangement of the stars bearing a similar message) would simply raise such emotional barriers, such waves of sullen resentment among the self-deceived, that there would be no hope of their eventually coming to perceive the power and deity of God in the ordinary, everyday operations of the things he has made?

Notes

LECTURE 1 THE PROBLEM OF EVIL AND THE ARGUMENT FROM EVIL

1. Lord Gifford's will is printed in Stanley L. Jaki, *Lord Gifford and his Lectures: A Centenary Retrospect*, 66–76. The quoted passage appears on pp. 72–3.

2. Ibid. 74. I should mention that various *obiter dicta* in his will suggest that Lord Gifford did not mean the intended subject-matter of the lectures he was endowing to be understood so narrowly as the two quotations, taken in isolation, imply.

3. According to Alvin Plantinga, who gives no citation. See *The Nature of Necessity*, 58. The rule is 'Possibly everything is F; *hence*, Everything is possibly F'. The counterexample is: Let 'is F' be 'is God'; suppose that God never created anything; then 'Everything is God' is true; but, although our supposition is false, it is *possibly* true; '*Possibly* everything is God' is therefore true (true in fact, true in actuality); but 'Everything is possibly God' is false (in actuality) because there are (in actuality) creatures and none of them is possibly God.

4. The former is edited by Marilyn and Robert Adams, and the latter by Michael L. Peterson. I concede that several of the readings in Part I of Peterson's collection are not addressed specifically to the argument from evil.

5. I don't know what to make of this fact, but there are three other "the problem of" phrases that are supposed to be the standard names of famous philosophical problems: 'the problem of universals', 'the problem of free will', and 'the mind-body problem', which, like 'the problem of evil', have no definite meaning: none of them is the name of a single, well-defined philosophical problem.

6. "Primarily" because what I am calling 'an encounter with evil' is usually, is in almost all cases, an encounter with a particular evil; but if we imagine a situation, and situations like this are not unknown, in which the evils of the world suddenly become "real" to a theist—a situation in which the theist learns no new fact about the evils of the world but in which the facts he had always known assume a new and horrible significance for him—that too would be a case of what I mean by 'an encounter with evil'.

7. I would distinguish the case, mentioned in the previous note, the case of the theist for whom the evils of the world at some point take on a new and

horrible significance, and the case of the theist who at some point comes to believe that the existence of evil confronts his beliefs with an intellectual challenge.

8. Indeed, an apologist might privately believe that he knew the real truth about why an omnipotent and loving God allowed evil to exist, and yet regard this real truth as unsuitable for apologetic purposes. Such an apologist would be like a defense counsel who thought that the real truth about the evidence that seemed to demonstrate the guilt of his client was so complex and involuted that he could better serve his client by avoiding all mention of it and telling instead a simple, plausible story that explained away the prosecution's apparently damning evidence, a story that was false in fact, but which the prosecution would be unable to disprove.

9. For a *very* different approach to the problem of evil see Marilyn Adams's *Horrendous Evils and the Goodness of God*. In this book Adams discusses both the purely intellectual problem considered in these lectures, and many other problems connected with trust in God and the very worst evils present in his creation. I find this book unpersuasive (as regards its general tendency and main theses; I think Adams is certainly right about many relatively minor but not unimportant points), but endlessly fascinating.

   For another important—and also very different—discussion of the problem of evil, see Eleonore Stump's Stob Lectures, *Faith and the Problem of Evil*.

10. The same point applies to those who think they are in possession of a theodicy: it would be a stupid and cruel thing for, say, Leibniz to tell the mother that the child's death was an essential component of the best of all possible worlds, or for Pope to tell her that whatever is, is right. And these responses would not be stupid and cruel because they rested on a false theodicy: even if—*per impossibile*, I want to say—the child's death *was* an essential component of the best of all possible worlds, it would be a stupid and cruel thing to respond to the mother's distress by telling her that truth. That something is true, and, to borrow a technical term from the philosophy of language, conversationally relevant, does not mean that it should be said.

11. See my essay "The Place of Chance in a World Sustained by God".

12. Elsewhere in the letter, Bilynskyj says that Christians to whom terrible things have happened often "wear themselves out" trying to find meaning in them. To learn that a terrible thing has no meaning can be a liberation for such Christians—not, of course, a liberation from the burden of their grief, but a liberation from a false burden that a wrong view of God's relations to the evils of the world has added to the burden of their grief.

13. J. L. Mackie, "Evil and Omnipotence". The quoted passage appears on p. 25 in Adams and Adams.

14. But here is a defense of the second thesis (I am quoting, with his permission, a paragraph of a letter from Alvin Plantinga):

I'm inclined to believe that there is a twofold problem of evil for atheists. First, I believe there wouldn't be any such thing as right and wrong at all, and hence no such thing as evil, if theism were false. (I know, I know, theism is if true, necessary.) But second, even if that weren't true (even if there could be such a thing as right and wrong, given atheism) naturalism can't accommodate genuinely horrifying evil, as in cases like "Sophie's choice". It's not just that we can't explain people's achieving that level of depravity in terms of ignorance, the struggle for survival, the reptilian brain, and so on (though it's true that we can't); it's rather that there couldn't be evil at that level if naturalism were true. (If naturalism were true, people might view such things as displaying the level of evil they actually do display; but they'd be mistaken.) There could be evil of that appalling degree only if something like the Christian story is true: there is such a person as God, who has displayed unthinkable love in the Cross (incarnation and atonement) in order to bestow a stunning benefit (a benefit that beggars both description and imagination) upon creatures who have turned their backs on him; but some of us, like Satan, take as our explicit goal destroying and defacing what God loves, and promoting and devoting ourselves to what God hates (as with Satan in *Paradise Lost.*) There is a level of evil only that sort of action and character can reach; and that level of evil isn't possible in a naturalistic universe.

Anthony Burgess was, I think, saying something similar—from the point of view of a lapsed Catholic—when he wrote, "There is no A. J. P. Taylor-ish explanation for what happened in Eastern Europe during the war" (quoted by Martin Amis in *Koba the Dread*, 196).

15. An analogy might be the relation between, on the one hand, philosophical problems about what metaphysicians call 'freedom' when they are discussing the ontological grounds of moral responsibility and, on the other, philosophical problems about what political philosophers call 'freedom' when they are discussing the limits a state should place on the actions of its citizens. What do these two classes of problems have to do with each other? Not nothing, maybe, but not a great deal either.

16. Here is a simple example of how one who embraced this method might report the "discovery" that the problems considered by two philosophers were the same. "Eighteenth-Century Jack thinks that existence is comprehensible only if there is a God, and he thinks that the Lisbon earthquake is prima facie incompatible with the existence of God. He believes, therefore, that evil (in the guise of the Lisbon earthquake) is a prima facie threat to the comprehensibility of existence. Twenty-First-Century Jill thinks that existence is comprehensible only if human behavior is intelligible, and she

thinks that the Holocaust is prima facie incompatible with the intelligibility of human behavior. She believes, therefore, that evil (in the guise of the Holocaust) is a prima facie threat to the comprehensibility of existence. So, you see, Jack and Jill are concerned with the same philosophical problem—admittedly in somewhat different forms."

17. I quote from memory. I no longer remember where I read this. I apologize to Dr Berlinski if I have misquoted him.

18. I have nothing to say about the philosophical value of the texts of Nietzsche and later thinkers that Neiman reads as contributions to a many-centuries-long discussion of an overarching problem of evil. I have nothing to say about the interpretive value of trying to read those texts as attempts to meet a threat to the comprehensibility of existence posed by radical evil. My only thesis is that it is *simply not true* that the authors of these texts (on the one hand) and the authors of *Theodicy* and parts X and XI of *Dialogues Concerning Natural Religion* (on the other) were engaged in a common project.

19. I could try this. Imagine a world in which the history of European thought is much like what it is in our world, but with the following minor differences: in that world, the word 'evil' has never meant anything but 'radical evil'; in that world, the traditional philosophical problem of the coexistence of God and bad things has always been known as 'the problem of bad things'; in that world, the phrase 'the problem of evil' was invented in the twentieth century by post-religious thinkers as a name for whatever problem it is they think the existence of radical evil poses. What plausibility would Neiman's thesis have in such a world? (How would one even state it in that world?) Yet European intellectual history in that world differs in no important way from European intellectual history in the actual world: European thinkers in the actual world and European thinkers in the imaginary world use a *word* differently.

20. A reader for Oxford University Press has made an interesting suggestion. There is, the reader suggests, a family of interrelated problems in the ontology of value that might be called "the metaphysical problem of good and evil". (Philosophers addressing this problem would attempt to answer such questions as "What *are* good and evil?" and "Could there be a world that contained good but no evil?—is that even metaphysically possible?") The reader goes on to suggest that the metaphysical problem of good and evil confronts both theists and atheists, although theists and atheists will no doubt see the problem very differently.

This may be right. And if it is right, it may be that the traditional problem of evil and the metaphysical problem of good and evil overlap to a considerable extent. (For example, an atheist's attempts to formulate the argument from evil or a theist's attempts to respond to the argument from evil may well incorporate theses the proper evaluation of which belongs to the metaphysical problem of good and evil.) However this may be, the problem of evil is not a special case of the metaphysical problem of good and evil: the problem of evil is not the "form" in which the metaphysical problem of good and evil confronts the theist. It would, moreover, be wrong to say that, because the atheist needs to find a solution to the metaphysical problem of good and evil—suppose for the sake of argument that that is so—the atheist, as much as the theist, needs to find a solution to the problem of evil. It remains true, it remains a very simple and obvious truth, that the existence of evil (the existence of bad things) poses at least a prima facie threat to theism and does not pose even a prima facie threat to atheism.

LECTURE 2 THE IDEA OF GOD

1. Why only the Middle Eastern or Abrahamic religions? Why not the Far Eastern religions? The short answer is that because of the intimate historical connections among the three Abrahamic religions, it is plausible to suppose that the meaning their adherents give to the word 'God'—when they are speaking English—is the same. Now suppose an adherent of some Eastern religion were to say, in English, "My co-religionists and I believe in God, but we do not, like Jews, Christians, and Muslims, believe that God is a person; we regard him rather as an impersonal first principle." I think it would be plausible to maintain that the person who said this was translating some Hindi or Pali or Sanskrit word into English as 'God' when he ought to be translating it in some other way. (And why *not* say this, if the history of the word he is translating as 'God' has no connection with the history of the English word or with the history of *Deus* or *theos* or *elohim*?)

2. Not so long ago, as time is measured in the history of thought, anyone who said that it was a mistake to regard *x* as F would have meant, and have been taken by everyone to mean, that *x* was *not* F. Not so long ago, if you had used the phrase 'object over against us', people would have stared blankly at you and have asked what you could possibly mean by it. Not so long ago, anyone who said that the items in a certain list of properties were not features of a particular being would have meant, and have been taken by everyone to mean, that nothing had the properties specified in the list. Not so long ago, everyone who said that nothing had the properties in the list 'aseity, holiness, omnipotence, omniscience, providence, love, self-revelation' would have proudly described himself as an atheist.

3. For my thoughts on the relation between the proposition 'God is a person' and the proposition 'In God there are three persons', see my essays "And yet They Are Not Three Gods but One God", "Not by Confusion of Substance but by Unity of Person", and "Three Persons in One Being: On Attempts to Show that the Doctrine of the Trinity is Self-Contradictory".

4. For more on this topic, see my essays "Ontological Arguments" and "Modal Epistemology"; see also the Introduction to *God, Knowledge, and Mystery*, pp. 11–21.

5. Compare Thomas Aquinas, *Summa Theologiae* 1, q.25, art. 3: "But if one were to say that God was omnipotent because he was able to do all things that were possible for a being with the power that was his, there would be a vicious circle in explaining the nature of that power. To say that would be to say only that God can do what he can do."

6. I'm helping Descartes out a bit here. The question Descartes actually raises (letter to Arnauld, 29 July 1648) is whether God "can make a mountain without a valley". But, of course, if God wishes to make a mountain without a valley, he need only place the mountain he has made in the midst of a plain. I take it that the words I used in the text do not misrepresent what Descartes had in mind. I am not going to enter into the intricate scholarly dispute about what Descartes meant by saying that God "creates the eternal truths". My interest lies in the "strong" theory of omnipotence and its implications, not in the question whether Descartes really did subscribe to that theory.

7. Here I follow common philosophical usage and speak of "believing" propositions. I feel compelled to apologize for this, if only to myself. I am uncomfortable with this usage; I much prefer to speak of *accepting* or *assenting to* propositions—or hypotheses, theses, premises,... (This preference is entirely a matter of English usage. No philosophical point is involved.) My scruples—which I have suppressed in the text because talk of believing propositions has certain stylistic advantages—could be accommodated by the following wording: A being is omniscient if, for every proposition, that being accepts either that proposition or its denial, and it is metaphysically impossible for that being to accept a false proposition.

8. Some philosophers have said that if I believe that, e.g., *I myself* am hungry, the content of my belief is a *first-person proposition* that only *I* can believe (or accept: see the preceding note). If this is true, then the second definition of omniscience (and perhaps the first as well; but this is less clear) faces an obvious difficulty. I will not discuss this (as I see it) purely technical difficulty—beyond the simple assertion that, in my view, the difficulty is only apparent and can be seen to be only apparent when it is viewed from the perspective of a correct understanding of first-person belief sentences.

9. See my essay "Ontological Arguments".

10. But suppose that someone maintains that the greatest possible being is not—or would not be if it existed—a person. (A Neoplatonist, or Plato himself, might maintain this, as would, perhaps, Spinoza and the British Absolute Idealists.) Those who accept the Anselmian account of the concept of God as the greatest possible being, I think, presuppose that the greatest possible being must be a person—that *of course* the

greatest possible being must be a person. (I myself would say, without the least immodesty, that I am greater than any possible non-person—simply because I am a person.) But this presupposition, some might contend, is a substantive metaphysical thesis, and should not therefore be presupposed by a definition. And others, I among them, would contend that personality is—non-negotiably—a component of the concept of God. The scruples of both these parties may be accommodated by the following statement. The concept of God should be understood in this way: the concept of God is the concept of a *person* who is the greatest possible being. (This is not the same as saying that the concept of God is the concept of a greatest possible person; someone might maintain that there is a greatest possible person and that some non-person is a greater being than that person.) I should be willing to count anyone who maintained that the greatest possible being was a non-person as an atheist. I should also be willing to count the following position as a form (a very unusual one, to be sure) of atheism: Some (existent) person enjoys—essentially—the highest degree of greatness that is metaphysically possible, *and*, in some other possible world, some other being enjoys that degree of greatness. (It is therefore conceptually possible—the concept 'atheist' does not rule out this bizarre possibility—that there should be an atheist who believes that the universe was created *ex nihilo* by an omniscient, omnipotent, perfectly good being who is the unique exemplar of these excellent features in every possible world in which it exists.) In sum: the concept of God is the concept of a person whose degree of greatness cannot be excelled *or equaled* by any other possible being. Anselm's Latin phrase (*aliquid quo nihil maius cogitari possit*) therefore needs to be revised: God is a person who is *aliquid quo nihil maius aut aequaliter magnum cogitari possit*. (I thank Christopher Hughes for getting me to see the need for the qualifications contained in this note.)

LECTURE 3 PHILOSOPHICAL FAILURE

1. László Kalmár, "An Argument against the Plausibility of Church's Thesis", in Heyting, ed., *Constructivity in Mathematics*, 72–80.
2. Philosophers often use the phrase 'the burden of proof' in a way illustrated by the following sentence: "The burden of proof falls on the realist, not the nominalist." This sentence, insofar as I am able to judge, seems to mean, or to be intended to mean, something like this: "Nominalism and realism are inconsistent theses; realism is prima facie much less plausible than nominalism; therefore, in the absence of a proof of (or at least of a very cogent argument for) realism, everyone should prefer nominalism to realism." I will call this (perhaps somewhat tendentiously) the Pointless and Vulgar Sense of 'the burden of proof'. The Correct and Proper Sense of the phrase is illustrated by this sentence: "In the criminal courts, the

burden of proof falls on the state." That is to say, in a criminal court, the state (or the Crown) bears a burden labeled 'proof' or 'having to prove things', and the defense does not. And this is not because a proposition of the form "The accused is guilty as charged" is always inherently less plausible than its denial (that, after all, is often not the case). It is because of a rule that rests on a moral, not an epistemological, foundation: the court presumes the accused to be innocent till proved guilty—and, in a trial by jury, instructs the jurors to presume the same. In our imaginary debate about the existence of God (in the part of it that figures in these lectures, the part in which Atheist attempts to turn the agnostics into fellow atheists by laying the argument from evil before them), the burden labeled 'proof' is carried by Atheist—and, as is the case with the counsel for the prosecution in a criminal trial, this is not because the proposition that is the conclusion of her argument is inherently less plausible than its denial. (Some will say it is, and some will say it isn't; *whether* it is, is irrelevant to where the burden of proof falls.) Unlike the rules that govern the procedures of a criminal court, however, the rules that govern our debate are not founded on moral considerations. The burden of proof, the burden of having to prove things (or at any rate of having to provide arguments for them), falls on Atheist, and does not fall on Theist (at this point in the debate), because it is she and not he whose job it is to change someone's beliefs.

3. But does 'agnostic' not mean 'someone who does not *know* whether God exists'? If we so understand 'agnostic', we must understand 'someone who does not know whether God exists' to mean 'someone who does not *profess* to know whether God exists'. (In the most literal sense of the words "knows whether", someone who knows whether God exists is someone who, if God exists, knows that God exists, and who, if God does not exist, knows that God does not exist. In the most literal sense of the words, therefore, if God exists, no atheist knows whether God exists, and if God does not exist, no theist knows whether God exists.) A person who does not profess to know whether God exists is a person who is willing to say (with perfect sincerity), "I do not know whether God exists." And anyone who is willing to say, with perfect sincerity, "I do not know whether God exists" will, unless that person is involved in some sort of pragmatic contradiction, neither believe that God exists nor believe that God does not exist. And anyone who neither believes that God exists nor believes that God does not exist, should be willing to say—prudential considerations aside—"I do not know whether God exists." I could present arguments for these assertions, but I will not, for it will make no difference to my larger argument whether they are true. Instead of defending them, I will simply *define* an 'agnostic' as someone who does not believe that—lacks the belief that—God exists and does not believe that—lacks the belief that—God does not exist. What I said about pragmatic contradictions and related

matters was said only to defend my application of the term 'agnostic' to people simply on the ground that they lack certain *beliefs*—an application that some might fault on etymological grounds. If the sense of 'agnostic' I have introduced by fiat is in any way objectionable, it is at any rate clear what I mean by the term, and that is all that really matters. (But I do think that it captures what most people today mean by the term, even if what they mean is not so noble as what its inventor, Thomas Henry Huxley, meant by it.) And, in any case, it is "agnostics" in just this sense who must make up my audience if I am to apply to arguments against the existence of God the criterion of success in philosophical argument that I have set out.

4. These arguments can be found in my book *An Essay on Free Will*.

5. If so, my proposed criterion of philosophical success and failure has the same consequence as the two criteria I have rejected: most if not all arguments for substantive philosophical conclusions are failures. And it was this consequence that was my reason for rejecting those criteria. Should I not, therefore, for just this reason, reject the proposed criterion and look for some more liberal criterion? Alas, there *is* no more liberal criterion. The criterion I have proposed is the most liberal possible criterion. (It *is* more liberal than the other two. It sets the philosopher seeking to offer a successful argument for a philosophical thesis an easier task than the other two do, even if that task is impossible. If it is objected that one impossible task cannot be easier than another, I reply that it is in a very obvious sense "easier" to convince 90 percent of the electorate to vote for one than it is to convince every voter to vote for one, even if, as things stand, it is impossible to convince 90 percent of the electorate to vote for one.) My position, then, is that, sadly, every known argument for a substantive philosophical position is a failure—by the most liberal (by the most possibility-of-success-friendly) possible criterion of success and failure.

LECTURE 4 THE GLOBAL ARGUMENT FROM EVIL

1. In the poem as it is printed in the novel there are (for reasons of the plot, as they say: the fictional author of the poem was an educated man who was attempting to disguise his authorship) several illiteracies (e.g. 'whose' for 'who's' in l. 1). I have "corrected" them—with apologies to Martin Amis, in whose opinion they are an important part of the intended effect of the poem on the reader (i.e. the effect Kingsley Amis intended the poem to have on the readers of *The Anti-Death League*). For Martin Amis's argument for this conclusion (and the poem without my officious corrections), see his memoir *Experience*, 188.

2. From ch. 4 ("Rebellion") of Book V (the quotation is from the Constance Garnett translation). Ivan is speaking. It is very nearly obligatory for writers on the problem of evil to quote something from this chapter.

3. *The Existence of God*; See pp. 145–8.
4. Pope, Epistle I, ll. 289 ff.
5. Well, not Surin—who is, after all, a Christian. I'm not sure how Surin supposes that a Christian (or Jewish or Muslim) theologian or philosopher should reply when an atheist attempts to convince theists or agnostics that there is no God by laying out the argument from evil and claiming for it the status of a proof of the non-existence of God. Perhaps like this: the philosopher or theologian simply "responds in faith"; that is, he or she proclaims that it is a matter of faith that there is a God despite the vast amount of evil in the world, and then proceeds to pour scorn on any apologist who responds to the atheist's argument in any other way—even if that way does not take the form of a theodicy (even if it consists, say, in pointing out some logical fallacy in the atheist's argument).
6. I'm going to assume that there is an objective moral standard, that this standard applies both to God and to creatures, and that it's possible for human beings to be mistaken about its demands. If this assumption is wrong, if there is no objective moral standard, then, presumably, there is no such property or attribute as "moral perfection". (When, in the text, I say that moral perfection is, non-negotiably, one of the divine attributes, I presuppose that it exists: *if* the words 'moral perfection' denote a property, they denote a property that God cannot possibly lack.) If there is no such attribute as moral perfection, it must, of course, be removed from the list of divine attributes (that is to say, the *words* 'moral perfection' must be deleted from our *statement* of the list of divine attributes). If there is no such attribute as moral perfection, the *aliquid quo nihil maius cogitari possit* will not be morally perfect—and not because it will be morally imperfect, but because there will not be any such thing for it to be. (Neither it nor anything else will be either morally perfect or morally imperfect, for a thing can no more be morally imperfect if there is no objective moral standard than it can be morally perfect.) But no doubt anyone who felt compelled to remove "moral perfection" from the list of the properties a "something" must have if it is to be a something than which a greater cannot be conceived (having been convinced by some argument or other that there was no objective moral standard) would want to "replace" it with some attribute whose existence did not presuppose an objective moral standard: "benevolent in the highest possible degree", perhaps, or "exhibiting perfect love toward all creatures". And, no doubt, the existence of vast amounts of truly horrible evil raises problems for those who believe in an omnipotent being who is benevolent in the highest possible degree (or whose love for all creatures is perfect) that are essentially the same as the problems it raises for those who believe in an omnipotent and morally perfect being

I should perhaps say something to those theists who resist the idea that there is an objective moral standard that "applies to God". I will say this.

I believe as strongly as you do in God's omnipotence and sovereignty; and, like you, I believe that he is *aliquid quo nihil maius cogitari possit*. Moreover, when I state these beliefs of mine, the words I use to state them are to be understood in the same senses as they have when you use them to state your beliefs. If you say that the thesis that there is an objective moral standard that applies to God is inconsistent with the beliefs I have professed, I will reply that I deny the inconsistency, and I will point out that your affirmation of the inconsistency is a philosophical thesis, not a part of the Christian faith. After all, Abraham said to God (Gen. 18: 25), "Far be it from thee to do such a thing, to slay the righteous with the wicked, so that the righteous fare as the wicked! Far be it from thee! Shall not the Judge of all the earth do right?" (RSV). If you say that you object only to the idea of a moral standard that is "external" to God, I will reply that I neither affirm nor deny that the moral standard whose existence I assert is external to God, for I have no idea what that means. I do affirm this: that general moral principles, if they have truth-values at all, are necessarily true or necessarily false, and that God *has no choice* about the truth-values of non-contingent propositions. If, for example, it would be wrong for God to slay the righteous with the wicked, that is something God has no choice about.

7. I have said that the critical responses of philosophers to the argument from evil usually consist in the presentation of defenses. There is, as far as I can see, only one other way for a philosopher who opposes the argument from evil to proceed: to present an argument for the existence of God that is sufficiently convincing that rational people who consider both arguments carefully will conclude either that at least one of the premises of the argument from evil must be wrong, or will at least conclude that one or more of its premises may well be wrong. In my view, however, this possibility is not a real possibility, for no known argument for the existence of God is sufficiently convincing to be used for this purpose. I would defend this thesis as follows. The only known arguments for the existence of God whose conclusions are inconsistent with the conclusion of the argument from evil are the various forms of the ontological argument. (Even if the cosmological and design arguments, for example, proved their conclusions beyond a shadow of a doubt, it might be that the First Cause or Great Architect whose existence they proved was not morally perfect. Strictly speaking, an atheist can consistently accept the conclusions of both those arguments.) And all versions of the ontological argument other than the "modal argument" are irremediably logically defective. As for the modal ontological argument, there seems to be no reason why someone who did not "already" believe in God should accept its premise (that the existence of a necessary being who possesses all perfections essentially is metaphysically possible).

8. See Antony Flew, "Divine Omnipotence and Human Freedom"; J. L. Mackie, "Evil and Omnipotence"; H. J. McCloskey, "God and Evil"; Nelson Pike, "Hume on Evil"; and Alvin Plantinga, "The Free Will Defense".

9. But there *are* other defenses, although none of them has been so carefully developed or extensively examined as the free-will defense. There is, for example, the "plenitude" defense: the Principle of Plenitude requires God to create all possible worlds in which good outweighs evil; the world we inhabit is one of these worlds; there are vastly many other created worlds, in some of which good outweighs evil much more decisively than it does in our world, and in some of which it only barely outweighs evil. Versions of the plenitude defense are presented in Donald A. Turner's "The Many-Universes Solution to the Problem of Evil" and in Hud Hudson's book *The Metaphysics of Hyperspace*. There is Alvin Plantinga's recent "felix culpa" defense, according to which the evils of the world are a necessary condition for the immeasurably great good of the Incarnation. (See his essay "Supralapsarianism, or 'O Felix Culpa'".) There is the "radical Calvinist" defense, according to which God decrees evil in order that his glory may be displayed in its final defeat; all created beings who suffer, suffer justly (the defense contends) because God has created them with evil wills—to demonstrate his glory and power by his ultimate victory over them—and their sufferings are an ordinate punishment for the evil actions that their evil wills lead them to perform. (A Notre Dame graduate student, Christopher Green, defended this view in a term paper in a seminar on the problem of evil, and made it seem more plausible than I should have thought possible. A later version of this paper, entitled "A Compatibi-Calvinist Demonstrative-Goods Defense", was read at the 2003 Eastern Division meeting of the Society of Christian Philosophers. It is as yet unpublished.) It may be that further development and discussion of these or other defenses would lead me to revise my judgment that the free-will defense is the only defense that has any hope of success

For recent work on the free-will defense, including the seminal work of Alvin Plantinga, see Adams and Adams, eds., *The Problem of Evil*, and Peterson, ed., *The Problem of Evil: Selected Readings*.

The free-will defense derives, at a great historical remove, from St Augustine. A useful selection of Augustine's writings on free will and the origin of evil (from *The City of God* and the *Enchiridion*) can be found in A. I. Melden, ed., *Ethical Theories*, 164–77.

Three important book-length treatments of the problem of evil, all in the Augustinian (or "free will") tradition, are C. S. Lewis, *The Problem of Pain*; P. T. Geach, *Providence and Evil*; and Richard Swinburne, *Providence and the Problem of Evil*.

10. Note that I do not say that affirmation of the truth of contradictions makes rational debate impossible. That may or may not be so, but to contend that it is so is not a part of my argument. Para-consistent logicians need not take offense. I said that someone who affirms the truth of contradictions *has the resources* to make rational debate impossible. Someone who affirms contradictions will no doubt affirm other things as well, and some of these things may forbid his making use of these "resources". Note, however, that the dialogue in the text does not represent the contradiction-affirming Cartesian theodicist as making use of the principle that anything follows from a contradiction. So far as I can see, he affirms nothing, takes no dialectical step, that could be disputed by the "friends of true contradictions".

LECTURE 5 THE GLOBAL ARGUMENT CONTINUED

1. The literature on the problem of free will is vast—even if one restricts one's attention to recent work by analytical philosophers. It is perhaps natural enough that I should recommend my book *An Essay on Free Will* as a point of entry into this vastness. More recent work, and comprehensive references, can be found in Laura Waddell Ekstrom, ed., *Agency and Responsibility: Essays in the Metaphysics of Freedom*; Robert Kane, ed., *Free Will*; and Gary Watson, ed., *Free Will*.

2. The two most important discussions of counterfactuals of freedom can be found in these splendid (but highly technical) books: Plantinga's *The Nature of Necessity* (ch. 9) and Thomas Flint's *Divine Providence: The Molinist Account* (chs. 2 and 4–7).

3. For references to Thomist and Jesuit theories of counterfactuals of freedom, see Flint, *Divine Providence*, chs. 2 and 4.

4. I have in mind the version of the free-will defense (*The Nature of Necessity*, ch. IX, sects. 7–9) that includes the proposition that "every creaturely individual essence suffers from trans-world depravity".

5. See Robert Merrihew Adams, "Middle Knowledge and the Problem of Evil" and "An Anti-Molinist Argument"; William Hasker, *God, Time, and Knowledge* and "Anti-Molinism is Undefeated!"; and my "Against Middle Knowledge".

6. The standard argument for the incompatibility of omniscience and free will depends on God's being "in time". In brief outline, it goes as follows. If God knew, and hence believed, at t (a moment in the remote past) that I should lie tomorrow, then I am able to tell the truth tomorrow only if I am able either to bring it about that God did not have this belief or that it was mistaken. And I am able to do neither of these things. I lack the ability to do the former because that ability would be an ability to *change*

the past. But if God is non-temporal, there is no *time* at which he believes that I shall lie tomorrow. The fact that he has this belief is therefore not a fact about the past, and an ability to bring it about that he does not have this belief is not an ability to change the past.

It is by no means clear that supposing that God is non-temporal solves the problem of reconciling divine omniscience and human freedom, for a non-temporal God has the power to reveal to temporal creatures—prophets—facts about what is to temporal creatures the future, and one can construct an argument for the incompatibility of non-temporal divine omniscience and human freedom by appealing to the possibility that he exercise this power: My ability to tell the truth (when a divinely inspired prophet has prophesied that I shall lie) must be an ability either to bring it about that this prophecy was never made—to change the past—or to bring it about that it was mistaken. Whatever the merits of this argument may be, however, it is certainly less straightforward than the argument that is based on the foreknowledge of a God who is in time.

7. I'm trying to avoid *merely* technical considerations in these lectures. I'll leave it to this note to point out that this statement needs qualification. For suppose that an omniscient being began to exist at *t*, and that, although there had been free agents before *t*, there would be no free agents at *t* or afterwards. That seems possible. But the qualification this would require is irrelevant to our purposes, since there never was a time when God was not. (The following two statements would seem to be true without qualification: no everlasting being is *always* omniscient in any possible world in which there are free creatures; if it is possible for there to be creatures with free will, no necessary being is essentially omniscient.)

8. Cf. Swinburne, *Providence and the Problem of Evil*, 133–4.

9. I will say this much. In every case in which the biblical narrative might seem to represent God as foreknowing the free actions of a human being, either the foreknown action is in fact not free, or the foreknowledge is to be understood as conditional: knowledge of what the consequences of a certain free choice would be if it were made.

10. In "The Christian Theodicist's Appeal to Love", Daniel and Frances Howard-Snyder defend the position that this thesis, the thesis that free will is necessary for love, is inconsistent with the Christian doctrine of the Trinity. The argument, stripped to its bare essentials, is this: according to that doctrine, the Persons of the Trinity love one another as a matter of metaphysical necessity. None of the Persons, therefore, has any choice about whether he shall love either of the others.

I would say this in reply. (I reply as a Christian. A Jew or a Muslim who wants to make use of the free-will defense in the text will not need to attend to the matters discussed in this note. But I should not like to think that the defense I am having Theist present was inconsistent with

Christianity.) Let us say that a being loves *perfectly* if it has the property *loving each thing* essentially. (For each object, there is a kind and degree of love appropriate to that object: a mother may love her child, her cat, and her parish church, but these three loves must differ in kind or degree, or something is very wrong. The property in question is that of loving everything in the right way.) Perfect love is obviously impossible for finite beings. For one thing, no finite being can be so much as *aware* of each thing, of every possible object of love. No finite being, moreover, can love even *one* thing essentially (not even given that thing exists). Even if Jill loves Jack as a matter of antecedent causal necessity, there will be, there must be, other possible worlds in which antecedent causes are arranged differently and in which (Jack exists and) she does not love Jack. There will be, there must be, (since this is possible) worlds in which she loves no one and nothing. Now suppose that finite Jill does love Jack. *Why* does she love Jack? One of three things must be true. Her love for Jack is a matter of external necessity; her love for Jack is a matter of chance (it just happened: it has no explanation whatever); her love for Jack is a matter of her own free choice. (No doubt her *feelings* for Jack will not be a matter of free choice, but there is more to love than feelings: one essential part of love consists in a certain orientation of the will.) In saying this, I am not presupposing that free choice is incompatible with external necessity per se. Everyone, I think, will agree that *some* kinds of external necessity are incompatible with free choice. (And everyone will agree that some kinds of chance are incompatible with free choice.) The reader should understand "external necessity" and "chance" in such a way that 'is a matter of external necessity', 'is a matter of chance', and 'is a matter of free choice' divide the possible explanations of Jill's love for Jack into three exhaustive and exclusive classes.

Now let us return to the concept of perfect love. I would maintain that perfect love is a property of God, and, since it is impossible for finite, imperfect beings, creatures, is a property of God alone. But let us ask this: How might creatures love one another (and God) in a way that best "imitates" perfect love? I would say, first, that creaturely love does not best imitate divine love if it is due to chance: that is the very opposite of the necessity that belongs to divine love. Would their love best imitate God's love if it were a matter of *external* necessity? No, for God's love (like all his properties) belongs to his essence, and therefore "comes from within": its necessity is *internal* to him. The best creaturely imitation of this internal necessity is love that is the consequence of free choice, for such love comes from within, and is not due to chance. Like God's love, it is neither the result of the operation of external forces (or if it is the result of the operation of external forces, it is so only to the extent that all free acts are: it is the result of the operation of external forces in the sort of way that does not violate the autonomy of the lover), nor something that "just happens". If this is right, it is at least true that the "best sort" of creaturely love, the love that is the best creaturely imitation of perfect love, involves free choice. This much would suffice for the free-will defense, for it would explain why God would give human beings free will even at a great price. (Given that the difference in value between the best sort of creaturely love and other sorts is great enough, a thesis that can be made a part of the defense.) I remain convinced, however, that love that is due to chance or external necessity is not love at all. (The logic of this last sentence is the same as that of "Love is not love that alters when it alteration finds".)

11. In what sense could these events be "random"? Can any event be "a random occurrence" or "due to chance" in a world created and sustained by an omnipotent and omniscient being? My answer to this question is Yes. For a technical discussion of the issues that the question involves, see my essay "The Place of Chance in a World Sustained by God". The essential point of the argument of the essay is this. First, God can, if he chooses, "decree" that it shall either be the case that p or [exclusive] be the case that q, without either decreeing that it shall be the case that p or decreeing that it shall be the case that q. Then it will either be the case that p or be the case that q, but *which* of the two will be a matter of chance. For example, although God said, "Let there be light", he could have said, "Let there be *either* light or darkness". If he had issued the latter decree, there would have been either light or darkness, and it would have been a matter of chance whether there was light or there was darkness. Secondly, God might have good reasons for issuing less-than-fully-specific decrees—explicitly disjunctive decrees like the one I have imagined, or decrees that are logically equivalent to disjunctions like "Let there be at least twelve major gods in the Babylonian pantheon—but not more than nineteen". One such reason might be this: God does not perform pointless acts, and if the exact number of hairs on my head makes no difference in the great scheme of things (a plausible enough thesis), it would be pointless for God to decree (or in any way to determine) that the number of hairs on my head shall be exactly 119, 202. And, if we have conceded that *some* states of affairs have not been decreed by God (and which he has therefore left to chance), the question "*Which* states of affairs has God left to chance?" must be conceded to be a matter for theological or philosophical speculation. It may well be, then, that such matters as whether a given person dies in some natural disaster is something God has left to chance. Whether this could be so is at any rate a matter about which philosophers and theologians can properly speculate.

12. For a more extensive discussion of the role of chance in the expanded free-will defense, see my essay "The Magnitude, Duration, and Distribution of Evil: A Theodicy".

LECTURE 6 THE LOCAL ARGUMENT FROM EVIL

1. This story has also been used by Marilyn Adams, both in her essay "Horrendous Evils and the Goodness of God" and in her book of the same title. My use of the story is independent of hers: I read the initial reports in the press of the appalling event recounted in the story (it happened in about 1980, I think) and have been using it as an example in my philosophy of religion classes ever since. I will also remark that, while both Adams and I use the word 'horrors', she uses the word in a special technical sense and I do not. Her meaning is "evils the participation in (the doing or suffering of) which gives one reason prima facie to doubt whether one's life could (given their inclusion in it) be a great good to one on the whole". I take no stand on the question of whether all or any of the events I call "horrors" have this feature.

2. Rowe, "Problem of Evil", 337; in Adams and Adams, 129.

3. See Isa. 30: 27–8 and 45: 7. The latter text reads, "I form the light and create darkness: I make peace and create [= cause, bring about] evil: I the Lord do all these things." According to Peter Baelz (*Prayer and Providence*, 64), J. S. Mill closed his Bible when he read these words. In the New Testament, see the story of the tower at Siloam (Luke 13: 1–9) and the story of the man born blind (John 9: 1–41).

4. Does it not then follow that, for any *n*, if the existence of at most *n* horrors is consistent with God's plan, then the existence of at most *m* horrors (where *m* is any number smaller than *n*, including 0) is consistent with his plan? No: mathematical induction is valid only for precise predicates.

5. Unless, as C. S. Lewis has suggested, pre-human animal suffering is ascribed to a corruption of nature by fallen angels. I will briefly discuss this suggestion in the seventh lecture.

LECTURE 7 THE SUFFERINGS OF BEASTS

1. I endorse an "abstractionist" modal ontology. That is to say, I apply the term 'possible world' to abstract objects of some sort—states of affairs, perhaps. (See my essay "Two Concepts of Possible Worlds".) I would, therefore, if this were a work of technical metaphysics, carefully distinguish "the actual world" from "the universe" (or "the cosmos"). I would point out that, while God has created the universe *ex nihilo*—and might have created a different one or no universe at all—the actual world is a necessarily existent (although contingently actual) abstract object, and that God has not *created* it but *actualized* it: indeed (I would point out), God has probably not done even that; probably he has actualized only some "large" state of affairs that it includes. I would point out that while God is not a part of the universe (nor does he share any part with it), he *exists in* the actual world (as he does in all possible worlds). In this work, I am not

going to point any of these things out. Ignoring these nice metaphysical points (in matters of verbal expression; they are of course present in my thoughts as I write) will not weaken my argument.

2. The laws of nature fail in a world if some of them are false in that world. (Whatever else a law of nature may be, it is a proposition, and thus has a truth-value.) For example, if "In every closed system, momentum is conserved" is a law of nature in the world w, and if, in w, there are closed systems in which momentum is not conserved, the laws of nature fail in w. For an account of laws of nature that allows a proposition to be both false in a world and a law of nature in that world, see my essay, "The Place of Chance in a World Sustained by God".

3. In this example, I assume that selection pressure is necessary if taxonomic diversification of the order exhibited by the terrestrial biosphere is to occur in the natural course of events (i.e. without miracles). This is certainly true for all anyone knows.

4. Note that propositions (1), (2), and (3) contain no element of the supernatural. They could be accepted without contradiction by the most fervent atheists and naturalists.

5. If you were asked to assign a probability to the hypothesis "The first ball drawn will be black" *before* the drawing of the number from the hat, you would know what probability to assign: it would be the average of the one-hundred-and-one probabilities that the hat-drawing will choose among: $(0/100 + 1/100 + 2/100 + \cdots + 100/100)/101$; i.e. 0.5. The thesis asserted in the text, however, is that *after* the number has been drawn from the hat, you will have no way to assign a probability to that hypothesis.

6. To make the case more realistic, we should say, "galaxies of the same age and type as our own Milky Way galaxy". Very "young" galaxies are unlikely to be "inhabited", and the same is true of older galaxies belonging to various specifiable types.

7. This statement requires one qualification. Someone might object that each of the four propositions that make up our defense is either necessarily true or necessarily false, whereas the propositions that figure in our examples are contingent. Here, then, is a third example: an example that involves a non-contingent proposition. Consider a certain mathematical conjecture: that there is a largest integer that has the property F. Suppose that all the mathematicians who fully understand the issues this conjecture involves are unwilling to commit themselves to its truth or its falsity—that none of them so much as *leans* toward saying that it is true or that it is false. Then the lay person who knows these things is in no position to ascribe a probability to the conjecture. One might of course say that, because the conjecture is either necessarily true or necessarily false, the lay person is in a position to *rule out* many probability assignments—in fact, almost all

of them: all of them but 0 and 1. (And one might go on to contend that the same was true of our defense.) On one understanding of probability ("objective chance" as opposed to "subjective probability"), this is correct. (In this note and in the text, I have been deliberately vague about "what kind of probability" I'm talking about—simply in order to avoid what I think would be an unnecessary digression.) But the following point remains, and it's the only point that matters: our lay person should be willing to say of the conjecture, "For all I know it's true, and for all I know it's false. I'm *completely neutral* as to its truth-value."

8. The two examples are isomorphic in structure. Let the urn contain as many balls as there are galaxies. (The number of balls in the urn is irrelevant to the force of the example.) Let the god who prepares the urn assign a galaxy to each ball, and let him turn a ball white if it corresponds to an inhabited galaxy and black if it corresponds to an uninhabited one. An urn prepared in this manner would be, from the point of view of someone in our epistemic condition who was asked to assign a probability to 'The first ball drawn will be black', indistinguishable from an urn containing the same number of balls in which the proportion of black balls was chosen by a random drawing.

9. For more on this topic, see my essay "Modal Epistemology".

10. For some of the facts about our world that should be appreciated by anyone engaged in world design, see Martin Rees, *Just Six Numbers*.

11. I doubt, however, whether the genesis of rationality involved only the operations of the laws of nature. I will say something about my reasons for skepticism on this point later in this lecture.

12. For evidence that supports this thesis, if evidence is needed, see Philip Yancey and Paul Brand, *The Gift of Pain*. Paul Brand is the physician who discovered that leprosy (Hansen's disease) does not, as had long been believed, "rot the flesh". The disease, rather, destroys the nerves that transmit pain-signals to the brain from many parts of the victim's body, particularly the hands and the feet; what observers had taken for rotting flesh was flesh that had been banged and pressed (unintentionally, by its "owners", who, unable to feel pain, were unaware of what they were doing to themselves) till lesions developed.

   The Gift of Pain is about the "function" of *human* pain, but—given that the book is right about human pain—it is hard to not to conclude that pain has the same function in the physiological economies of apes and beavers. I particularly commend to readers of the present book the authors' discussion (pp. 191–7) of "why pain has to hurt so much"—i.e. their presentation of convincing empirical evidence for the thesis that not particularly unpleasant signals of incipient peripheral damage (a loud buzzer, say) or only slightly unpleasant signals (like a mild electric shock) are ineffective means of protecting an organism from inadvertent self-injury.

13. Many critics of theism make much of the "waste" or "profligacy" that is to be found in nature and which is no doubt a necessary consequence of any evolutionary process in which natural selection plays a significant role. (Consider, to take just one example, the countless species—classes, orders, even a few phyla—that have perished "without issue". All the clever modifications that time and chance worked on the genetic material of these species are *gone*: thousands of ingenious and useful solutions to a wide range of problems of biological design have been, as it were, accidentally deleted from Nature's hard drive.) This waste and profligacy should be considered as one aspect of the "patterns of suffering of the actual world".

14. In my view, it is fair to compare him to a Christian Scientist who believes both that all sickness is an illusion and that cigarette smoking causes lung cancer.

15. My answer to this question contained the following statement:

Unless one proceeds in this manner, one's statements about what is intrinsically or metaphysically possible—and thus one's statements about an omnipotent being's "options" in creating a world—will be entirely subjective, and therefore without value.

In saying this, I "in effect" advocated a form of modal skepticism, because "proceeding in this manner" is not something anyone has ever done; nor is it at present possible.

16. This "quotation" is not a continuous passage but a selection of scattered verses from Job 38 (verses 3, 4, 21, 31, 33).

17. For a discussion of God's "leaving things to chance", see my "The Place of Chance in a World Sustained by God".

18. And also because I'm very strongly inclined to think it's true. More precisely (for the case is, by its nature, imaginary, and asking whether it has this feature is therefore like asking whether Lady Macbeth had three children), I'm very strongly inclined to think that there *have been* cases in which beasts who existed long before there were human beings died in agony and "no good came of it".

19. It might be, e.g., that the world is "nearly regular" (the "opposite" of 'massively irregular': 'nearly regular' stands to 'massively irregular' as 'very tall' stands to 'very short'), and that that is a great good. No doubt the world would still have been nearly regular if God had miraculously saved the fawn. And, therefore, if regularity is the only good "in play" in this case (and irregularity the only evil), no good was achieved (and no evil averted) by his allowing the fawn to suffer and die. If, however, God had miraculously eliminated *all* instances of intense suffering from the natural world, the good of near regularity would have been lost. And it would have been lost if he had eliminated all but one of them, all but two of them, all but three of them . . . .

20. One might, however, wonder how much pain is felt by the victims of predators. Here is a famous passage from the first chapter of David Livingstone's *Missionary Travels*:

> When in the act of ramming down the bullets, I heard a shout. Starting, and looking half round, I saw the lion just in the act of springing upon me. I was upon a little height; he caught my shoulder as he sprang, and we both came to the ground below together. Growling horribly close to my ear, he shook me as a terrier dog does a rat. The shock produced a stupor similar to that which seems to be felt by a mouse after the first shake of the cat. It caused a sort of dreaminess, in which there was no sense of pain nor feeling of terror, though I was quite conscious of all that was happening. It was like what patients partially under the influence of chloroform describe, who see all the operation, but feel not the knife. This singular condition was not the result of any mental process. The shake annihilated fear, and allowed no sense of horror in looking round at the beast. This peculiar state is probably produced in all animals killed by the carnivora; and if so, is a merciful provision by our benevolent Creator for lessening the pain of death.

Commenting on this incident in his 2003 Reith Lectures, the eminent neuroscientist Vilayanur S. Ramachandran says:

> Remember the story of Livingstone being mauled by a lion. He saw his arm being ripped off [Livingstone's injury was not quite that bad, but the bone of his upper arm was crushed and he suffered deep and serious wounds from the lion's teeth.—PvI] but felt no pain or even fear. He felt like he was detached from it all, watching it all happen. The same thing happens, by the way, to soldiers in battle or sometimes even to women being raped. During such dire emergencies, the anterior cingular in the brain, part of the frontal lobes, becomes extremely active. This inhibits or temporarily shuts down your amygdala and other limbic emotional centers, so you suppress potentially disabling emotions like anxiety and fear—temporarily. But at the same time, the anterior cingular makes you extremely alert and vigilant so you can take the appropriate action.

The Reith Lectures are delivered on BBC Radio 4. This passage is from Lecture 5, "Neuroscience—the New Philosophy". The text of the lecture can be found at <http://www2.thny.bbc.co.uk/radio4/reith2003/lecture5. shtml>.

21. C. S. Lewis, *The Problem of Pain*, 121–4.
22. See Geach, *Providence and Evil*, 79–80.
23. In 1973, I heard Geach deliver a series of lectures that contained much of the material that later appeared in *Providence and Evil*. If my memory does not play me false, in those lectures he presented an argument that does not

appear in the book, an argument that is addressed to exactly this question. The argument, as I remember it, was this, or something very like it:

Human beings and beasts share the same animal nature; human beings can therefore sympathize with beasts and are consequently subject to (certain severely limited) moral obligations pertaining to their welfare. God and human beings share the same rational nature; God can therefore sympathize with human beings and is consequently subject to (certain severely limited) moral obligations pertaining to their welfare. But no nature is common to God and beasts, and he therefore cannot sympathize with them, and is therefore subject to no moral obligations pertaining to their welfare.

(The first and third sentences of this argument correspond closely to the argument in the text. It is the second sentence that is "addressed to exactly this question".) Whether this is Geach's argument or not, it does not meet the case. Whatever merits the argument may have, it does not even claim to show that an obligation to attend in any way to the *physical sufferings* of human beings is among the moral obligations pertaining to human welfare that God is said to be subject to. And, indeed, the opposite seems to be true: however deeply God may sympathize with those aspects of the human condition that involve only our rational nature, he cannot sympathize with our physical sufferings, and (if the larger argument is correct) cannot be subject to any moral obligation that is grounded in sympathy with physical suffering.

LECTURE 8 THE HIDDENNESS OF GOD

1. This argument does not appeal to the validity of "Absence of evidence is evidence of absence" as a general epistemological principle. And that is to its credit, for that principle is wrong: we have no evidence for the existence of an inhabited planet in the galaxy M31, but that fact is not evidence for the non-existence of such a planet. For a discussion of this principle and arguments for the non-existence of God that appeal to it, see my essay "Is God an Unnecessary Hypothesis?" If the present argument appeals to any general epistemological principle, it is this rather obvious one: If a proposition is such that, if it were true, we should have evidence for its truth, and if we are aware that it has this property, and if we have no evidence for its truth, then this fact, the fact that we have no evidence for its truth, is (conclusive) evidence for its falsity.

2. Those who wish to learn more about the problem of the hiddenness of God should consult Daniel Howard-Snyder and Paul K. Moser's *Divine Hiddenness: New Essays*. The present lecture is an expanded version of my own contribution to that volume, "What is the Problem of the Hiddenness of God?"

3. Those who think that the sufferings of non-human animals that are unrelated to the acts of human beings are relevant to "the problem of the hiddenness of God" should feel free to imagine that our invented world is one in which beasts in the state of nature never suffer. As I said in the previous lecture, it is not easy to imagine in any detail a biologically rich world without animal suffering unless one imagines it as a world of ubiquitous miracles—a world in which, for example, fawns are always miraculously saved from forest fires. The imaginer who has recourse to a vast array of miracles had better take care to make them "unnoticeable" (at least in those epochs and places in which there are human beings to notice them), for if the ubiquitous miracles were *obviously* miracles, this would defeat our purpose in trying to imagine a utopia in which "the problem of the hiddenness of God" could be raised.

4. I can imagine someone in the actual world (a reader of this book) protesting, "This metaphysical argument confuses the God of the Philosophers with the God of Abraham, Isaac, and Jacob. For the prophet Isaiah says (45: 15), 'Verily, thou art a God that hidest thyself, O God of Israel, the Saviour' ". In my view, however, Isaiah is simply calling attention to the fact that God has revealed himself to the Hebrews alone, and not to the great nations of Egypt and the Fertile Crescent. (In the Vulgate, incidentally, Isa. 45: 15 is rendered as "Vere, tu es Deus absconditus, Deus Israel, Salvator". This is the source of the phrase 'Deus absconditus'—'the hidden God'—that often occurs in discussions of the problem of the hiddenness of God.)

5. This argument is, of course, modeled on the central argument of Hume's unjustly celebrated essay "Of Miracles" (*An Enquiry concerning Human Understanding*, sect. X).

6. Atheist's statement is reminiscent of a famous statement of Norwood Russell Hanson's ("What I Don't Believe", 322):

I'm not a stubborn guy. I would be a theist under some conditions. I'm open-minded. . . . Okay. Okay. The conditions are these: Suppose, next Tuesday morning, just after breakfast, all of us in this one world are knocked to our knees by a percussive and ear-shattering thunderclap. Snow swirls, leaves drop from trees, the earth heaves and buckles, buildings topple, and towers tumble. The sky is ablaze with an eerie silvery light, and just then, as all of the people of this world look up, the heavens open, and the clouds pull apart, revealing an unbelievably radiant and immense Zeus-like figure towering over us like a hundred Everests. He frowns darkly as lightning plays over the features of his Michelangeloid face, and then he points down, *at me*, and explains for every man, woman, and child to hear: "I've had quite enough of your too-clever logic chopping and word-watching in matters of theology. Be assured Norwood Russell Hanson, that I do most certainly exist!"

7. By 'signs and wonders' I mean "visible" miracles, events that are on the face of it contraventions of the natural order of things. ("The raising of a house or ship into the air is a visible miracle. The raising of a feather, when the wind wants ever so little of a force requisite for that purpose, is as real a miracle, though not so sensible with regard to us" (Hume, "Of Miracles," n. 1).) To use this biblical term in this sense is by no means an anachronism. "Law of nature" may be a modern concept (it would have been difficult indeed to explain to anyone in the ancient world what Hume meant when he said that the raising of a feather by the wind might be a violation of the natural order—if the wind *did* raise the feather, how could it have wanted, to any degree, a force requisite to that purpose?; what could that *mean?*), but people in biblical times were well aware that the truth of certain reports would entail the existence of violations of the natural order, for those reports are reports of things that "just don't happen". See, e.g., the reaction of Porcius Festus, procurator of Judea, to Paul's confession of faith before King Agrippa (Acts 26: 24). Festus was a first-century man of affairs, not a post-Newtonian philosopher, but his reaction to Paul's speech evidences a position that is as "Humean" as those differences from Hume permit: it is more reasonable to believe that Paul is mad than it is to believe what he says, for the kinds of things that Paul has described are kinds of things that just don't happen—and a learned man's being driven mad by his great learning *is* a thing that has been known to happen.

8. These words are from a manuscript that, as far as I know, is unpublished. They are quoted in Robert Bartlett, *England under the Norman and Angevin Kings*. I take them from a review of the book by John Gillingham. Here is a second quotation from the book by the reviewer: "simple materialism and disbelief in the afterlife were probably widespread, although they leave little trace in sources written by clerics and monks". (No page citations are given in the review.)

9. In the "American undergraduate" version, Russell went on to say: "Then God will say to me, 'Good for you, Bertie; you used the mind I gave you. Enter into the Kingdom of Heaven.' And you, young man, you he will send straight to Hell."

10. This is the translation of the Jerusalem Bible. Here is a more literal translation: "Do you believe that God is one? You do well. The demons also believe, and they shudder."

11. Is there any evidence that *A Christmas Carol* was influenced by Luke 16? I should like to know.

12. Wisd. 1: 16–2: 11. The phrase "they have made a covenant with death" occurs in Isaiah (28: 15), but in that verse, I believe, a different sort of covenant is intended.

13. "For whoever would draw near to God must believe that he exists (*hoti estin*) and that he rewards those who seek him" (Heb. 11: 6, RSV). Note

that the first conjunct is (logically) redundant: one who believes that God rewards those who seek him *ipso facto* believes that God exists. Note also that even the more inclusive belief—that God rewards those who seek him—is represented as having merely instrumental value: what is of intrinsic value is drawing near to God.

14. If Descartes's account of intellectual error was right, this epistemic defect wasn't innocent, for it involved an abuse of free will (but I don't suppose that his account was right).

Works Cited

Adams, Marilyn McCord, "Horrendous Evils and the Goodness of God", *Proceedings of the Aristotelian Society*, suppl. vol. 63 (1989): 297–310. Reprinted in revised form in Adams and Adams.

_____ *Horrendous Evils and the Goodness of God* (Ithaca, NY: Cornell University Press, 1999).

_____ and Adams, Robert Merrihew, eds., *The Problem of Evil* (Oxford: Oxford University Press, 1990).

Adams, Robert Merrihew, "An Anti-Molinist Argument", *Philosophical Perspectives*, 5: Philosophy of Religion (1991): 343–54.

_____ "Middle Knowledge and the Problem of Evil", *American Philosophical Quarterly* 14 (1977): 109–17.

Amis, Kingsley, *The Anti-Death League* (New York: Harcourt, Brace, and World, 1966).

Amis, Martin, *Experience* (New York: Hyperion, 2000).

_____ *Koba the Dread: Laughter and the Twenty Million* (New York: Talk Miramax, 2002).

Baelz, Peter, *Prayer and Providence: A Background Study* (London: SCM Press, 1968).

Bartlett, Robert, *England under the Norman and Angevin Kings, 1075–1225* (Oxford: Clarendon Press, 2000).

Black, Max, ed., *Philosophy in America* (Ithaca, NY: Cornell University Press, 1965).

Craig, William Lane, ed., *Philosophy of Religion: A Contemporary Reader* (Edinburgh: Edinburgh University Press, 2004).

Dole, Andrew, and Chignel, Andrew, eds., *God and the Ethics of Belief: New Essays in the Philosophy of Religion* (Cambridge: Cambridge University Press, 2005).

Ekstrom, Laura Waddell, ed., *Agency and Responsibility: Essays in the Metaphysics of Freedom* (Oxford: Westview Press, 2001).

Flew, Antony, "Divine Omnipotence and Human Freedom", in Flew and MacIntyre, 144–69.

_____ and MacIntyre, Alasdair, eds., *New Essays in Philosophical Theology* (London: William Clowes and Sons, 1955).

Flint, Thomas P., *Divine Providence: The Molinist Account* (Ithaca, NY: Cornell University Press, 1998).

Gale, Richard M., and Pruss, Alexander R., eds., *The Existence of God* (Aldershot: Ashgate, 2003).

Geach, P. T., "Omnipotence", *Philosophy* 48 (1973): 7–20.

_____ *Providence and Evil* (Cambridge: Cambridge University Press, 1977).

Gillingham, John, review of Bartlett, *England under the Norman and Angevin Kings, 1075–1225*, *Times Literary Supplement*, 5 May 2000, p. 26.

Hanson, Norwood Russell, "What I Don't Believe", in Toulmin and Woolf.

Hasker, William, "Anti-Molinism is Undefeated!", *Faith and Philosophy* 17 (2000): 126–31.

_____ *God, Time, and Knowledge* (Ithaca, NY: Cornell University Press, 1989).

Heyting, A., ed, *Constructivity in Mathematics* (Amsterdam: North Holland, 1959).

Howard-Snyder, Daniel, and Howard-Snyder, Frances, "The Christian Theodicist's Appeal to Love", *Religious Studies* 29 (1993): 185–92.

_____ and Moser, Paul K., eds., *Divine Hiddenness: New Essays* (Cambridge: Cambridge University Press, 2002).

Hudson, Hud, *The Metaphysics of Hyperspace* (Oxford: Oxford University Press, 2006).

Jaki, Stanley L., *Lord Gifford and his Lectures: A Centenary Retrospect* (Edinburgh: Scottish Academic Press, 1986).

Kane, Robert, ed., *Free Will* (Oxford: Blackwell, 2002).

Lewis, C. S., *The Problem of Pain* (London: Macmillan, 1940).

Livingstone, David, *Missionary Travels and Researches in South Africa* (Philadelphia: J. W. Bradley, 1860).

Mackie, J. L., "Evil and Omnipotence", *Mind*, n.s. 64 (1955): 200–12. Reprinted in Adams and Adams.

Matson, Wallace I., *The Existence of God* (Ithaca, NY: Cornell University Press, 1965).

McCloskey, H. J., "God and Evil", *Philosophical Quarterly* 10 (1960): 97–114.

Melden, A. I., ed., *Ethical Theories*, 2nd edn. (Englewood Cliffs, NJ: Prentice-Hall, 1955).

Mill, J. S., *Three Essays on Religion* (New York: Henry Holt and Company, 1878).

Morris, Thomas V., ed., *Divine and Human Action: Essays in the Metaphysics of Theism* (Ithaca, NY: Cornell University Press, 1988).

Neiman, Susan, *Evil in Modern Thought: An Alternative History of Philosophy* (Princeton, NJ: 0Princeton University Press, 2002).

Padgett, Alan, ed., *Reason and the Christian Religion* (Oxford: Clarendon Press, 1994).

Peterson, Michael L., ed., *The Problem of Evil: Selected Readings* (Notre Dame, Ind.: University of Notre Dame Press, 1992).

Pike, Nelson, "Hume on Evil", *Philosophical Review* 72 (1963): 180–97.

Plantinga, Alvin, "The Free Will Defense", in Black, 204–20.

_____ *The Nature of Necessity* (Oxford: Clarendon Press, 1974).

_____ "Supralapsarianism, or '*O Felix Culpa*'", in van Inwagen, ed., *Christian Faith and the Problem of Evil*, 1–25.

Rees, Martin, *Just Six Numbers: The Deep Forces that Shape the Universe* (New York: Basic Books, 2000).

Rowe, William L., "The Problem of Evil and Some Varieties of Atheism", *American Philosophical Quarterly* 16 (1979): 335–41. Reprinted in Adams and Adams.

Stewart, M., ed., *The Holy Trinity* (Dordrecht: Kluwer, 2003).

Stump, Eleonore, *Faith and the Problem of Evil* (Grand Rapids, Mich.: Stob Lectures Endowment, 1999).

——and Murray, Michael, eds., *The Big Questions: Philosophy of Religion* (Oxford: Blackwell, 1999).

Surin, Kenneth, *Theology and the Problem of Evil* (Oxford: Basil Blackwell, 1986).

Swinburne, Richard, *Providence and the Problem of Evil* (Oxford: Oxford University Press, 1998).

Toulmin, Stephen, and Woolf, Harry, eds., *What I Do Not Believe, and Other Essays* (Dordrecht: D. Reidel, 1972).

Turner, Donald A., "The Many-Universes Solution to the Problem of Evil", in Gale and Pruss, 143–59.

van Inwagen, Peter, "Against Middle Knowledge", *Midwest Studies in Philosophy* 21 (1997): 225–36.

——*An Essay on Free Will* (Oxford: Clarendon Press, 1983).

——*God, Knowledge, and Mystery: Essays in Philosophical Theology* (Ithaca, NY: Cornell University Press, 1995).

——"Is God an Unnecessary Hypothesis?", in Dole and Chignel, 131–49.

——"The Magnitude, Duration, and Distribution of Evil: A Theodicy", *Philosophical Topics* 16, 2 (1988): 161–87. Reprinted in Stump and Murray, in Feinberg and Shafer-Landau, and in Craig.

——"Modal Epistemology", *Philosophical Studies* 92 (1998): 67–84. Reprinted in van Inwagen, *Ontology, Identity and Modality*.

——"Not by Confusion of Substance but by Unity of Person", in Padgett, 201–26. Reprinted in van Inwagen, *God, Knowledge, and Mystery* and in *The Philosopher's Annual*, 17 (1994).

——"Ontological Arguments", *Noûs* 11 (1977): 375–95. Reprinted in van Inwagen, *God, Knowledge, and Mystery*.

——*Ontology, Identity and Modality* (Cambridge: Cambridge University Press, 2001).

——"The Place of Chance in a World Sustained by God", in Morris, 211–35. Reprinted in van Inwagen, *God, Knowledge, and Mystery*.

——"Three Persons in One Being: On Attempts to Show that the Doctrine of the Trinity is Self-Contradictory", in Stewart, 83–9.

——"Two Concepts of Possible Worlds", *Midwest Studies in Philosophy* 11 (1986): 185–213. Reprinted in van Inwagen, *Ontology, Identity, and Modality*.

_____ "What is the Problem of the Hiddenness of God?", in Howard-Snyder and Moser, 22–32.

_____ "And yet They Are Not Three Gods but One God", in Morris, 241–78. Reprinted in van Inwagen, *God, Knowledge, and Mystery.*

_____ ed., *Christian Faith and the Problem of Evil* (Grand Rapids, Mich.: Eerdmans, 2004).

Watson, Gary, ed., *Free Will*, 2nd edn. (Oxford: Oxford University Press, 2003).

Yancey, Philip, and Brand, Paul, *The Gift of Pain* (Grand Rapids, Mich.: Zondervan, 1997).

Index

If one of the lectures that make up this book is devoted entirely or primarily to a certain topic, and if that fact is evident from the title of the lecture, that topic does not appear in the index unless it is also discussed in other lectures. In the latter case, the page numbers of the lecture devoted to that topic do not appear in the index. There is no entry 'God', for the simple reason that God's presence in these lectures is as pervasive as his presence in the world.